TECHNOLOGY OF MAIZE AND ALLIED CORN PRODUCTS

TECHNOLOGY OF MAIZE AND ALLIED CORN PRODUCTS

Written By :

EIRI Consultants and Engineers

ENGINEERS INDIA RESEARCH INSTITUTE

4449, Nai Sarak, Main Road, Delhi-110 006 (India)

Ph. : 91-11-23918117, 23916431, 23840361

Fax : 91-11-23916431, 23918117

✶ **E-Mail :** eirisidi@bol.net.in

✶ **Website :** www.eiriindia.org

Sole Distributors :

INDIAN INSTITUTE OF CONSULTANTS

4/54, Roop Nagar, Delhi-110007

Printed and Published by :

ENGINEERS INDIA RESEARCH INSTITUTE

4449, Nai Sarak, Main Road, Delhi-110 006 (India)

Ph. : 91-11-23918117, 23916431, 23840361

Fax : 91-11-23916431, 23918117

* **E-Mail :** eirisidi@bol.net.in
* **Website :** www.eiriindia.org

Distributed by :

SMALL INDUSTRY RESEARCH INSTITUTE
INDIAN INSTITUTE OF CONSULTANTS

ISBN : 978-81-89765-17-0

Printed in New Delhi (India)

Rs. 650

Printed and Published by Sudhir Gupta for "Engineers India Research Institute", 4449, Nai Sarak, Main Road, New Delhi-110 006 and Printed at Swastik Offset, Delhi

Preface

According to one study, there are more than 250 races of corn inabout 14 racial groups. Maize or Corn products have got tremendous demand in India and in overseas countries. Now-a-days many eatable products are being produced from maize. To consider the demand of these products EIRI have recently published a unique book on its subjects.

The book **'Technology of Maize and Allied Corn Products'** covers various methods including Corn, Types of Corn, Botany of Corn, Cultivation Practices, Carbohydrats and Related Compounds, Quality Factors, Traditional Food Products from Corn, Corn Milling, Products and their Uses, Processing Ready-to Breakfast Cereals, Popcorn, Formulated Puffed Snacks, Manufacturing Corn Chips, Maize Products, Maize Starch, Sweet Corn, Baby Corn, Extruding Snacks, Corn Flakes, Liquid Glucose, Maize/Corn Oil, Malto Dextrin from Maize, Plant Economics of Non-Roasted Corn Flakes (POHA), Starch from Maize, Snack Food, Yeat Dry Powder from Maize, Suppliers of Maize/Corn Processing Machineries, Present Manufactuers/Exporter/ Suppliers of Maize and Maize Products.

The book has been written for the benefit and to prove an asset and a handy reference guide in the hands of new entrepreneurs and well established industrialists.

Director

ENGINEERS INDIA RESEARCH INSTITUTE

Nai Sarak, Main Road,
Delhi-110 006 (India)
E-mail : eirisidi@bol.net.in

CONTENTS AND SUBJECT INDEX

1

Corn

INTRODUCTION

Corn *(Zea mays* L.) originated in the Western hemisphere. It was the only cereal systematically cultivated by the American Indians although some other grains were harvested from the wild state. Columbus found com being cultivated on Haiti, where it was called mahiz. From this Arawak Indian word was derived the name maize that is used in Europe to distinguish this cereal from other grains which were called "com" (Hunt 1915). Locations which have been suggested as possible centers of origin of com are central America (including southern Mexico) and the highlands of Peru.

Since the grain-bearing part of corn is inclosed in tenacious leaf sheaths, it is incapable of reseeding itself. Wild forms do not exist. The evolutionary path leading to modem corn is not clear, but archeological findings have partially explained its development. Mangelsdorf *et al.* described an evolutionary sequence based on about 24,000 maize specimens found in five caves in the Tehuacan Valley of southern Puebla and northern Oaxaca, Mexico. Some of these specimens were nearly 7,200 years old. It was deduced that wild com probably had a one-inch ear with two husks borne high on the stalk. At maturity, the husks opened to permit dispersal of the seeds. Above the ear was a male spikelet, about 1 to 2 inches in length. The kernels were rounded and either brown or orange. Repeated selection of seed from plants with larger kernels, more kernels on each cob, and other desirable features led to corn as we now know it.

It is apparent that this distant ancestor of modern com no longer exists. Either it was completely displaced by domesticated com which was sowed in all places suitable for the plant, or cultivated com hybridized with the wild com rendering the latter incapable of independent propagation. Over the several thousand years of its evolution under cultivation, there has been no change in the fundamental botanical characteristics of the com plant. That is, the changes which have occurred were in the size of the parts of the plant and in productivity.

The tribe Tripsaceae to which com belongs differs substantially from the tribe Hordeae, to which the other common cereal grains (wheat, rye, and barley) belong. In the same tribe with corn are teosinte *(Euchiaena mexicana* Schrad., a subtropical plant regarded by some botanists as the ancestor of com, gama grass *(Tripsacum dactyloides* L.), and adlay or Job's tears. Attribution of teosinte to the genus *Euchlaena* has been questioned.

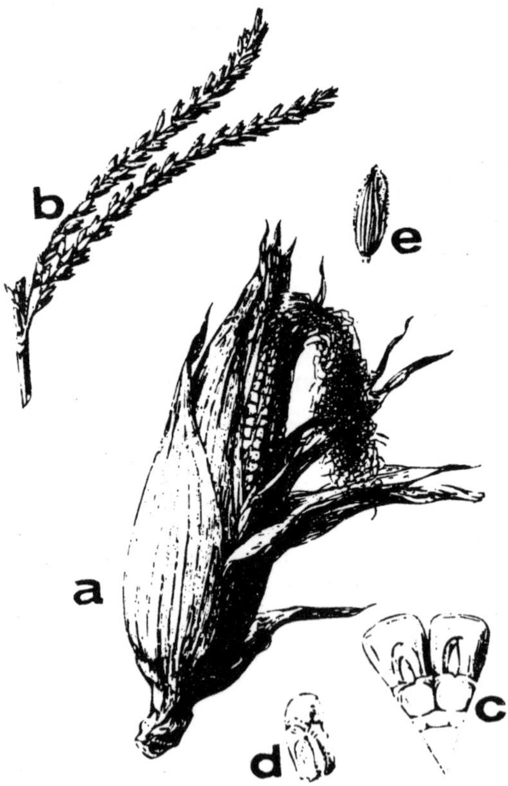

Fig. 1.1 Corn structures.

The wild annual form of teosinte has the same chromosome number as corn *(2n=2x=20)* and appears to be its close relative, even if not the the ancestor of *Zea*. Corn can be crossed with teosinte and some of the hybrids are even fairly fertile '.These "tripsacoids" apparently became the most common maize in the period from about 1,000 to 200 BC, according to the Tehuacan valley specimens. The tripsacoid complex eventually gave rise to Nal-Tel and Chapalate, two Mexican corn races which still exist, and to another type called late tripsacoid.

Some of the earlier theories on the origin of corn were well summarized by Wallace and Brown (1956). Weatherwax (1954) and other authorities favored the hypothesis that corn, teosinte, and tripsacum evolved from a single ancestral stock by ordinary divergent evolution. Other botanists, on the basis of genetic evidence, consider *Zea* to be older than teosinte, the latter having arisen from a relatively recent cross of corn with gama grass.

2

Types of Corn

There are more than 250 races of corn in about 14 racial groups, according to one study. The classification into races was based on: (1) recognizable characteristics of the plant tassel and ear, (2) physiological, genetic, and cytological differences, (3) cytological differences, and (4) geographic origin of the variety. Racial groups were based on further examination of the ear and kernel characteristics. Most of these races are grown in very small amounts in restricted areas of Central and South America. By far the greatest Production of corn is field corn of the dent and Pint types, with the former greatly predominating in this country. When the unqualified term "corn" is used, it is this kind of corn that is generally meant. Sweet corn and popcorn are also of considerable economic importance in the U.S.

Dent and flint corn

The vast quantities of dent corn which are produced in the U.S. and in some other countries are extremely important to food, feed, and industrial processors. Dent corn was not known to the American Indians; it originated in the early nineteenth century, purportedly as a cross between Virginian Gourdseed corn and a Northeastern Flint variety. Present day dent cultivars are the end result of nearly two centuries of intensive selection, breeding, and, eventually, hybridization. The superior qualities of dent for feed and industrial use, its very high yields under satisfactory conditions, and its relatively good resistance to disease and pests, have caused it to displace other types of field corn.

Of course, dent corn is quite specialized in some respects. It is not usable as popcorn, and it is not very suitable as a sweet corn substitute, though some immature green corn is undoubtedly used for the latter purpose, but as a feed materiaf and a source of raw material for food and for processing into starch and sweeteners, dent corn is in a class by itself. Some of the most popular varieties of the open-pollinated (before hybrid) dent corn were called Reid Yellow Dent, Krug Yellow Dent, Leaming, Midland Yellow Dent, Lancaster, Boone County White, Johnson County White, and Minnesota 13. Southern dents constituted ° a race which was at one time very important to U.S. agriculture and included the major varieties Hickory King, Gourdseed, and Mexican June. In the northernmost states, a race of flint corn adapted to the shorter seasons became prominent with the early settlers and included the varieties Longfellow, Smutnose, and New England Flint. Table 2.1 presents some important physical properties of dent corn. Kernels can vary in color from white to dark red or brown, in unusual cases dark blue. The weights of dent variety kernels will range from about 150 to 600 mg, with an average of about 350 mg.

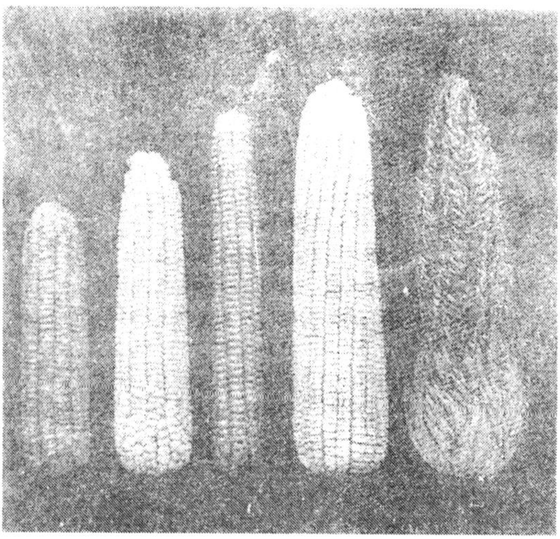

Fig. 2.1 Types of Corn, Left to Right : Representative Ears of Pop, Sweet, Flour Flint, Dent and Pod Corn.

Much field corn is used as feed for animals on the farm where it is grown, but far larger amounts are manufactured into mixed feeds by formula feed manufacturers, feedlot operators, and the like. Dent corn is also the basis of an enormous sweetener manufacturing business which has encroached on many uses formerly reserved for cane and beet sugar. It provides the raw material for food and industrial starches which are found in thousands of products.

Table 2.1 Some Physical Properties of Dent Corn

Property and Unit	Typical Value	Range
Kernels per ear	800	500-1,200
Kernels per pound	1,300	900-1,800
Bulk density, lb/bu	58.3	52-60
Bulk density, lb.cu.ft.	45.4	40-46
Specific gravity	1.26	---
Void volume, %	42.3	---
Thermal conductivity	1.22	---
Specific heat	0.1	
Heat energy content, Btu/lb	8.075.	
Angle of repose, degrees	35.	34-43.5

1. Modified from watson (1987). Mature grain of 15% moisture content. "Typical value" represents the "most protable median value."
2. Thermal conductivity units are Btu/(hr) (ft^2) (°F/in)

The originators of maize, the American Indians, used it primarily as the basis of tortillas and all the myriad permutations they developed of that simple product. The making of tortillas starts with the preparation of nixta mal, which is corn kernels that have been soaked for several hours in hot lime water. Nixtamal becomes masa when it is ground into a paste using a stone hand mill. Masa is formed into flat thin cakes, more or less circular, which are baked on a heated stone surface (or skillet or griddle, nowadays) until the dough has lost considerable water and achieved sufficient cohesiveness to allow it to be folded around food or otherwise manipulated. The completed assembly may be further cooked by pan frying, deep frying, or baking. Furthermore, rolled up tortillas without filling may be sliced and used as an ingredient in soups, stews, etc. A later development is the wheat flour tortilla, which differs in several respects from" the masa tortilla and will not be discussed at this point.

Lye hominy is also prepared by soaking whole field corn kernels in hot alkaline solution. The loosened husks are then removed by washing, and the whole kernels used as a cooking ingredient without particle size reduction. It is not clear that the American Indians used this process.

Sweet corn

Sweet corn differs from field corn in that a large proportion of the carbohydrates of the kernel is present as dissolved or dispersed glucose polymers of fairly low molecular weight rather than as starch granules. As a consequence, the kernels of sweet corn retain their tender and succulent texture, and their sweet taste, for a longer period of time during their development. In dent corn development, the amount of carbohydrates present as sugars at any one time is relatively small. most of these molecules being quickly incorporated into the starch granules which will make up the bulk of the endosperm. Sweet corn kernels, when allowed to mature and then dried, are nearly as hard as those of dent corn, although they have a wrinkled surface rather than the smooth contours of a field corn kernel. On the other hand, certain varieties of field corn are often sold in their immature stages as sweet corn. This is particularly true in the southern U.S., where the greater susceptibility of sweet corn to disease and insect infestation has placed constraints on its economical production.

Sweet corn has been regarded by some botanists as a distinct species or subspecies *(Zea mays saccharata)* extant since prehistoric times, while other authorities consider it to be a field corn mutation of fairly recent origin. The latter view is the one which prevails today. The mutated gene, which has been named *su* (*Su* is the field corn gene), is located on the fourth chromosome. It is presumably one of the genes responsible for initiating the mechanisms whereby the carbohydrates of the maturing kernel are transformed into granules containing high molecular weight branched starches. There are other gene combinations that give sweet corn, but the common commercial type is due to mutation of *Su* Single kernels having the characteristics of sweet corn can be observed on ears of flint corn grown under controlled pollination.

It is noteworthy that sweet corn differs from field corn in several respects. Sweet corn is more susceptible to attacks by pathogens, for example. These additional differences could result from the operation of the same mutant gene which interferes with starch granule production or from linked genes controlling susceptibility. The mere presence of additional water, and more readily available nutrients, in sweet corn kernels during a longer period of its development would seem to make it more susceptible to microbiological invasion. It is tempting to speculate that the sweet corn gene is the most ancient form and that pressures from pathogens led to the survival and eventual predominance of corn that could produce forms of its storage carbohydrate (Le., starch granules) which were more resistant to the attacks of microorganisms.

Most of the sugar in sweet corn is sucrose, but there are significant amounts of maltose, glucose, and fructose; all of which contribute to the desirable sweet flavor of this vegetable. The creamy appearance and texture of the kernel, which also have an important effect on sweet corn's acceptability, are largely due to the accumulation of phytoglycogen, which may form as much as 25% of the dry weight. This polysaccharide consists of glucose molecules linked by-D-(1,4) bonds, with branching at ∝-D-(1,6).

The first variety of sweet corn acquired by European settlers was Papoon, obtained from the Iroquois in 1779. The first known listing by seed growers was in 1828, and it was called "sweet corn" at that time. The most important early cultivar of open-pollinated sweet corn was Golden Bantam, first offered to the public in 1902. Work on hybrid sweet corn led to the successful introduction of these types in the 1930s, actually before the commercial availability of hybrid field corn. Standard sweet corns are described as "normal," "traditional," "standard," "conventional," and "sugar." A type of sweet corn called Xtrasweet was introduced about 30 years ago by scientists at the University of illinois. It is genetically homozygous for a mutant gene called sh which blocks all starch synthesis. The kernels contain 35% sucrose at milk stage and maturity. The problems associated with high sugar varieties include decreased eating consistency or texture and the extremely short duration of peak quality in the field, as short as one day for some cultivars. A mutant called sugary enhancer, homozygous for gene *se* increases sugar while maintaining many of the desirable characteristics of standard sweet corn. These varieties are of good texture when cooked and maintain good quality for relatively long times after being harvested. The improved results are apparently due to development of increased amounts (compared to high sugar cultivars) of phytoglycogen.

A characteristic of sweet corn affecting the consumer's perception of quality is the color of the silks. Whether the corn is prepared in the home for immediate consumption or in a factory for canning, it is almost inevitable that some of the silks will carry through to the finished product, no matte!" how intensive an effort is made to remove them all. If the silks are dark in color, they are perceived as impurities and adversely affect some consumers' enjoyment of the product. It is desirable, then, that the silks be as light in color as can be obtained. The color is under genetic control and considerable success has been achieved in matching the hue to that of the kernels.

Seed-bed preparation, planting, and cultivation of sweet corn are similar to these procedures as used for field corn. Harvesting is usually performed by machines which cut the ears off the stalk so that bruising of the tender kernels is kept to a minimum. The time of harvesting is quite critical and is usually about 18 days after silking. Even the most tolerant varieties retain satisfactory canning quality for a period of only 6 to 8 days. In other varieties, this period of optimum quality may be as short as two days. Sweet corn yields only about one-half to two-thirds as much food product dry matter per acre as do the best varieties of field corn under similar conditions. Most aspects of sweet corn growing and processing have been excellently presented by Huelsen.

Sweet corn is marketed fresh, frozen, or canned. A very .small proportion is also dehydrated by methods giving a product which has a characteristic flavor and can be rehydrated by cooking. Fresh corn is sold at roadside stands by growers and through the usual distribution channels for fresh vegetables going to grocers and other retailers.

Nearly all canned corn is sweet corn. The amount of field corn canned as such, excluding that made into lye hominy, is negligible. Sweet corn cannot be made into lye hominy. Most canned corn is prepared either as cream style or as whole kernel, although a small amount of combination items, (e.g., corn with peppers) is canned. Cream style corn includes portions of kernels cut from the cob combined with the scraped-off residue of the kernel portions which remained on the cob. Small amounts of corn or wheat starch, natural or modified, may be added to thicken the can contents. Salt is usually added and, sometimes, a sweetener. There have been a few attempts to can corn-on-the-cob, but this proved to be totally impractical so far as quality and economics were concerned.

Sweet corn for canning is grown under contract with a processor. The canner provides ~e farmer with treated seed and designates the date of planting. When it ,has been harvested, the corn is purchased at a price which may be fixed at the signing of the contract or be related by some factor to the price, of field corn at the time of delivery. The contractual arrangement is necessary because the factory must have a constant flow of raw material over an extended canning period, and the farmer must have an assured outlet for this very perishable crop.

At the time of harvest, sweet corn from the currently popular cultivars should fall in a moisture content range of 76 to 79%. These are the so-called shrunken sweet corns of very high sugar content. Standard sweet corns have an optimum moisture range of 70 to 72% at harvest. The shrunken sweet corn loses only about 0.25% of moisture per day at the optimum level, while standard sweet corn loses about 1% per day, making the harvesting period about four times as long for the new varieties. More details about these recent developments can be found in the excellent review of Marshall.

Corn is received at the cannery with the husks retained on the ears. The ears are fed from the trucks into chutes leading to machines which cut off the ends of the cobs and strip the freed husks from the ears. Washing by high pressure jets of water removes most of the debris and many of the silks. There are U.S. Standards for Grades of Canned Cream Style Corn and for Grades of Canned Whole Kernel (or Whole Grain) Corn. Grading factors for cream style corn include color, consistency, absence of defects, tenderness and maturity, and flavor. The Grades are Grade A (Fancy), Grade B (Extra Standard), Grade C (Standard), and Sub-standard. For whole kernel corn, the grade designations are the same, and grading factors include colour. cut, absence of defects, tenderness and maturity, and flavour.

Large quantities of sweet corn are frozen. Most frozen sweet corn is sold as whole kernel corn. At one time there was a frozen counterpart of cream-style corn, but this seems to have disappeared. Various combinations with other vegetables, such as corn with peppers or beans (succotash) are produced in limited amounts. Some frozen packs include butter sauces, cheese sauces, or other condiments. Tressler *et ai.* (1968) gave a thorough review of methods for preparing these items. Improved canning processes have reduced the differences in quality at the serving level of frozen and canned whole kernel corn to the point' where there is little or no real incentive for the average consumer to purchase the frozen product unless it has been combined with sauces or other adjuncts not readily compatible with the canning process. The market for frozen corn on the cob has increased in an irregular pattern for three or four decades, and has received renewed impetus in the last few years from improved quality, packaging of the more convenient partial ears, and emphasis on microwave cooking of the corn. Large quantities of frozen corn-on-the-cob are sold by foodservice distributors, primarily for preparation by fast food restaurants.

Popcorn

The use of expanded or puffed kernels of corn as food is very ancient. Examples of grain suitable for preparation in this way have been found not only in the Toltec pyramids of Central America, but also in 4,000 year old deposits in the Bat Cave of New Mexico. Popcorn was not widely used in colonial America, but, by the late 1800s the popping of corn was a widespread domestic culinary practice, and the growing of popcorn was becoming commercially important. Popcorn has always been predominantly an American food, although fairly large quantities of it are sold in England and other European countries, principally as caramel-coated confections.

Popcorn has been described as a small flint corn type containing a high proportion of horny (corneous) endosperm. Cultivation procedures for popcorn are not much different from those used for other corn crops. Time of seeding, optimum soil and climate conditions, diseases, and harvesting procedures are much the same as for dent corn. Popcorn growers usually have more trouble with weeds because their crop grows more slowly than dent corn and the plants are smaller in stature at maturity. Herbicides alleviate this problem considerably. Common row widths for planting popcorn in the corn belt are 30, 36, and 38 inches, with individual plants placed equidistant in the row. Plant densities are probably higher for popcorn than for dent corn, on the average.

Popcorn has long been a favourite crop with home gardeners, but it is also an important commercial crop. Commercial growers of popcorn almost always operate under a contract with a large merchandising concern which provides them with seed and offers an assured outlet for the grain. Because of this close control by relatively few persons, annual production figures for popcorn are subject to large fluctuations as compared with the figures for field corn, the production of which is determined by decisions of a large number of independent growers. Popcorn sells for considerably more per bushel (i.e., 70 lb of ear corn) than does field corn, but the yield per acre is lower for popcorn and cultivation procedures are more labor intensive..

Prior to 1940, open-pollinated varieties were used in most commercial production. The first hybrid popcorn seed was released in 1935 by the Minnesota Agricultural Experiment Station, but it was adapted only to the northern edge of the corn belt and was not widely used by commercial growers. The first hybrids adapted to the central corn belt areas were released by the Indiana and Kansas Agricultural Experiment stations in the early 1940s. Most commercial popcorn hybrids are three-way crosses, with a few single crosses also being used. Hybrids are evaluated for yield per acre, lodging tendencies, disease resistance, and amount of expansion of the kernels. High popping expansion is dependent on the presence of probably four or five major genes, with a number of minor genes contributing to such other characteristics as hull thickness and flavor. The development of superior inbred lines involves the combining of many of these genes into each line. Hybrids are then produced by crossing the inbred lines, and these are tested over several years at different locations to identify the best combination.

Popcorn is planted at the same time field corn would be planted in the area. Temperatures of 50° to 52°F in a loam soil are adequate, while clay soil should be a degree or so higher and sandy soil a degree or so lower. Readings should be taken between 7:00 and 8:00 AM at a depth between 2 and 4 inches Rate of planting can be heavier than for field corn. Grower experience indicates that, given fertile soil and normal rainfall, seeds can be planted as close as 7 or 8 inches. Experiment station tests have shown that, where moisture is adequate, corn planted one inch deep out yields corn planted deeper. Because seed size varies greatly with different hybrids, it is important to have the right planter plate for the seed being used. Planter plates for popcorn can be obtained for most makes of planters, but if they are not available it may be possible to substitute sorghum plates. About 6 to 10 pounds of seed are required to plant an acre, the optimum amount depending on size of seed and rate of seeding.

Rainfall and temperature during the ten days before and the twenty days following tasseling have more to do with yield than the weather at any other period. There should be 4 to 5 inches of rainfall during this thirty-day period, and the mean temperature should fall between 72° and 74°F. Temperatures above 96°F at tasseling time have an adverse effect on yield.

Popcorn is attacked by the same insects that harm field corn. Because popcorn grows slower than field corn early in the season, making the stalk and ear shank weaker, damage from these pests maybe greater in popcorn. Popcorn is relatively resistant to disease, but hybrids differ greatly in their response to the various organisms. Planting popcorn hybrids resistant to diseases known to be endemic in the area is the best way to forestall heavy losses. Seed treated with fungicide is good protection against seed rot and certain seedling diseases, but will have essentially no effect on smut, leaf blights, rust, ear or stalk rots, crazy top, and bacterial wilt.

Harvesting should be delayed until the corn has dried down to at least 22% and preferably 20% moisture content, unless the corn is to be dried artificially. Com should be harvested promptly if it falls below 18% moisture, because there is a danger that a spell of hot weather may cause it to become too dry if it is left in the field. There may also be considerable loss from ear drop and broken stalks in excessively dry corn.

There is the question as to whether to shell the grain as it is picked. When picker-shellers became available, most growers started harvesting popcorn with these machines. Since it is difficult to moisten shelled corn, the crop must be at about the correct moisture content before it is harvested. If corn is harvested when it is too wet, there will be some damage to the kernels, and this damage will-cause significantly reduced expansion. On the other hand, if the corn is too dry, it must be moistened before it is marketed. It is said that more damage occurs to the kernels when the picker-sheller is used as compared to storing the whole ears and shelling as required. Some sellers of popcorn advertise "cob cured" grain as an indication, they say, of better quality.

A problem faced by developers of hybrid popcorn is the need to have ears with sufficient diameter at the butt so the ears will not be drawn into the snapping rolls and crushed or carried through to the ground during harvesting. Hybrids now available can be harvested with mechanical pickers and will stand up well enough so pickers can be used.

Since the correct moisture content is essential for achieving maximum popping expansion, the entire container (silo, bin, etc.) of grain should have free access to moving air so as to obtain rapid and uniform drying and prevent the development of moldy areas. Corn should be quickly brought to 14% moisture content, or less, before long term storage. Drying popcorn at temperatures below 120°F does not lower popping volume provided the corn did not start with more than 25% moisture.

3

Botany of Corn

The appropriate tribe is the Tripsaceae (Maydeae) and includes not only com but teosinte, gama grass, adlay, and some other less well known genera. A distinguishing characteristic of this tribe is the presence of male and female !flowers in separate spikelets on the same plant. This tribe is similar to the sorghum group Androponeae from which it differs principally in the suppression of certain floral parts.

The genus *Zea* has the pistillate spikes grown together fonlrlng an ear, the grains at maturity much exceeding the glumes. According to the most prevalent taxonomic view, only one species, *mays,* is included in the genus. Some taxonomists have been of the opinion that several species, or at least subspecies, should be included in this genus. For example, Sturtevant classified sweet com as *Zea saccharata,* and elevated other types to the level of species.

The major varieties of com are pod corn, flint corn, dent corn , sweet corn, popcorn, flour corn, and waxy corn. All of these types have the normal *2n* chromosome number of 20. The characteristics rendering the variety distinguishable are usually endosperm differences depending on the operation of a single gene. For example, the "sweet" phenotype depends upon a single recessive gene.

Pod corn is presumably a primitive type. Each kernel is enveloped by a fibrous husk. This character can appear in any of the other com types described here. Flint com has very hard kernels, as the name indicates.

This characteristic is due to a rather thick layer of hard starch and protein just under the bran layer. Most flints are early maturing and have a certain popularity among farmers for this reason. The texture may adversely affect their value for feeding livestock, but presumably does not affect their milling utility. Flints are grown largely in Argen.tina and Africa.

Dent com comprises the largest com crop in the U.S. The crown of the kernels exhibits a pronounced concavity at maturity due to shrinkage of the endosperm as moisture is lost. Though the grains are hard, they are not as hard as those of flint com. Flour com is grown in South and Central America to a considerable extent. The grains are large and soft, and the endosperm is very friable. These characteristics permit easy grinding of the grain into meal, an advantage in home preparation methods.

Waxy corn does not contain wax as such but owes its texture to the presence of relatively large amounts of the amylopectin fraction of starch. It has important food and industrial uses.

Description of the Plant

Zea is a robust, erect annual grass. Some varieties may reach 15 it or more in height, while others rarely exceed 1.5 it at maturity. The plant has broad leaves arranged in two vertical ranks. Its inflorescences are monoecious. The flowers of the staminate tassel are borne in many spikelike racemes which together form large spreading panicles terminating the stems. A pistillate inflorescence is borne on one or more spikes of the leaves. There are eight or more rows of spikelets on a greatly thickened axis (cob) and the whole is inclosed in foliaceous bracts (husks). Protruding from the tops of these bracts are the styles called silks. The styles are long and slender and may be fertilized throughout their length. Except in pod com, the floral bracts on the axis do not envelope the kernels. The spikelets are unisexual. The pistillate spikelets occur in pairs, both members of which may be fertile, but, more commonly, one member is fertile and one is sterile. The glumes are broad and rounded at the apex. Staminate spikelets are two-flowered and are arranged in pairs on the side of a continuous rachis, one member of the pair being sessile and one pedicillate. The glumes are membranaceous, acute, and covered with short hairs. Hyaline palea and lemma are present.

Genetically Engineered Corn

Development of gene-modified corn began in the late 1980s. Scientists demonstrated that corn plants possessing an artificially-inserted gene could be stable, fertile, and capable of transmitting the gene to the next generation.

The ultimate goals are the production of new races of corn that are 'more resistant to insect attack, yield better, or have better nutritional properties. For example, it would be a significant achievement if a gene encoding high levels of the amino acid lysine could be inserted, assuming it would function without lowering yield or otherwise damaging the race.

4

Cultivation Practices

Corn can be grown in a wide variety of climates and on very diverse kinds of soils as indicated by the geographical distribution of its production. for maximum yields, however, it does require deep dark silt loam, good drainage, abundant moisture, and moderately high temperatures for maximum yields. The ideal soil should have a pH of about 6.5, an exchange capacity of about 20 meq per 100 gm soil, a percentage base saturation of 75 to 90% (with less than 10% of the bases being sodium), a water-holding capacity of about 2 inches of water in available form per foot of soil, and a bulk density of not more than 1.3.

Sandy soils are less suitable for production of corn because they do not retain moisture for a sufficient length of time. In addition, sandy soils often contain low concentrations of nutrients needed by the plant. The latter condition can, of course, be corrected temporarily by fertilization, but excessive leaching of the fertilizer by rainfall may make this practice uneconomical. Clay soils also give relatively low yields because they are liable to be too compact to allow maximum root proliferation and may have inadequate drainage.

The mean maximum temperature, the mean relative humidity, and the evaporation in the month of pollination are closely related to corn yields. Each of these factors is more closely correlated with yields than is the amount of rainfall of any period of the year. The number of rains in June showed a higher correlation with yield than did any other rainfall factor considered in one study. Under normal conditions in the corn belt, moisture requirements of corn plants exceed the precipitation during the peak growth period.

The rather indirect relationship of rainfall in any short period to yield may be partially explained by results of another study which showed that corn utilized water to a depth of 5 ft or more in a deep Brunizem soil in Illinois, while rainfall and irrigation affected the soil moisture profile to a depth of only 2 ft on both corn and fallow plots. It also appears that corn yields are closely related to the reserve soil moisture conditions at the beginning of the growing season and to the soil moisture stress to which the plant is subjected during the growing season. The moisture stress effect on growth is-closely related to the seasonal weather. Efficiency of water use is strongly conditioned by soil temperature. Both soil moisture tension and oxygen concentration of the root atmosphere have imp/?rtant effects on growth.

Notwithstanding the apparent tolerance to short-term deficits in precipitation, an extended drought can have disastrous consequences on corn yield. The 1988 drought was a principal cause of the drop in corn yields from record levels of 119.4 bushels per acre in 1987 to 84.6 bushels per acre in 1988, this being one of the largest percentage declines of the century. An unusual feature of the 1988 drought was the severity of early-season weather through June. Results of past drought seasons indicate there is little carryover effect from the dry year; the following year typically gives yields near trend levels. Timely rains in July are the most critical factor in restoring yields, with July temperatures next in importance in most years. Other results show that' average weather is not necessarily optimal for yields, and that there are more chances than yield will be decreased downward than upward by weather fluctuations.

When corn seedlings were grown in temperature controlled greenhouses and in field plots where the temperature was adjusted by underground heating, the rate of corn growth seemed to be approximately in accord with the Van't Hoff law, the Q_{10} of the law being from 2.0 to 2.8.

This relationship applied in the range of 60° to 80°F. The most favorable soil temperature at the four inch depth for corn grown in central Iowa appeared to be about 75°F. The time between silking and maturity was reduced by increased soil temperature.

Corn is grown in many areas where the temperature and soil requirements for optimum yield cannot be expected. Use of hybrids selected to fit the limitations of the soil and climate where optimum conditions do not exist helps to reduce but does not eliminate the decrease in yield resulting from these limitations. Proper selection of planting time, to take advantage of a soil temperature of at least 60°F is also helpful, but this procedure has obvious limitations.

Authorities recommend that hybrids be planted as early as soil conditions and climate permit. Later plantings tend to give lower yields, have higher moisture content, at harvest, and suffer more insect damage. . The improvement due to early planting is usually attributed to improvement in available soil moisture at critical growth periods.

Varieties

Hybrids, which constitute the majority of corn seed now used in the U.S., vary considerably in their growth rate, resistance to disease and insects, ratio of stover to ear, etc. It is evident, therefore, that the hybrid selected for seed will have a considerable effect on yield per acre. Appropriate hybrids are those which allow weather, technology, and management to be fully expressed in high yields.

Information on yield and lodging resistance of hybrids can often be obtained from the corn yield tests conducted in many states. It is also desirable to know about insect and disease susceptibility, suitability for combining, maturity rating, and dry-down characteristics. Such data can sometimes be obtained from representatives of the companies supplying the seed.

Recently, two biotechnology teams have successfully inserted foreign genes into corn plants capable of forming viable seeds. So far as is known, inserting new genes into fertile plants had previously been successful only for dicotyledons such as tomatoes, tobacco, and rapeseed. In one case, the gene conferred a resistance to the herbicide bialaphos. Another group of researchers transferred a gene that allowed cells to grow in the presence of an inhibitor and another that caused luminescence. None of these test genes have any immediate practical importance for growers or users of corn, but the work suggests that such applications will be possible in the near future.

Rotations and Fertilizer

Rotations.-USDA surveys indicated that there are two common cropping patterns in the ten major corn producing states. These are continuous corn production and corn-soybeans-corn rotations. The continuous corn pattern was the most common in Nebraska, where 62% of the total corn land was monocultured. Fixed investment in irrigation and heavy participation in government commodity programs probably contribute to the lack of crop diversity. Continuous corn cropping consumes greater amounts of insecticides and fertilizers than corn rotated with legumes.

A corn-soybeans-corn rotation pattern dominates in Iowa (89%), Indiana (46%), and Minnesota (40%). In the dairy state of Wisconsin (about 17% of the land used to grow corn in 1988 had been planted to alfalfa in the previous two years. Alfalfa serves the same purpose ans soybeans in a rotation and provides feed for dairy cattle. In South Dakota, where lack of moisture is a problem, 36% of the 1988 corn acreage had been planted in wheat or oats during the previous year. With the exception of Michigan and South Dakota, over 90% of the 1988 corn acreage was used in rotations involving wheat, alfalfa, corn, or soybeans.

Fertilization.-Corn extracts enormous quantities of nutrients from the soil. In fact, it is the cereal crop most destructive to soil fertility. One set of investigators found that a 50-bu per acre corn crop removed from each acre of soil 78.4 lb of nitrogen, 27.6 lb of phosphorus, 55.2 lb of potassium, 14.7 lb of calcium, and 5.6 lb of magnesium. For this reason, heavy fertilization is essential if corn is to be grown several years in succession on the same acreage. On the Morrow field plots of the University of Illinois, where corn had been grown continuously for about 40 years, the yield showed a steady (though uneven) decrease through the years, falling from an initial value of about 54 bu per acre to about 24 bu per acre. When oats were grown in alternate years, corn production held up slightly better, showing a decrease from about 50 to about 28 bu per acre. A corn-oats clover rotation gave much better results, with only a slight decline throughout the test. period. The corn-oats-clover pattern, together with applications of manure and phosphated lime actually showed a significant increase during the earlier years and subsequent maintenance of production at a high level.

In another study of yields of corn grown continuously for 30 years on plots at St. Paul, Minnesota, the data showed a somewhat erratic trend, but yields near the end of the study were not much different from the earliest figures when the plots were manured at the rate of two tons per acre. On plots where a corn-oats-wheat-hay rotation had been maintained for over sixty years, it was shown that (1) lime alone does not increase yields, (2) high yields can be maintained indefinitely with inorganic commercial fertilizers, (3) manure should be reinforced with superphosphate, and (4) fertilizers alone cannot compensate for the problem of an acid soil, but the addition of lime can increase the efficiency of fertilizers on these soils up to 300% as measured by yield.

Protein content of the kernels tends to increase with increasing nitrogen supply in the soil. The oil content may also increase slightly as the result of fertilizer additions. There seems to be a direct relationship between the amount of nitrogen applied to the soil and the contents of crude protein, zein, and leucine in the grain. Increasing the rate of nitrogen results in an increased percentage of leucine in the grain and in the crude protein. On the other hand, increasing the number of plants per acre decreases the total leucine content, but the decrease is not proportionately as great as the decrease in crude protein. There is not much effect of nitrogen fertilization, as related to plant population, on tryptophan content. On the other hand, another set of experiments showed that application of 50 lb of nitrogen under certain conditions actually resulted in a lowering of the protein content of the grain, although protein content of the stover increased. Evidently, conditions must be properly chosen if grain of higher protein content is to result from applications of nitrogenous fertilizers.

Plant Population

It might be expected that grain yield would reach a peak and then decline as the plant population per unit area was increased over a wide range. This effect does exist, at least under some circumstanr:As. When com was planted in rows 8.5 ft apart to reduce row competition *w* a low level, and the within-row spacings of plants varied, there was httle difference between total plant weights per acre as the within-row spacing was varied from 1 to 4 inches, but the closer spacings increased the stover to ear ratio. Ear com yield per acre was greatest at a plant spacing of about 4 inches. Another test showed that planting at 16,000 per acre resulted in higher protein content of the grain than did planting at 10,000 plants per acre. Oil content of the kernels was virtually the same at both levels of population.

It was found that the log of the average yield of individual com plants making up a population bears a linear relationship to the population, at least between 5,000 and 25,000 plants per acre. Therefore, only two. yield population values are needed to estimate yields at any other population within the linear range, according to the investigator.

When phosphorus and potassium are not limiting, the average weights of ears of com decrease as the planting rate increases, and this trend is not reversed by application of nitrogenous fertilizers.

Tillage

Tillage practices intended to optimize conditions for germination and to prevent competition by weeds have undergone some changes in recent years. These changes, mainly aimed at reducing the amount of labor required to secure maximum yields, have been made possible by the availability of new kinds of equipment and by the development of selective herbicides.

Weeds compete with the crop for moisture, nutrients, and solar energy. It has been shown that weeds compete strongly with com at all rates of fertilizer (N, P, or K) application, and suppress growth and yield of corn. It does not appear to be possible to maintain high corn yields in the presence of competing weeds by increasing the rate of fertilization. On the other hand, some weeds are much more adversely affected by inadequate essential nutrients than is corn. Thus, in some tests, corn with weeds yielded better when no fertilizer was applied.

Weed growth is conventionally controlled by turning over or breaking up the soil with disk harrows or field cultivators. There are definite possibilities of eliminating the usual primary tillage and post-planting tillage in certain types of soil when weed growth is reduced by the use of selective herbicides applied at carefully chosen times. Such techniques are by no means universally applicable, however, and require an initially good soil condition.

Diseases and Pests

Insects.-Insects which are primarily destructive to the seed are seed corn maggots *(Hylema platura* Meigen), seed corn beetles *(Agonoderus lecontei* Chaudoir), thief ants *(Solenopsis molesta* Say), and wireworms *(Elateridae* spp.) Chemical controls are usually effective. Timing of planting to insure rapid germination will minimize loss of seed to these pests.

Damage to corn roots is usually the result of the activities of corn rootworms *(Diabrotica* spp.), grape colapsis *(Colapsis flavida* Say), Japanese beetle *(Papilla japonica* Newman), white grubs C *Phyllophaga* spp.), annual white grubs *(Cyclocephala* spp.), and corn root aphid C*Anuraphis maidiradicis* Forbes). Most of these insects, except annual white grubs, can be partially reduced by crop rotation, but use of insecticides is generally the method of choice for control.

Among the insects which feed on the underground portion of the stalk are the sod webworn *(Crambus* spp.), the black cutworm *(Agrotis ipsilon* Huffnagel), and billbugs *(Sphenophorus* spp.). Crop rotation and improvevement in drainage are cultural methods which have been suggested for control.

Exposed corn leaves are attacked by many insects, such as corn flea beetles C *Chadocnema pulicara* Melsheimer), yellow and black grass thrips *(Anaphothrips obscuras* and *Frankliniella tenuicornis),* corn blotch leaf miners

(Agrnmyza parvicornis Loew), yellow-striped armyworm *(Prodenia ornithogalli* Guenee), two-spotted spider mite *(Tetranychus urticae* Koch), true armyworms *(Pseudaletia unipuncta* Haworth), caterpillars *(Simyra henrici* Grt.), grasshoppers *(Melanopus* spp.), chinch bugs *(Bliss us leucopterus* Say), corn leaf beetles *(Oulema melanopus* L.), and corn leaf aphids *(Rhopalosiphum maidis* Fitch). Control is generally by insecticides.

Insects feeding on the whorl, stalk, or ear include European corn borers *(Ostrinia nubilaiis* Huebner), the southwestern corn borers *(Zeadiatraea graniosella* Dyar), southern corn stalk borers *(Diatraea crambidoides* Grote), common stalk borers *CPapaipema nebris* Guenee), fall armyworms *(Spodoptera frugiperda* J. E. Smith), corn earworms *(Heliothis zea* Boddie), corn sap beetles *(Carpophilus dimidatus* Fabricius), and scavenger beetles *(Glischrochilus quadrisignatus).*

For further details on the insect pests of corn, the specific damage attributable to them, and methods of control, the reader should consult the very thorough report of Petty and Apple (1967), on which the preceding discussion is largely based.

Diseases.-Corn seems to be relatively resistant to diseases, as compared to other grain crops. The yearly loss from this cause in the U.S. has been estimated at from 2 to 7% of the crop. In some cases, localized losses due to leaf diseases may be as high as 60%.

Corn is subject to parasitic diseases causes by fungi, bacteria, and viruses, and to nonparasitic diseases such as those caused by nematodes and by nutrient element deficiencies. Seed rots and seedling blights can be caused by *Pythium* spp., *Diplodia maydis, Gibberella zeae, Penicillium oxalicum,* and *Rhizoctonia batatola.* Stalk rots can also be caused by *D. maydis* and G. *zeae.* Charcoal rot of stalks and roots is due to *R. bataticola.*

The two smut diseases infecting corn are known as head smut and common (or boil) smut. The latter is due to *Ustilago maydis,* and it may invade corn plants which have been injured by cultivation, hail, or other agencies. It causes large galls or tumors. Head smut is caused by *Sphacelotheca reilana,* and sometimes damages corn in Texas, seldom elsewhere in the U.S. Damage can be reduced by using resistant hybrids, although there are none which are immune.

A number of fungi and bacteria cause leaf diseases. The only diseases of this type which are of economic importance in the U.S. are northern corn leaf blight *(Helminthosporium turcicum),* southern corn leaf blight

(Helminthosporium maydis), and bacterial wilt *(Erwinia stewartiO.* The latter severely affects many sweet corn hybrids and is starting to affect dents. Control is achieved through planting resistant hybrids, if they are available.

There are three rust diseases infecting corn: common corn rust *(Puccinia sorghi,* southern corn rust *(Puccinia polysora),* and tropical corn rust *(Physopella zeae).* The last two are seldom seen in the U.S. Common, rust is widespread here but causes very little damage. It can be recognized by the circular brownish pustules which form on the leaves. There has been very little effort devoted to breeding resistant cultivars, apparently.

Several downy mildew diseases of corn are known. Downy mildew is most severe in tropical countries. The diseases found in the U.S. are crazy top *(Sclerophthora macrospora),* green ear *(Sclerospora graminicola),* and sorghum downy mildew *(Sclerospora sorghi).* The latter is the most important of these. Some resistant inbred varieties of corn are available.

Maize dwarf mosaic and maize chlorotic dwarf are the most important virus diseases of corn known to occur in the U.S. They are especially prevalent where corn is grown adjacent to johnsongrass, which is an overwintering host for these viruses. Dwarf mosaic causes mottling of young leaves, stunting, proliferation of adventitious buds, and barreness. Chlorotic dwarf results in disappearance of the chlorophyll between the veins of the leaves and stunting of the plant.

STRUCTURE AND COMPOSITION

Figure 4.1 is a drawing of a section of a mature corn kernel. The four principal parts are the tip cap, germ, hull, pericarp, and endosperm.

An intensive investigation of the com kernel's structure was reported by Wolf *et ai.* (1952A, 1952B, 1952C, and 1952D). In their introduction, these investigators say, "The kernel of com is a fruit composed of a thin pericarp enclosing a single seed. The pericarp is the mature ovary wall and comprises all of the outer cell layers down to the seed coat. Along its inner surface, it adheres closely to the seed coat. The latter in turn encloses the germ and the endosperm, the three forming the seed. This type of singleseeded fruit, in which the pericarp does not open on drying to liberate the seed, is characteristic of cereal grains. It is" known as a caryopsis."

Table 4.1 lists the average proximate analysis of the kernels of sweet com, hybrid popcorn, inbred dent com, and hybrid yellow dent com.

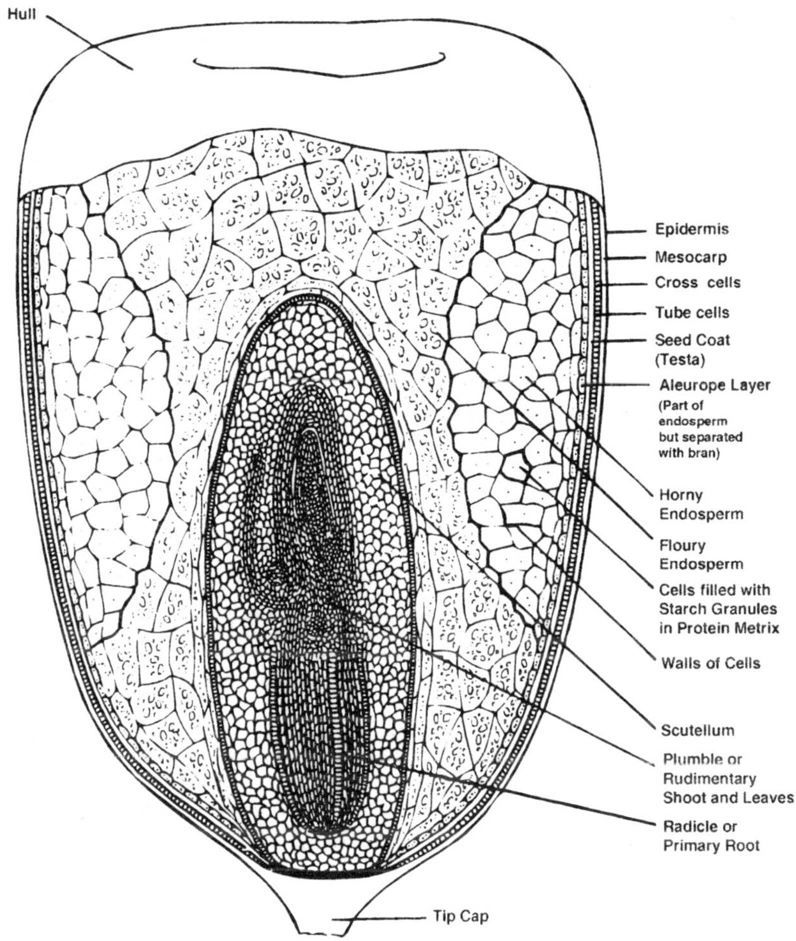

Fig. 4.1 Longitudinal section of a corn kernal. Source : Wheat Flour Institute

These data are on an "as is" basis, and it can be seen that the sweet corn values refer to a dried kernel rather than to the "fresh" or succulent form in which this food is usually consumed. Flint and flour corn can be expected to have compositions somewhat similar to dent. Notable differences between the varieties are apparent in the ether extract values, which are relatively high for sweet corn.

Table 4.1. COMPOSITION OF WHOLE CORN KERNELS

Content, in percent

Component	Sweet corn	Hybrid popcorn	Inbred dent corn	Hybrid yellow dent
Protein	10.88	10.69	8.31	8.06
Ether extract	8.18	3.69	3.90	3.94
Crude fiber	1.99	2.25	1.74	2.09
Moisture	10.10	9.78	11.46	10.12
Ash	1.83	1.45	1.18	1.40
N-free extract	67.02	72.14	73.41	74.39

Based on data of Fan et al.

Distribution of some of the components within the dent corn kernel is given in Table 4.1. There is a characteristically high level of oil in the embryo and of starch in the endosperm. There are also relatively high concentrations of sugar and ash in the embryo.

5

Carbohydrates and Related Compounds

Starch is the predominant component of corn kernels. Other carbohydrates are present in relatively small amounts. In waxy varieties, close to 100% of the starch will be in the branched molecule form, i.e., amylopectin. In ordinary varieties, a sustantial amount of amylose is present. The proportion of amylose averages about 27% and seems to vary within a rather narrow range. In a series of nonwaxy varieties comprising 190 samples from the U.S. and 167 varieties from abroad, the amylose content of the starch was found to vary from 20 to 36%. Varieties containing from 55 to 80% of the total starch as linear fraction have been developed.

Table 5.1. DISTRIBUTION OF COMPONENTS OF YELLOW DENT CORN KERNELS AMONG THE FRACTIONS

	Endo-sperm	Embryo	Peri-carp	Tip cap
	%	%	%	%
Proportion of the part to the whole kernel	82.	11.6	5.5	0.8
Protein	73.1	23.9	2.2	0.8
Oil	15.0	83.2	1.2	0.6
Sugar	28.2	70.0	1.1	0.7
Starch	98.0	1.3	0.6	0.1
Ash	18.2	78.5	2.5	0.8

Based on data of Earle et al. (1946).Percentages may not total 100% because of rounding.

Starch from dent com includes rounded granules from the floury endosperm and polyhedral granules from the horny endosperm. The latter show pronounced pressure facets which are attributed to tension developed during field drying. Diameter of the granules lies between 2 and 30 microns. The hilum is centrally located, the lamellae indistinct or invisible, and the polarization crosses are of moderate intensity. High-amylose varieties tend to have grossly irregular granules which show little or no birefringence and are usually smaller than normal. Waxy constarch granules are similar to those of ordinary cornstarch except that the maximum diameter of the waxy granules may be a few microns larger.

Cell walls of the pericarp contain quite a bit of fibrous material. Cellulose and pentoglycan, in about equal amounts, are the principal constituents. Pentoglycan, when isolated, forms viscous pastes in water and may have some commercial use. It contains residues of D-xylose, L-arabinose, DL-galactose, D-glucose, and glucuronic acid in highly branched molecules.

About 0.1 to 0.3.% raffinose, 0.9 to 1.9% sucrose, 0.2 to 0.5% glucose, 0.1 to 0.4% fructose, and smaller amounts of myo-inositol and glycerol are present in sound corn kernels. Maltose and probably other saccharides appear during germination while raffinose disappears.

Nitrogenous Compounds

As might be expected, most of the nitrogen of the com kernel is present in the form of protein. The proteins can be separated into various fractions based on their solubility in different reagents. The significance of such fractionations can be debated, but the predominant protein of com, zein, is a prolamine; that is, it is soluble in dilute alcohol. Most of the proteins, including zein, are located in the endosper'm. The hull contains little protein. Germ protein usually accounts for between 15 and 25% of the total protein of corn and may contribute 25 to 40% of the total kernel lysine.

Relatively small amounts of nonprotein nitrogen are found in corn. The amounts of amino acids, quaternary-N compounds, nucleosides, purines, and pyrimidines in germ, endosperm, and bran fractions were measured by Christianson *et al.* It appears that ove 50% of the nonprotein nitrogen in whole corn is in the form of amino acids, and they are distributed almost equally between the endosperm and the germ fractions. Their percentage concentration in the germ is, however, several times that in the endosperm. The quaternary-N and heterocyclic-N compounds are found primarily in the germ.

Table 5.2. AMINO ACIDS IN PROTEIN OF MAIZE KERNELS

Amino Acid	Content	Amino Acid	Content
Tryptophan	0.067	Valine	0.477
Threonine	0.355	Arginine	0.470
Isoleucine	0.337	Histidine	0.287
leucine	1.155	Alanine	0.705
Lysine	0.265	Aspartic Acid	0.655
Methaionine	0.197	Glutamic acid	1.768
Cystine	0.170	Glycine	0.386
Phenylalanine	0.463	Proline	0.822
Tyrosine	0.383	Serine	0.477

Amount as grams per 100g of the edible portion.

Lipids and Related Compounds

Analyses of a series of 125 inbreds showed oil content of the whole kernel to vary between 1.2 and 5.7% (Quackenbush *et al.* 1961). Varieties developed particularly for high oil content are known to yield as much as 14% of this constituent. Fatty acids which have been reported by various investigators are 56% linoleic, 30% oleic, and 0.7% linolenic, while stearic, palmitic, arachidic, and others were present in relatively insignificant amounts. The content of lipid by class in three strains of corn is shown in Table 5.2. Strain A was identified as "IHO," or illinqis high oil and contained 13.8% oil; B was strain H51 with 5.3% oil; and C was strain K6, with 2.7% oil content.

The study by Quackenbush and associates reported iodine values from 111 to 151, and tocopherols from 0.03 to 0.33%. Appreciable amounts (around 1%) of phosphatides are present. Lecithin content is about 0.5%.

The oil from the total kernel takes on many of the characteristics of the germ lipids, of course, since the embryo is the preponderant source of fatty material. Although few studies have been published on the subject, it appears that the endosperm oil is similar in most respects to germ oil.

Com oil is one of the seed oils known to have a hypocholesterolemic effect in man and animals. The property of reducing cholesterol in the blood is evidently due, at least in part, to the large amounts of plant sterols, such as ß-sitosterol, in com oil.

Table 5.3. LIPID CONTENT BY CLASS IN THREE CORN STRAINS

Lipid class	Content of class as percent of total oil		
	Strain A	Strain B	Strain C
Hydrocarbons + sterylesters	1.5	2.9	3.4
Triacylglycerols	88.1	79.0	75.8
Free fatty acids	0.4	1.0	1.1
Sterols	2.5	4.5	4.6
Diglycerides + monoglycerides	3.0	3.9	2.1
Phospholipids + glycolipids	4.5	8.7	13.0

Based on data of Weber for corn kernels.

Vitamins and Minerals

The distribution of minerals in the fractions of com kernels is shown in Table 5.4. Since it is known that phytate affects the absorption of some of these minerals, and thus controls their biovailability to a considerable extent, the content of phytate is also shown in this table. Most of the phosphorus is present as the phytate and nearly all of the phytate is present in the germ.

Table 5.4. MINERAL AND PHYTATE CONTENT OF CORN KERNELS

Element or compound and unit	Content in kernel or part			
	Entire kernel	Germ	Endosperm	Hull
Total P,%	0.30	2.04	0.05	0.13
Phytate P, %	0.25	1.80	0.01	0.02
Zn, ppm	18.8	106.	6.66	20.3
Fe, ppm	20.9	145.	10.7	31.8
Mn,ppm	5.20	34.6	2.25	15.8
Cu, ppm	1.50	7.28	0.87	7.2
Ca, ppm	44.0	109.	29.5	582.
Mg, %	0.11	0.84	0.02	0.08
K, %	0.35	1.69	0.07	0.25

O'Dell et al. 1972. Kernels contained 12% germ, 82% endosperm, 6% hull. Data reported on an air dry basis.

Table 5.5. VITAMIN CONTENT OF DENT CORN KERNELS

Nutrient and unit	Average Content
Vitamin A, mg/kg	2.5
Vitamin E, IU/kg	30.
Thiamine, mg./kg	3.8
Riboflavin, mg/kg	1.4
Pantothenic acid, mg/kg	6.6
Biotin, mg/kg	0.08
Folic acid, mg/kg	0.3
Choline, mg/kg	567.
Niacin, mg/kg	28.
Pyridoxine, mg/kg	5.5

Based on data compiled by Watson. Dry weight basis.

Corn is not a particularly good source of vitamins. Although yellow corn is a good source of vitamin A, and is important in animal feeding for this reason (among others), white corn has little or none of this fat-soluble vitamin. Of course, most of the vitamin A is found in the oil, and therefore the germ is the principal depository for this nutrient. Table 5.5 summarizes the vitamin content of corn.

Other Constituents

A compilation summarizing typical values for most of the commonly analyzed components in corn grain will be found in Table 5.6.

A topic of considerable interest to many cereal scientists is the subject of pigments in corn. The system of carotenoid pigments in yellow corn grain is quite complex, and separation of the original compounds has proved to be difficult. When fractions are eluted ,from a magnesia column, spectrophotometry of these fractions provide values for three provitamins as well as eight carotenoids with little or no vitamin activity. In addition to *cis* isomers of the major polyenes, a number of minor components were observed. This method showed that wide differences exist in carotenoid and tocopherol distribution in 125 different inbred lines of corn. Provitamin A ranged from a trace to 7.3 ppm. Lutein, the predominant xanthophyll, ranged from 2 to 33 ppm. The total tocopherol content was found to fall between 0.03 and 0.33%.

Xanthophylls of typical double-cross hybrid yellow dent corns varied from 10 to 30 ppm and carotenes from 1 to 4 ppm. Some exotic strains from

Table 5.6

NUTRIENTS AND OTHER COMPONENTS IN CORN *(Zea mays L.)* [1]

	Unit	Amount
Proximate :		
Water	*g*	10.37
Food energy	*kcal*	365.
	kj	1,527.
Protein (N x 6.25)	*g*	9.42
Total lipid (fat)	*g*	4.74
Carbohydrate, total	*g*	74.26
Crude fiber	*g*	2.90
Ash	*g*	1.20
Lipids :		
Fattyacids :		
Saturated, total	*g*	0.667
16:0	*g*	0.569
18:0	*g*	0.075
Monounsatured, total	*g*	0.251
16:1	*g*	0.004
18:1	*g*	1.247
Polyunsaturated, total	*g*	2.163
18:2	*g*	2.097
18:3	*g*	0.065
Vitamins :		
Ascorbic acid	*mg*	0.
Thiamin	*mg*	0.385
Riboflavin	*mg*	0.201
Niacin	*mg*	3.627
Pantothenic acid	*mg*	0.424
Vitamin B-6	*mg*	0.622

	Unit	Amount
Amino acids :		
Tryptophan	*g*	0.067
Threonine	*g*	0.354
Isoleucine	*g*	0.337
Leucine	*g*	1.155
Lysine	*g*	0.265
Methionine	*g*	0.197
Cystine	*g*	0.170
Phenylalanine	*g*	0.436
Tyrosine	*g*	0.383
Valine	*g*	0.477
Arginine	*g*	0.470
Histidine	*g*	0.287
Alanine	*g*	0.705
Aspartic acid	*g*	0.655
Glutamic acid	*g*	1.768
Glycine	*g*	0.386
Proline	*g*	0.822
Serine	*g*	0.447
Minerals :		
Calcium	*mg*	7.
Iron	*mg*	2.71
Magnesium	*mg*	127.
Phsophorus	*mg*	210.
Potassium	*mg*	287.
Sodium	*mg*	35.
Zinc	*mg*	2.21
Copper	*mg*	0.314
Manganese	*mg*	0.485

[1] Amounts of nutrients in 100 grams, edible portion. From USDA Handbook 8-20. Where nutrients are not indicated, they are either present in amounts to small to be significant or data are not available.

South America contained about 60 ppm, the highest found up to that time. Analyses of several samples indicated that xanthophylls and carotenes may be independently inherited. Outward appearance of the seed was not correlated with xanthophyll content.

Samples of yellow dent corn, representative of those processed by wet-millers, showed a 3- to 4-fold variation in xanthophylls (about 10 to 30 ppm) and carotenes (1-4 ppm). Variation in total carotenoid content (247 to 379 ppm) of two commercial samples of com gluten containing 60 to 70% protein was of the same magnitude as the differences in carotenoid level (19 to 30 ppm) of the whole com used for processing. The total carotenoid content of gluten feed (21% protein) varied from 14 to 34 ppm and that of gluten meal (41% protein) from 65 to 253 ppm. The gluten fractions contained larger quantities of noncarotenoid pigments than did the whole corn.

6

Quality Factors

In discussing the factors affecting quality of com, it is necessary to keep in mind that the analytical values given the most weight will vary depending upon the intended use of the grain. For example, many of the quality factors important in sweet corn will obviously be quite different from those looked for in field com, and both field and sweet com will have different requirements from popcorn. On the other hand, some specifications will remain the same, for example, freedom from significant mold damage and from rodent contamination would be required for all food items and most industrial raw materials. Some of the specifications for field com and sweet com will be discussed in the following paragraphs, but popcorn quality will be covered in the chapter on snack foods.

Field Corn

Federal grain standards.-Field com is a standard item of commerce and closely defined classes and grades have been established by the Federal government. The commercial quality of com as grain cannot be discussed intelligently without consideration of these basic specifications. For the purposes of the Official Grain Standards of the United States (Anon. 1990C), "com" is any grain which consists of 50% or more of the whole kernels in the dent or flint variety of *Zea mays* L. and not more than 10.0% of other grains for which standards have been established under the U.S.

Grain Standards Act. The balance may be made up of other varieties of maize. Other important terms are defined as follows:

(a) "Broken com" is all matter 'that passes readily through a 12/64 round-hole sieve and over a 6/64 round-hole sieve when tested according to procedures described in the Federal Grain Inspection Service (FGIS) instructions.

(b) "Broken com and foreign material," hereafter abbreviated BCFM, is all matter that passes readily through a 12/64 roundhole sieve and all matter other than com that remains in the sieved sample after sieving according to procedures in the Federal Grain Inspection Service (FGIS) instructions.

(c) "Damaged kernels" are kernels and pieces of corn kernels that are badly ground-damaged, badly weather-damaged, diseased, frost-damaged, germ-damaged, heat-damaged, insect-bored, mold-damaged, sprout-damaged, or otherwise materially damaged.

(d) "Foreign material" is all matter that passes readily through a 6/64 ro~d-hole sieve and all matter other than corn that remains on top of the 12/64 round-hole sieve according to procedures given in the FGIS instructions"

(e) "Heat-damaged kernels" are kernels and pieces of corn kernels that are materially discolored and damaged by heat.

(f) "12/64 round-hole sieve" is a metal sieve 0.032 inch thick with round perforations which are 0.1875 (12/64) inch in diameter and spaced 0.25 inch from center to center.

(g) "6/64 round-hole sieve" is a metal sieve 0.032 inch thick with round perforations which are 0.0937 (6/64) inch in diameter which are 5/32 inch from center to center. The perforations of each row shall be staggered in relation to the adjacent row.

Color of the grain furnishes the basis for three fundamental market classes of corn. Yellow corn includes all varieties of yellow and may not include more than 5% by weight of kernels of other colors. A slight tinge of red on kernels which are predominantly yellow shall not affect their classification as yellow corn. White corn must contain at least 98% by weight of white kernels. Grains showing slight tinges oflight straw color or of pink shall be graded white. Mixed corn includes lots of corn not falling into the classes of white or yellow.

These three basic classes are further qualified as Flint, if 95% of more of the kernels by weight are of the flint varieties. If it meets this requirement, the grain would be classed as Yellow Flint Corn, White Flint Corn, or Mixed Flint Corn, as appropriate. "Flint and Dent Corn" is a mixture of the flint and dent varieties which includes from 5 to 95% flint. Dent com requires no modifying adjective signifying the variety.

Each named category must also be classified into 1 of 5 numerical grades or into Sample grade according to the criteria listed in Table 6.1. Grade designations include (in the following order): (1) the letters "U.S.", (2) the abbreviation "No." and the number of the grade or the words "Sample grade", (3) when applicable, the subclass, (4) the class or kind of grain, (5) when applicable, the special grades, and (6) when applicable, the word "dockage" together with the percentage thereof. When applicable, the remarks section of the certificate will h'1clude in the case of a mixed class, the name and approximate percentage of the classes.

A special grade serves to draw attention to a special factor or condition present in the grain and, when applicable, is supplemental to the grade assigned on other bases. Multiple special grade designations will be listed in alphabetical order. Special grades for com are Flint, Flint and Dent, and Waxy Corn. Dent com does not require any statement of clarification. Waxy Com is com that consists of 95% or more waxy corn, when evaluated according to procedures prescribed in FGIS instructions. Popcorn or sweet corn kernels in dent corn are graded as foreign material. Only the test required for fixing the lowest possible grade need be made. Thus, corn which is sour or musty immediately falls into Sample grade and the tests for damaged kernels, bushel weight, foreign material, etc., need not be considered, at least as far as the United States Standards are concerned.

It can be seen that quality of corn of commerce, so far as the U.S. Standards are concerned, is based primarily on: (1) variety, (2) color, (3) test weight per bushel, (4) moisture, and (5) amount and kind of material other than kernels of corn which have not been heat-damaged. Until late in 1985, moisture content was one of the grade determining factors, but it is now only a standard, the amount of which must be shown on the invoice.

Many of the tests required in the Standards can only be applied by visual inspection, or their performance with the aid of complex instrumentation is neither necessary nor desirable. Since they are subjective evaluations, their application requires the services of qualified inspectors, and, in case of litigation, based on a difference of opinion (such litigation is rather rare), the final decision must of necessity be based on a weighing of the evidence of two or more experts. Tests of this sort are less satisfactory from a theoretical standpoint than are more objective criteria, but they seem to function well in practice, perhaps because the vendor is generally disinclined to. employ an expert of his own.

The typical procedure followed when grading a lct of shelled corn, is to

Table 6.1

GRADES AND GRADE REQUIREMENTS FOR CORN

Grade	Minimum test weight per bushel (pounds)	Maximum limits of— Damaged kernels: Heat damaged kernels (percent)	Maximum limits of— Damaged kernels: Total (percent)	Maximum limits of— Broken corn and foreign material (percent)
U.S. No. 1	56.0	0.1	3.0	2.0
U.S. No. 2	54.0	0.2	5.0	3.0
U.S. No. 3	52.0	0.5	7.0	4.0
U.S. No. 4	49.0	1.0	10.0	5.0
U.S. No. 5	46.0	3.0	15.0	7.0

U.S. Sample grade—

U.S. Sample grade is corn that :

(a) Does not meet the requirements for the grades U.S. Nos. 1,2,3,4 or 5; or

(b) Contains 8 or more stones which have an agreegate weight in excess of 0.20 percent of the sample weight, 2 or more pieces of glass, 3 or more crotalaria seeds (*Crota'aria* app) 2 or more castor beans (Ricinus communis L.), 4 or more particles of an unknown. substance(s) or a commonly recognized harmful or toxic substance(s), 8 or moroe cockleburs (Xanthium spp.) or similar seeds singly or in combination, or animal filth in excess of 0.20 percent in 1000 grams;or

(c) Has a musty, sour or commercially objectional foreign odour; or

(d) Is heating or otherwise of distinctly low quality.

insert a trier or probe into the bulk material and draw out a fair average sample. Automatic proportioning devices may also be used to withdraw a small fraction of a flowing stream of the grain. If it is noticed that the interior of the grain is appreciably warmer than the surroundings, the grain is said is said to be "heating" and the whole batch is graded "Sample grade."

Grain removed by the probe is examined carefully for insects. If insects (or their larvae) of kinds that are mown to be destructive to grain are found, the word "Weevilly" is added to the grain grade. Accidental contamination with insects of other types (e.g., ants) may be ignored. The odor of the sample is noted. If it smells musty or sour, indicating extensive microbiological activity, it is graded "Sample grade." The same rating may be assessed if it smells noticeably of insecticides, hydrocarbons, or other foreign odorants.

Weight per bushel is determined by weighing a known volume (rarely a bushel) of grain and calculating the weight of 2,150.42 cubic inches, i.e., the volume of a Winchester bushel. Test weight per bushel is recorded in whole and half pounds, with a fraction of a half pound disregarded. Test weight for corn is determined on the original sample; for some other grains it is determined on a cleaned sample. For the purposes of buying and selling corn, quantity is determined by weight, and a bushel is 56 pounds of corn.

A sieve with round holes 12/64 inch in diameter is used to remove cracked corn and foreign material. Any material other than corn remaining on top of the sieve is removed and added to the screenings. The material is removed and that passing through the screen is weighed and the percentage by weight is calculated to determine the cracked corn and foreign material.

Kernels which have been damaged mechanically or by heating are manually separated from a 250-gm portion of the cleaned corn and are weighed and the percentage calculated. Heat-damaged kernels are segregated from the total damaged portion and weighed separately. Heat damage is manifested by a darkening of the germ and other changes. It destroys the viability of the grain and reduces its milling quality.

A water oven method of determining moisture percentage is the legally prescribed technique, but in practice, moisture may be determined in several ways.

Aflatoxin.-A very serious quality problem that affects corn is aflatoxin contamination. This can be so severe that the grain is unsuitable for any use connected with food or feed. Aflatoxin is a metabolite elaborated by the fungus *Aspergillus flavus* as it grows on corn in the field. There are several types, and some of them are among the most potent carcinogens known and can, in addition cause acute symptoms of poisoning. High temperatures accompanied by drought type conditions during maturation of the corn kernel favor the growth of the mold and production of the poison.

Aflatoxin contamination of corn has proved to be a very difficult regulatory problem. It is fairly common for part of the corn crop in the Southern and Southeastern U.S. to contain these substances at levels exceeding FDA guidelines. This creates conflicts between regulatory authorities and corn growers, corn merchandisers, and corn users who suffer economic damage, often severe, when their grain becomes contaminated through no fault of their own. It seems to be a practical impossibility to remove the toxic materials without irretrievably damaging the food. Furthermore, it is possible for a grain merchant to buy a lot of com in good faith, only to have a government agency with access toa more sensitive testing instrument than he has tell him his property must be destroyed.

Current testing technologies are not adequate (Anon. 1989A). The rapid tests used at the country elevators and terminals are usually based on examining a sample of grain which is being illuminated in a dark cabinet by an ultraviolet lamp. This is merely a screening method which does not quantitate the toxin. Although contaminated corn will have spots on the kernel that will glow a bright greenish-yellow when so tested, false positives are possible. Other tests involve the use of a Holaday-Velasco minicolumn or thin-layer chromatography methods. The mini column test takes about 45 minutes to conduct, and will give an indication of whether or not the content of aflatoxin exceeds the 20 parts per billion guideline established by the FDA. A test using thin-layer chromatographic methods will give quantitative estimations of aflatoxin levels, but requires 3 to 4 hours to perform.

Recently, several new methods based on enzyme immunoassay have been developed to detect aflatoxin in a commercial environment with a minimum chance for false positives. In some cases, they also give rapid results and can be performed by persons with little technical training.

Aflatoxin appeared in a large part of the U.S. com crop harvested in 1988. This was a change from the situation existing for many years, and was due to the extremely dry weather conditions prevalent over much of the com belt in 1988.

Agricultural experts were expecting an aflatoxin outbreak in the south during 1990 because severe hot and dry conditions damaged part of the com crop. In September, roughly half of the com samples examined by Texas state chemists showed more than 20 ppb aflatoxin.

Dry milling quality.-The dry millers of com are insistent on having supplies as free as possible of certain contaminants. Among these unwanted inclusions are insects, the excreta of rodents and birds, toxic weed seeds, kernels invaded by mold growth, and soybeans. The latter are undesirable because they follow the process all the way through and appear in prime grits causing interference with the processing into food or beverage products. The com should not show excessive levels of such physical damage as split and broken pieces because they pick up moisture at a faster rate than whole kernels in the tempering process and thus give an inconsistent and non-uniform response to subsequent treatment. It is not desired to have a large proportion of small kernels. Tough bran which is difficult to break from the endosperm is objectionable. Color is important for most uses of the meal or grits, but special precautions must be taken if the com is destined for alkali-treatment (as for tortilla chips) because the high pH the com encounters during processing affects the pigments.

A procedure for estimating dry-milling quality without going to the expense of a full-scale pilot test was developed by Strohshine *et ai.* 1986. Com is conditioned to 24% moisture content in three stages then degermed in a horizontal drum degerminator, screened, and aspirated to remove hulls.

The material which remains is dried to 17% moisture content and sieved through a screen stack containing 3½W, 5W, 7W, IOW, and 16W sieves.

The fractions are aspirated and suspended in a sodium nitrate solution of 1.275 specific gravity. The pieces of germ float and are removed. Endosperm fractions are dried and weighed. A calculation gives a so-called milling evaluation factor (MEF) which is said to correlate highly with test weight, density, percent floaters, kernel length, horny:floury endosperm, and breakage susceptibility.

Quality for wet milling.-Several laboratory wet-milling procedures have been described. In a recent version (Brown *et ai.* 1982) used a set of artificially dried com samples to compare three factors (viability, test weight, and stress crack intensity) with results from a "steeping index (S1) test." To determine the SI, test samples of com were placed in wire baskets, which were then immersed in commercial corn steeps for the normal 32 hr of the process. The steeped material was evaluated for degree of kernel softening. The S1 was highly correlated with commercial starch recovery but was not well correlated with results from the three quality tests made on the corn before steeping.

The buyers for wet milling companies base their purchases largely on U.S. grade with the bulk of requirements being for U.S. No.2. Undesirable properties are high levels of BCFM, breakage susceptibility, and damage. Broken pieces interfere with processing because they hinder the flow of steepwater through the bed olcorn,;md also the starch and protein emitted from broken surfaces cause gelling problems during steepwater evaporation. The processor can remove broken corn and dust by aspiration, but these materials then go to the feed-product fraction which commands a lower price than the food products obtained from the whole kernels.

Wet millers reject corn that tests positive for mycotoxins. Moldy corn is undesirable because germ recovery and crude oil quality are relatively low from corn with fungi-damaged germ. The germ is also likely to be high in free fatty acids. Contaminating materials such as mycotoxins (as well as insects, debris, etc.) tend to become concentrated in the feed fractions of the wet-milling process, to the detriment of those materials.

Feed grain quality.-The quality requirements specified by the feed manufacturer are to some extent dependent on the type of feed in which the corn will be used. Corn with excessive BCFM can be tolerated in mash or pelleted feeds because the nutrient content in such material is close to that of corn, but if a rolled or flaked product is being made, excessive fines may give the feed an appearance that could be undesirable to a person feeding animals by hand.

All food manufacturers want their ingredients to be reliable sources of the nutrients for which they are being used. Corn is generally the lowest priced source of energy, but this is a factor that is difficult to measure. It will also be used as a source of protein and B-vitamins, and, if it is yellow corn, as a contributor of I3-carotene and xanthophylls. The manufacturer will want the corn to have a moisture content lower than 15.5%, because that level is too high to guarantee storage stability of the grain and the feed made from it (Watson 1987).

Energy content is decreased by low test weight, excessive levels of damaged kernels, and excessive foreign materials such as cobs, husks, etc. Protein contributed by the corn is an important consideration to the miller and the rapid measurement made possible by NIR instruments has encouraged many manufacturers to determine the protein content of each lot of corn rather than rely on published tables for these values.

Feed manufacturers have become highly sensitized to the dangers of mycotoxin contamination in grain supplies. It is unfortunately true that there is always a danger of mold growth and the consequent development of mycotoxins in stored grains. It is also possible for fungi to grow in mixed feeds, altering nutrients and producing odors and flavors which may reduce the product's acceptance by animals. Many feed manufacturers now examine incoming corn supplies, or corn withdrawn from their own storage facilities, with ultaviolet irradiation to detect the bright greenish yellow fluorescence characteristic of certain kinds of mycotoxny.

7

Traditional Food Products From Corn

Bulgur

Traditionally, bulgur is made with wheat; a method for preparing wheat bulgur has been given in the preceding chapter. It appears that corn is being used as a raw material for bulgur in Turkey, and perhaps in other countries (Elgun *et al.* 1990), although there is no commercial production of the material. Corn bulgur is a parboiled whole or crushed kernel corn made by a process generally resembling that used for wheat bulgur. Corn is cooked on the cob and dried. The kernels are shelled from the cob and milled into coarse particles on a stone mill. It is said the nutritive value of corn is increased by this method because the water dissolves vitamins and minerals from the outer layers of the kernels and carries them into the endosperm, similarly to parboiled rice. The product has good storage life because enzymes have been inactivated and it is resistant to attack by insects because of its hard structure. Bulgur made from corn processed in the milky stage is reported to have better flavor than product made from fully mature corn kernels. Sweet corn has been used as a raw material for bulgur. Corn bulgur is prepared for the table in any of the ways used for the wheat version, i.e., as a substitute for rice in pilaf, and as an ingredient in soups. Corn bulgur flour, the finer material resulting from the milling step, is used as an ingredient in several cooked and baked sweet foods.

Tortillas

In some "underdeveloped" areas of the world, corn constitutes a substantial part of the diet of most of the population. For a period of some decades, this was the situation throughout much of the southern U.S., and health of the consumers suffered because of the poor nutrient profile of com. Economic improvement and education on dietary factors gradually reduced and finally eliminated the problem. In South and Central America, com is still the staple food. Physiological disorders attributable to nutritional deficiencies can be observed in these populations. As a result, considerable effort has been devoted to the study of the nutritional' adequacy of com. It has been well-documented that the limiting factor in the growth promoting ability of com protein is its relatively low content of lysine residues, while niacin is the limiting vitamin.

In Central and South America, corn is generally consumed in the form of tortillas, Le., flat thin disks of baked masa. Preparation of masa involves heating and soaking whole kernels of corn in lime water, washing the cooked kernels to remove most of the lime, and grinding the softened endosperm to a paste or dough.

In a typical procedure, one unit volume of corn kernels will be added to two volumes of a lime solution. The mixture of lime water and corn is heated to about 180°F for 20 to 45 minutes, and then allowed to cool. After the mixture has stood overnight, the fluid is decanted and the corn washed 2 or 3 times with water. The germ is generally not removed in this step. The washed kernels are then ground to a fine dough called "masa" which is shaped into patties of perhaps 50 gm weight. These raw tortillas are cooked on both sides on a hot iron plate until some browning of the high spots occur and the piece develops sufficient strength to hold together during subsequent handling.

It has been shown that substantial percentages of nutrients are lost during the preparation of masa. For white corn, the combined physical and chemical losses average 60% of the thiamin, 52% of the riboflavin, 32% of the niacin, 44% of the ether-extractables, and 10% of the nitrogenous substances. Comparative figures for yellow corn are 65%, 32%, 31%, 33%, and 10%, respectively. Yellow corn also loses 21% of the carotene originally present. 'The hot lime water treatment does, however, increase the rate of release of most of the essential amino acids.

Several workers have confirmed that alkali-treated corn, when fed to rats *ad libitum* will prevent the development of the symptoms of niacin deficiency which are associated with consumption of untreated grain. The beneficial effect of alkali treatment is evidently due to the release of niacin from a protected, bound, or otherwise unavailable form. The "potential" niacin can also be released by prolonged boiling.

Reports on the effect of supplementing corn protein with purified amino

Table 7.1

NUTRIENTS AND OTHER COMPONENTS IN CANNED LYE HOMINY

	Unit	Amount
Proximate :		
Water	g	82.53
Food energy	kcal	72.
	kj	300.
Protein (N x 6.25)	g	1.48
Total lipid (fat)	g	0.88
Carbohydrate, total	g	14.26
Crude fiber	g	0.45
Ash	g	0.86
Lipids :		
Fatty acids :		
Saturated, total	g	0.123
16:0	g	0.105
18:0	g	0.014
Monounsaturated, total	g	0.231
16:1	g	0.001
18:1	g	0.230
Polyunsaturated, total	g	0.399
18:2	g	0.387
18:3	g	0.012
Vitamins :		
Ascorbic acid	mg	0.
Thiamin	mg	0.003
Riboflavin	mg	0.006
Niacin	mg	0.033
Pantothenic acid	mg	0.154
Vitamin B-6	mg	0.005
Folacin	mcg	1.

	Unit	Amount
Amino acids :		
Tryptophan	g	0.008
Threonine	g	0.050
Isoleucine	g	0.058
Leucine	g	0.202
Lysine	g	0.033
Methionine	g	0.031
Cystine	g	0.033
Phenylalanine	g	0.076
Tyrosine	g	0.056
Valine	g	0.077
Arginine	g	0.068
Histidine	g	0.045
Alanine	g	0.107
Aspartic acid	g	0.115
Glutamic acid	g	0.299
Glycine	g	0.052
Proline	g	0.138
Serine	g	0.065
Minerals :		
Calcium	mg	10.
Iron	mg	0.62
Magnesium	mg	16.
Phsophorus	mg	35.
Potassium	mg	9.
Sodium	mg	210.
Zinc	mg	1.05
Copper	mg	0.030
Manganese	mg	0.070

[1] Amounts of nutrients in 100 grams, edible portion. From USDA Handbook 8-20. Where nutrients are not Indicated, they are either present in amounts to small to be significant or data are not available

acids confirmed that lysine is the first limiting amino acid. Other workers stated these results might have been more informative if the total nitrogen intake had been maintained at an optimal level or if the effect of nonesssential amino acid intake on the nitrogen retention had been followed. It was shown that the nitrogen retention of adult men fed isocaloric diets was significantly greater when white corn meal provided 8.0 gm nitrogen per subject per day than when lower amounts were ingested. When a, suboptimal amount (6.0 gm N/subjectJday) was fed, the optimal Nretention level could be re-established by the addition of 2.0 gm nitrogen from any of several purified essential amino acids or even certain other purified sources of nitrogen. Therefore, it appears that nitrogen from any metabolically usable source is the first limiting nitrogenous factor in corn protein, as determined by nitrogen retention in adult men.

In an investigation of the factors influencing the estimation of - availability to rats of threonine, isoleucine, and valine in corn, it was shown that availability of threonine was influenced by changes in composition of the basal diet and by the amounts of protein and calories in it. Interaction between the calorie and protein levels, as indicated by growth rate, was eliminated by calculating availability values from a standard curve based on the amount of amino acids consumed rather than the amino acid content of the diet. Low utilization of zein and corn gluten, when assessed by the growth method was found to be due mainly to antagonism between leucine and isoleucine in the experimental diet. Elimination of this antagonism resulted in higher availability values. Although a considerable amount of valine was excreted in the feces of rats fed zein, the values for availability assessed by the growth method increased when the leucine content of the experimental diet was decreased.

Further work evaluated factors affecting availability of lysine in corn and rice, as determined by growth and fecal analysis methods. In general, the lysine of proteins obtained from these two grains was found to be highly available. Values obtained by the growth method were influenced by changes in the composition of the diet and the method of calculating availability. Data were most reproducible and least influenced by other factors when availability was calculated as a function of lysine consumption rather than a function of the lysine level in the diet. The fecal analysis method gave somewhat lower values for corn products.

Lye Hominy

Lye hominy is prepared somewhat like nixtamal, in that the initial step involves soaking whole dent corn kernels in hot alkaline water. Lime water does not, however, make acceptable lye hominy. The loosened hulls and other debris are washed from the kernels, and the alkali is washed and soaked out. The swollen kernels, moderately soft but cohesive and retaining their original shape, are canned in water containing a little salt. About 1.6 million cases of this delicacy were canned in 1982, less than 3% of the total for canned sweet corn.

An old explanation of a commercial procedure for canning lye hominy includes the following directions. Use white dent corn of the broad-type kernel, hard and flinty. Typical equipment would include a round tank about four feet deep, equipped with a circular stirrer. Add 400 lb of clean corn to the tank, and pump in enough water to cover six inches above the top of the corn. Turn on the steam and have the water boiling before attempting to start the agitator, as the corn packs very closely on the bottom, making it almost impossible to start mixing unless the corn is stirred or agitated first.

After the agitator is started, add enough lye to make a two percent solution. The higher the concentration, the shorter the time needed to remove the hulls and the less absorption of lye into the kernels. Care must be taken when adding the lye to the hot water to prevent splashing aqd foaming. First add the lye to cold water and then add this solution to the tank, a small quantity at a time. The corn is often added to a boiling two percent lye solution and kept boiling for about forty minutes. Where fresh corn is used, the temperature can be reduced.

Some manufacturers prefer to use one percent and give the corn a longer cook, as they believe the lye is not absorbed as readily and is more easily removed. The weaker the lye, however, the longer the time required in handling. Less than a two percent solution requires too long a cooking time, while over two percent is apt to cause discoloration due to lye burning.

After removing the lye by boiling the kernels in fresh water several times, the hominy can be bleached to make a white product by using 1.5 ounces of sodium bisulfite for each bushel of corn and then boiling 15 to 20 minutes. The bisulfites should be removed by washing in at least three changes of fresh water. As soon as the hulls are loos~ned, the corn must be passed to the hulling machine. Delay in removing the surplus lye will cause the corn to soften.

A tomato pulping machine with an 8-mesh wire sieve may be used for this purpose after attaching an inch perforated pipe by means of a hose to the top of the cover of the machine. Start the water in the pulping machine and draw off the corn from the lye tank, passing it through the pulper and to the cooking tank. Fill the wash tank with fresh water to within a few inches from the top. Start the agitator, turn on the steam, and cook until the corn is soft enough to mash between the teeth. This will require from 1 to 1.5 hours cooking. Fill 13.5 to 14 oz into #2½ enamel cans. Cover with either hot brine or hot water. Exhaust can for three minutes and process 70 minutes at 240°F. Cool rapidly to avoid discoloration.

There are yellow and white varieties of lye hominy made, of course, from yellow and white corn, respectively. Lye hominy is used in recipes somewhat like pasta, rice, or potato chunks as a basis for casseroles, as an ingredient in soups, or as a staple accompanying the entree. A home method of preparing lye hominy for the table consists of draining the hominy, and frying it with onion pieces in bacon grease until the kernels become firm through loss of Bome of their water. content, then seasoning the mixture with salt and pepp\r. Apparently, there are no frozen versions of this item. Lye hominy is totally different from hominy grits (which is nothing more than coarsely ground corn endosperm), and both of them are totally different from hominw feed (which is a combination of by-products from the milling operation}- except that all are made from corn.

The contents of nutrients and other components to be found in typical examples of canned lye hominy have been assembled in Table 7.1.

8

Corn Milling

INTRODUCTION

There are two distinct types of corn milling operations. In the oldest type of corn processing, dry milling, the field corn of commerce is reduced in size and separated into components to make different kinds of meal, somewhat like wheat is milled, though corn milling is much the simpler procedure. In wet milling of corn, a more complete separation of the kernel's components is achieved, with starch and oil as the derivatives of major economic importance. Starch can be further processed into corn sweeteners while oil goes through a series of purifications and treatments which render it useful for a number of different applications, although its primary use is as a food ingredient. Wet milling and dry milling will be discussed separately in this chapter.

DRY MILLING OF CORN

There is a fairly large consumption of dry milled corn products in the world. The consumer contacts these ingredients mainly in three different products: (1) corn bread and muffins, which are chemically-leavened baked products containing corn meal with some wheat flour added to give structure, (2) grits, a coarsely ground meal which is cooked with water to give a product used either as a breakfast cereal or in the same applications as mashed potatoes, and (3) snack foods of the corn chip or corn puff type. There is also a large usage of corn in tortillas, for which the kernels must be alkali-treated before use; if the traditional method is followed, whole kernels are treated, not flour, so the process is outside the scope of this section. It is known, however, that some housewives use corn meal instead of masa and add a pinch or two of lime with the water to simulate the familiar masa flavor. There is also a alkali-treated meal called masa harina which is sold at retail for home use. The following discussion will be restricted to the grinding of dry field corn kernels.

Corn was originally ground on buhr mills, just as wheat and rye were. A very few of these mills still remain, furnishing corn meal for those folks who like the old-time flavor. The chief note in the old-time flavor is rancidity, since corn meal ground on buhr mills contains all the germ and the oil therein, so that oxidation of this unstable fat progresses rapidly once the kernel is ground. Removal of the germ before grinding is an essential feature of all modern corn milling. When wheat is ground on roller mills, the germ is flattened and the mostly intact piece can be removed quite easily by sieving and air separation methods. The germ of corn is, however, relatively large (12% of the kernel cornpared to 3% for wheat) so that it tends to break up into small pieces when sheared between rollers. These fine chunks are hard to remove by the methods and machinery used for wheat millipg, so a different approach is required. The Beall degerminator was developed specifically for dislodging the germ of corn without breaking it into pieces. This machine is described in more detail in a subsequent section.

The Dry Milling Process

The dry milling process consists of the following steps: (1) cleaning, (2) conditioning, (3) degerming, (4) drying, (5) cooling, (6) grading, (7) aspirating, (8) grinding, and (9) sifting and classifYing. From mill to mill, there may be different arrangements of these steps, with some omitted and others added, but the basic flow plan will remain the same since there are certain operations which must always be accornplished to yield the desired end products. Typical yields of products are shown in Table 8.1.

Table 8.1 Dry Milling Products From Corn.

Product	Typical Yield, %
Flaking, grits	12
Brewers, grits	28
Fine grits, meal & flour	20
Corn oil	1
Hominy feed	37
Shrinkage	2
Whole Corn	100

Cleaning and conditioning.-When corn is received at the mill, it is cleaned by both dry and wet processes. Many of the dry cleaning steps are similar to those used for any other grain. They involve sieving, separating particles by shape and density, and removing ferromagnetic metals by permanent magnets. A problem which is peculiar to corn is the need for giving special attention to the removal of rat pellets, many of which are similar in size and weight to corn kernels. Electrostatic separators are used to insure cornplete removal of these contaminants; these devices usually follow the reels and disk separators and are positioned before the wet stoner and washer.

Next, the cleaned corn is conditioned, which basically means that water is added and the moisture allowed to equilibrate within the kernels. Objectives of conditioning are to: (1) loosen the germ, (2) moisten the germ more than the endosperm, making the germ more flexible and easier to separate, and (3) loosen the bran and toughen it, making it easier to remove in large pieces. Tempering or conditioning may consist of 1, 2, or 3 stages. A moisture content of 21% is considered optimal. This is considerably higher than the 15% typical of wheat tempered for milling because the germ of corn tends to be more fragile than the germ of wheat and if the corn germ is too dry it will break into small pieces later in the process. The extra moisture toughens both the germ and the bran without having deleterious effects on the endosperm. Conveyors and whizzers are the principal types of equipment used in the conditioning process.

Degermination.-Degerming by Beall degerminators or Entoleters is the next step. Beall degerminators are attrition mills. There are different designs in use. One of the cornmon types consists essentially of a cast iron inner cone which rotates inside a conical housing. The rotor has knob-like protrusions on its outer surface and the housing has perforated screens. The end of the rotor and housing are also provided with knobs, giving additional attrition. Corn kernels are fed into the space between these cones, at the smaller end. As they move by gravity to the larger end of the mill, toward the base of the cones, they are rubbed and struck by the projections. When the kernel finally reaches the bottom of the cone, it has been dehulled and the germ knocked loose. The smaller pieces of corn and germ pass through the perforated housing. If the screen has openings of 18/64 or 20/64 inch, the fraction which passes through will usually amount to 60 to 80% of the total. The larger pieces. will exit at the end, through a weighted gate which can be regulated to restrict the flow and to some extent control the action of the degermer. To give greater control, the rotating cone can also be moved back and forth~o adjust its clearance relative to the outer cone.

Entoleters, which are impact mills rather than attrition mills, can also be used for dehulling and degerming. These machines consist of a circular chamber housing a rapidly rotating disc to which are affixed several steel pins or small rods. Grain falls through an central opening in the roof of the enclosure and lands on the rotating disk. Centrifugal force flings the kernels with considerable velocity on to the pins and on to the wall of the chamber. These multiple impacts, with minimal shear, dehull and degerm the kernel.

The large particles which corne out of the tail of the degermer are called tail stock or hominy stock. They are used primarily for flaked breakfast cereals. The finer particles of broken corn and germ which pass through the screen perforations are called through-stock. In large mills these two streams are kept separate until a later stage in the process. The tail stock is dried, cooled, aspirated, and sifted. If it is not required for flaking grits, it is sent to conventional roller mills where it is reduced in particle size by a series of grinding, sifting, and aspirating steps.

Reduction and classifying.-So that the intermediate products can be handled on roller mills and sieves, the through stock must be dried to 15 to 18% moisture following the degerming operation. Drying is performed by conventional rotary steam tube dryers of inclined drum configuration, while cooling is done by either rotary cereal coolers or fluid bed coolers using ambient air. After drying and cooling, the through-stock is sifted or classified by particle size and enters into a conventional long reduction system having the function of removing bran and germ while releasing a maximum amount of clean large grits. After the first sifting operation, this material may be processed over gravity tables to insure a more cornplete separation of the large germ from the larger grits before the grits are sent on to the aspirators, grinding rolls, and sifters. The germ which is removed in all of these steps is collected for further processing in the oil mill.

The milling operation consists of the steps of grinding, sifting, classifying, purifying, aspirating, and, in some cases, final drying. The normal flow is through break rolls and then to plansifters. Fines go to the next break roll and coarse particles to purifiers and then to the germ rolls. The germ rolls flatten the germs so that they are readily removed by sifting. The break rolls are followed by reduction rolls which grind the endosperm to the desired particle size. In a corn mill, the break system is longer than the reduction system. Since corn flour is not as important a product as corn grits or corn meal, a long reduction system is not needed to make a product of very fine particle size.

Corn flour is produced in limited amounts on the long reduction system handling the through stock and in the system handling the large hominy grits. This is an inadvertent consequence of the endosperm fracture occurring during the reduction operation. If corn flour is required in large quantities, it is frequently made by breaking down the grits in impact mills or other high speed grinding equipment.

The tip caps found at the pointed end of the corn kernel create a problem peculiar to corn milling. Since they are an intense black colour, they show up very clearly in corn meal and flour; they are greatly disliked by consumers because they give the impression of being contaminants. The tip caps are removed with the corn bran by aspirators.

Gentle treatment of the germ is achieved by a special system of rolls which is reserved for cleaning this fraction of the. kernels. Since the germ is about 12% of the kernel and contains about 34% oil, it is an economically important by-product. Oil extraction processes cannot operate efficiently if the germ they receive contains substantial amounts of foreign material, therefore careful cleaning of the germ fraction is essential. Every dry corn milling plant has an oil extraction system connected with it.

The yield of endosperm products will fall between 65 and 70% of the whole kernel. Other milling processes have been devised to improve purity of the meal. For example, one modification involves a two-step tempering of the grain followed by an abrasive removal of bran by wire brushes before the kernels are ground and sifted.

Hominy feed is the principal by-product made in the dry corn mill. It will contain the bran, tip caps, ground cake from the oil mill, and the tailings streams from the grit reduction system. Hominy feed will contain about 5% fat and 10% protein. It is used by formula feed manufacturers.

Uses and specifications of products.-The coarsest product of the dry milling process is generally called hominy grits or flaking grits. These are the major ingredients used in making the breakfast cereal known as corn flakes. Their particle size or granulation is usually described as being 100% through a No. 3.5 mesh screen and 100% retained on a No.6 screen. A series of granule sizes ranging from coarse grits (through a No. 10 and retained on a No. 12) to fine grits (through a No. 16 and retained on a No. 20 or No. 30 screen) can be sold separately or blended for sale to manufacturers of breakfast cereals and snack foods. Brewers grits also fall in this size range. All of these grits flow readily, have good colour, are generally free from dust and bran contamination, and will contain less than 1% fat and less than 14% moisture.

Most products identified as corn meal will pass through a No. 20 mesh screen and be retained on a No. 45 mesh sieve. This is the product sold in consumer size packages and used in many bakery mixes, as for pancakes, corn bread, and muffins. It can range in fat content up to 1.5%.

Corn cones is a finer granulation of corn meal that mostly passes through a No. 45 sieve and is collected on a No. 80 screen. This fraction contains much of the vitreous starch of the kernel and has a fat content of about 0.7 to 1.5%. Corn cones have a rather unique, almost round shape and are used both in bakery mixes and breakfast cereals. Corn flours are simply ground products that are too fine to be sold as meal. They will, in most available forms, pass through a No. 80 mesh sieve. They are used in bakery mixes of several types, as coatings on foods to be baked or fried, in baby foods, as fillers, binders, and carriers in sausages and the like, as ingredients in breakfast cereals, and as fermentation substrates. In the U.K., and perhaps elsewhere, corn flour is often understood to mean corn starch, which is, of course, an entirely different product from the corn flour being considered here.

Table 8.2 shows the typical cornposition of dry milled corn product streams. It should be noted, however, that these streams are not usually sold as separate finished products (except for hominy feed), but are cornbined with broken corn and subsequently dried and hammer milled together to produce hominy feed. The germ cornposition refers to the material before removal of the oil by pressing or solvent extraction.

Further Processing

A group of so-called "specialty products" are produced by heattreating grits. A large amount of this material is used in non-food applications, as for-foundry core binders and in wallpaper paste, but some is also used in foods and beverages. Raw corn grits are processed by steaming them and applying heat and pressure, as in a roller mill. The purpose is to gelatinize, or partially gelatinize, the starch and to convert the grit to a shape which is more suitable for its intended application. The steel flaking rolls are usually either 20 inches in diameter by 24 inches in length or 32 X 40 inches, and are heated externally by gas flames. For some purposes, the flakes are finely ground after processing, but confectionery flakes and brewer's flakes are not ground. The products produced in these systems are gelatinized or dextrinized to a specific point determined by the heat and moisture conditions. Reduction of moisture will cause the starch to be dextrinized to a greater extent while reducing the gelatinization. This condition will yield a product with high adhesive

Table 8.2. TYPICAL COMPOSITION OF DRY-MILLING BY-PRODUCT STREAMS

Component	Standard meal	Corn germ	Corn bran	Hominy feed
	%	%	%	%
Moisture	14.0	9.6	10.0	13.5
Protein	11.0	15.8	8.0	8.0
Fat	4.5	23.8	4.5	3.4
Crude fiber	2.5	5.7	12.0	4.7
Ash	2.0	6.7	2.5	2.0
Starch	60.0	18.4	35.0	61.0
Other polysaccharides	6.0	20.0	28.0	7.4

[1] Alexander (1987). Percentages reported on "as is" basis.

quality but low absorption. Increase of moisture during heat processing will yield high absorption and lower adhesive properties, qualities desirable in brewer's flakes and confectionery flakes.

WET MILLING OF CORN

History

Starch was separated from other grains and from root vegetables such as potatoes long before corn was used as a raw material. Doubtless the development of wet milling was based on the observation that a white, insoluble granular material settled to the bottom of the pan when quantities of cut tubers were washed. The first starch factory in the U.S. was established in 1802-it used potatoes as raw material. In 1842,Thomas Kingsford founded the cornstarch refining industry. He was the first person to extract starch from maize on a commercial basis. The basic principles relied upon by Kingsford are still used in the wet milling industry, though of course many technical improvements have been made. Some other grains are wet-milled today, but corn far exceeds the combined total of all other cereals given this treatment.

In the original process, corn was placed in wooden, flat bottomed tanks, covered with warm water and allowed to stand. After the corn was softened throughout, the kernels were ground in stone mills and sieved and washed on silk-screened shakers powered by reciprocating engines. The slurry that was washed through the sieves was put in wooden tubs, treated with caustic soda, and allowed to settle. After settling, the effluent was sent to the sewer, taking with it all of the gluten and soluble materials. This settling process was repeated three times for each batch.

Yield calculations were not made in those days (or, at least, not recorded) but it seems probable that the starch recovery could not have been much above 50% of the total available starch. No chemical tests were run in the plant, but an effort was made to control the alkalinity of the settling tanks. Key employees were trained to test the slurry in the settlers, and they either approved the batch or caused more caustic soda to be added. When the starch was hydrolyzed to convert it to "glucose." tasters who had no other responsibility judged the cornpleteness of the conversion.

The need to improve the yield, to reduce the discharge of high solids sewage, and to gain better control of product quality has spurred the development of many improvements in corn refining processes. Marked increases in efficiency have led to low priced products which have opened many new markets for starch derivatives. New products, especially high fructose corn syrups, have brought prosperity to existing cornpanies and supported the construction of many new plants. The oil side of the mill has perhaps not benefited as much from technological advancement, although a steady' improvement in quality and efficiency can also be noted in these operations.

Table 8.3 Wet Milling Products from Corn

Product	Typical Yield, %
Starch	67.50
Crude Oil	3.86
Germ cake	3.64
Solubles	7.60
Fiber	9.50
Gluten meal	5.80
Other	2.10
Whole Corn	100.00

Liverzey (1982), Yield expressed on the dry basis.

Modern Processes

In a conventional wet-milling operation, the final products and by products will normally be starch, crude oil, germ cake, solubles, fiber, gluten meal, and "other." The germ cake, fiber, and solubles are usually cornbined and sold as gluten feed. Table 8.3 gives representative yield figures.

Cleaning.-Corn wet-millers use only shelled corn and primarily No. 2 yellow dent corn. The grain is shipped into the plants at a typical rate of about 260 carloads per day, and it is immediately transferred from the railcars to cleaners and then to temporary storage bins to await further handling. The moisture content of the grain which cornes into the receiving area of the plant varies from 10 to 25%.

The cleaning operations involve passing the corn past powerful magnets which remove scrap iron, steel, nails, or other ferromagnetic tramp metal which has been introduced into the corn by previous handling. After it passes the magnets, the grain is weighed on scale hoppers and sampled for quality.

Fig. 8.1 Softened corn kernels droping out of steeping tanks.

After sampling and weighing, the corn is further cleaned by passing it over perforated screens. The upper screen has holes just large enough to let corn and smaller particles through while the lower screen holds back the corn but lets smaller pieces of chipped corn, cobs, sticks, and stones pass through. Next, the corn is contacted with high velocity air which removes low density materials and delivers them to cyclone dust collectors. Because the corn itself is considerably agitated by the air, a further separation of the higher density materials occurs at this point, and these materials are removed from the bottom of the flowing stream of corn.

Steeping.-The cleaned kernels are transferred to "steep" tanks holding 2,000 to 3,000 bushels. Here they are soaked for 36 to 48 hr in water at about 120° to 130°F. The added water contains a slight amount of sulfur dioxide to prevent germination and to retard fermentation and other undesirable microbiological changes. It also appears that the sulfur dioxide weakens the protein which binds the starch grains together. Although many microorganisms are inhibited by these conditions, lactic acid producing bacteria can grow and the acid they produce buffers the pH and assists in softening the kernel. Corn refiners have traditionally manufactured their own sulfur dioxide by burning sulfur in rotary ovens.

In the early days of wet-milling of corn, batch methods were used in steeping. In the other steps of processing, water was discarded. The result was a large demand for water, and large amounts of product were lost in the waste water discharged from the plant. From the early days of the industry, corn wet-millers had been concerned about the waste water problem. They recognized that the wastes produced pollution and odor problems and that part of their raw material was being lost. In addition, there was a desire to cut down on the water requirements, which sometimes outran the available supply. In the period from 1925 to 1937, several inventors obtained patents dealing with the "bottling up" or "corking up" of the corn refining process; these were plans for recycling the water. Changes of this general type increased the yield of starch from 90 to almost 100% of the theoretical, greatly improved the efficiency of the entire process, reduced the waste disposal problems, and saved water, thus lowering the operating costs.

As a result of these developments, wet-milling is now conducted as a countercurrent system. The freshest water passes over corn which has been steeped the longest, assuring removal of the maximum amount of soluble material. About 10 gallons of fresh water are used per bushel of corn to wash the separated starch at the end of the process. This water then flows countercurrently back through the separation system and finally goes to the steep tanks at about 1% solids. About 40% of the initial intake, or about 4 gallons per bushel, are absorbed by the corn in the tanks, while the remainder is withdrawn as "light" steepwater containing about 5% dry substance-solubles leached from the corn. This steepwater is subsequently concentrated by evaporation to a slurry of about 54% dry matter. There are about 3 pounds of solubles per bushel of corn.

Figure 8.1 shows corn being dropped out of a steeping tank. It will be carried by a vibrating type conveyor to the grinding department.

In the early days of the industry, steepwater was discarded, but its nutritive value was eventually recognized and the wetmillers then started to concentrate it and add gluten and bran to make corn gluten feed. Steepwater is excellent for growing acid-producing bacteria, and these bacteria are beneficial when fed to ruminants.

Degermination.-Corn which has been softened by the steeping process is ready for the first milling operation. This step, called "degermination," separates the oil rich germ from the starch, gluten, hulls, and fiber. The softened corn is first passed over shakers in a second cleaning operation which removes any foreign material which has escaped the first series of cleaning operations or has been picked up in subsequent handling.

Fig. 8.2 View of an opened degerminating mill.

The corn is then ground in attrition mills. These units consist of two circular plates with teeth or cogs projecting from their facing surfaces. Some models have the two plates rotating in opposite directions, while others have one stationary plate and one rotating plate. The spacing between the plates and other conditions are adjusted so that the rubbery germ is torn from the rest of the kernel without fragmenting the germ. Figure 8.2 shows the inside of a degerminating mill, giving a view of the teeth or knobs which tear apart the softened corn kernels.

Slurry from the attrition mills, consisting of endosperm, germ, and fiber, is diluted with a carefully controlled amount of process water. In the older style of factory, this mixture was transferred to a series of long troughs which served to separate the lighter oil-bearing germs from the rest of the material. There was an agitator in the lower part of the troughs which kept the products mixed and helped to free any germs which might have been entrapped. In modern plants, the mixture is fed to a battery of hydroclones. The germ, being lighter, is spun off at the top while the heavier endosperm and fiber flow out the bottom. The germ is washed free of starch, dewatered, and dried before being sent to the oil extraction and refining plant.

In the old method, germs were removed from the top of the tanks along with some of the slurry. The germ-slurry mixture was then transferred to reels or shakers where the slurry was washed off and returned to the starch-gluten stream. At the same time that the germ was leaving the top of the tank, the mixture of starch, gluten, hulls, and fiber was leaving at the bottom and being sent to reels and shakers where most of the water and soluble materials were removed. Quality control tests were run to insure that the germ was cornpletely separated from the starch and gluten, and, if not, the degermination process was repeated on the solids remaining after the starch-gluten slurry was passed over the reels and shakers.

Separation of hulls and fiber.-The wet mash of fiber, hulls, gluten, and starch which remains on the reels and shakers is fed to mills which grind the materials to a very small particle size. Hulls and fibers are not reduced in size as much as the starch and gluten in this milling process. The industry used roughened flat mill stones for many years. These buhr mills were circular and rotated at fairly high speeds over stationary stones. This process reduced the charge to a fine slurry. Eventually, the buhr mills were replaced by stainless steel vertical mills which perform the same function but require less maintenance and last longer.

In the older plants, the hull and fiber particles were removed from the mill effiuent by a series of reels (rotating hexagonal screens of copper) and shakers (flat nylon sieves). Modern plants separate fiber and hull from starch and gluten by screening the mixture over a series of D.S.M. (Dutch Slate Mines) screens. These have replaced all shakers and reels.

Gluten-starch separation.-The corn refining industry has always used gravitational methods for separating starch and gluten. In. the earliest plants, large wooden tubs were used to hold the slurry until the starch settled to the bottom. These tubs were replaced by long, narrow, slightly inclined wooden troughs called starch tables which permitted a constant flow of the starch-gluten slurry.

The starch tables were about two feet wide and 100 feet long. They had a pitch of about five inches which caused the slurry to flow slowly down them. The tables were almost always wooden although other materials such as concrete and slate have been used. For each 1,000 bushels of corn that were ground, about 3,000 square feet of table area were required. Since many plants mill upwards of 50,000 bushels per day, the space required for tabling starch was enormous. In fact, the table house was usually the largest building in the refinery.

The starch-gluten slurry flowed slowly down the tables and sedimentation occurred with the heavier starch depositing on the bottom and the gluten being removed at the top of the lower end ofthe tables. The first tabling operation produced starch containing small percentages of gluten and gluten containing larger percentages of starch. Further purification of the starch was accomplished by repeating the tabling operation or by washing the starch on rotary vacuum filters.

Development of the tabling separation method played a major role in improving the yield of products and lowering their cost. It did result in the loss of some starch in the effiuent, however, and centrifuges were first introduced to recover additional starch and to raise the protein content of the gluten fraction. In the 1940s, centrifuges began to replace tables for the primary starch-gluten separation. Large highly efficient continuous centrifuges now take the starch-gluten slurry, handle large volumes of materials, and yield products of high purity. The tremendous floor space required for the tables is no longer needed. In modem plants, the entire operation is now inclosed and a major source of air contamination in the plant has been eliminated. Figure 8.3 is a photo of a primary separation centrifugal, opened to show the rotor.

The starch stream from the centrifuges contains about 1 to 2% protein. It is further purified to less than 0.3% protein by passing it through many

Fig. 8.3 A primary centrifugal separator for corn starch.

small hydro clones. This is the only point in the entire wet-milling process where additional water is needed (i.e., subsequent to the steeping operation). The extra water must be added to wash out the last traces of the solubles in the starch. Normally, it takes 7 to 10 gallons of water per bushel of corn.

Wet starch from the hydroclones is dewatered on rotary vacuum filters, moving belt filters, or basket centrifuges. The final drying takes place in tunnel (kiln) driers, continuous belt hot air driers, or in spray driers. After centrifugation, the gluten fraction is a thin slurry that is either separated by sedimentation in large tanks or, more often, is dewatered and de starched in another centrifuge, then filtered and dried. It is then ready to be used as corn gluten meal or corn gluten feed, or processed to recover the protein, zein, which has some nonfeed uses.

Recent Developments

In an attempt to simplify the separation of starch from the other fractions of the corn kernel, the effect of high-pressure disintegration of suitably prepared raw materials was investigated. The intent of this study was to replace the attrition-, pin-, and disc-mills currently used for grinding the soaked kernels with a high-pressure homogenizer. In a pilot plant operation, about ten tons per hour of coarse degerminated maize material was ground in a homogenizer which, though not described in cornplete detail in the referenced article, appeared to have some basic resemblances to the machines used to homogenize milk. The corn had" been steeped for twelve hours at atmospheric pressure before grinding. Disintegration is caused mainly by pitting (probably meaning cavitation), with assistance from shearing action and collisions. Valve geometry exerts a decisive influence on the efficiency of the grinding. Trials in which maize was steeped both with and without application of pressure and sulfur dioxide, and then homogenized after degermination, showed that endosperm so prepared could be selectively disi,ntegrated. Thorough soaking of the endosperm was a necessary pre-condition to releasing starch granules from the matrix in high purity. Cell disintegration through homogenization had a positive effect on starch yield but starch from the limited tests contained a rather high amount of protein.

Wet-milling Other Grains

Grain sorghum can be processed in much the same way as corn to yield a starch that is about the equal of cornstarch in most of its important characteristics. Although wet-milling of the whole wheat kernel to produce starch is technically feasible, it is believed that most current wheat starch production methods are based on the initial formation of a dough from lowgrade wheat flour. Most wheat starch is the by-product of a gluten separation process. Rice can also be processed by wet-milling techniques to produce a fine quality starch, but the high cost of the raw material makes the starch uneconomical except for a few very specialized uses, such as a cornponent of face powder. Rice starch or rice powder has been used as a cosmetic for a long time.

STARCH CONVERSION

The factor that has impelled the great increase in corn wet-milling during the past few decades has been the seemingless limitless market for the hydrolysis products of corn starch. Always predominant among these products are the several kinds of sweeteners (corn syrups of many different varieties, dextrose, etc.), but there are a few bulking agents of low or no sweetness which fill certain specialized niches in food formulation.

Acid Hydrolysis

A large part of the cornstarch that is produced is further processed to make corn sweeteners. This process, called "conversion" by the industry, involves catalyzed hydrolysis of the starch. In the conversion process as well as in dextrinization, starch modification, and starch derivative formation, the nature of the manufacturing operation undergoes an profound change. The wet-milling process is almost entirely mechanical in nature and has many resemblances to other milling operations, differing from them mainly in the large amounts of water which are used. Conversion and the other processes mentioned above are largely chemical in nature.

Starch is made up of two forms of glucose polymers: amylose, the linear fraction, which is a chemical cornpound cornprised of many D-glucose molecules linked at the 1 and 4 positions, and amylopectin, a branched molecule which includes not only the 1-4 bonds but also a significant number of bonds at the 1 and 6 positions. There is about one branch for each 25 to 30 glucose units in amylopectin. There are probably very small numbers of other linkages in the starch molecule. In chemical hydro1ysis, it appears that the 1-4 and 1-6 linkages are cleaved at about the same rate. When enzymes are catalyzing the hydrolysis, however, the rates are very different.

When starch is hydrolyzed with water and an appropriate catalyst, the elements of water are added to the starch molecules. This means that a given amount of starch will yield a larger amount of hydrolytic products. The extreme case is the conversion of starch to the ultimate product, dextrose. The relationship is shown in the equation

$$\underset{\text{starch}}{(C_6H_{12}0_5)n} + \underset{\text{water}}{nH_20} = \underset{\text{glucose}}{n(C_6H_{12}0_6)}$$

Theoretically, 162 grams of starch will react with 18 grams of water to produce 180 grams of dextrose. Lesser degrees of hydrolysis, which produce maltose and other polysaccharides, will result in smaller weight gains.

The rate of hydrolysis of starch is increased by raising the temperature and by increasing the acid concentration. Because glucose can react under these conditions to produce a disaccharide, and because this is an equilibrium reaction, the overall rate of reaction appears to be slower at higher starch concentrations. These l:lide reactions as well as the Maillard browning reaction and oxidation, which results in the production of furfural-type products, are all undesirable. They all lead to decreased yields of desirable products. and increased production of materials which have a deleterious effect on the flavor and color of the desired products. For these reasons, conditions of hydrolysis are usually chosen and controlled so as to minimize undesirable side reactions.

The cornmercial hydrolysis of starch is carried out in such a way that two main classes of materials are obtained. The first class includes the more cornpletely hydrolyzed products which are crystallizable. These are the corn sugars-mainly D-glucose and low molecular weight polysaccharides. The other class consists of the materials called corn syrups and maltodextrins; they contain glucose, the disaccharide maltose, and larger polymers of glucose. Since the hydrolysis proceeds slowly at temperatures below 212°F, the reaction is carried out in pressure vessels at higher temperatures. These vessels hold a charge of between 3,000 and 4,000 gallons of starch suspension.

Progress of the hydrolysis may be followed by measuring the dextrose equivalent (DE) of the solution. This factor is a measure of the reducing substances present, calculated as glucose. Since the technique for directly measuring reducing substances is time-consuming, a derived relationship between dextose equivalent and specific rotation is used. The specific rotation starts at +200 degrees and gradually decreases during the course of the hydrolysis. Pure glucose has a specific rotation of +52.5 degrees and the solution approaches this value as a limit. When the specific rotation reaches the desired value, the acid is neutralized with soda ash and the hydrolysis stops. Acid-enzyme syrups will vary considerably in specific rotation from acid hydrolyzed syrups of the same DE because of differences in their carbohydrate cornposition.

The neutralized syrup or sugar solution is filtered, passed over absorbent charcoal or an ion-exchange resin to remove colored substances and other impurities, and then concentrated to the desired solids content by evaporators.

The starch hydrolysis process is now being performed in some plants by means of continuous pressure converters. The quality of the syrup made in this fashion is superior because the conditions can be more closely controlled

Enzyme Hydrolysis

Because of the undesirable secondary reactions which occur at high starch and high acid concentrations, there was from the start an interest on the part of corn sweetener manufacturers in having a process which used milder conditions and which was more specific. These advantages were obtained through the use of enzymes.

One of the earliest processes making use of specific amylolytic enzymes for corn sweetner production was the patented method of Dale and Langlois (1940). In this invention, an acid hydrolysis is carried out until the desired DE has been reached. The acid is then neutralized and the syrup filtered and conce~trated. An enzyme is added and it further hydrolyzes the syrup oligosaccharides. This type of process produces syrups which are sweeter and less viscous &..an the syrups made entirely by the acid hydrolysis procedure. In addition, secondary reactions are greatly reduced and some off-flavored products are eliminated.

The distribution of saccharides in corn syrup (i.e., the relative proportions of mono-, di-, and tri-saccharides as well as larger molecules) is related to the dextrose equivalent and will also vary according to the conditions of hydrolysis. Production of AyrupS having special characteristics can be attained by use of appropriate enzymes, or enzyme and acid hydrolyis cornbinations. For example, in the production of high maltose syrup, the acid conversion is halted at a point where the glucose concentration is negligible. Then the maltose producing enzyme (j3-amylase) is added and the conversion continued under appropriate conditions. Finally, the enzyme is deactivated and the operations of purification, clarification, and concentration performed.

In multiple enzyme processes, after the starch granqles are gelatinized, all of the starch splitting, or depolymerization, is brought about by amylase enzymes rather than wholly or partially by means of acid. Enzyme inactivation, purification, and concentration of these syrups are conducted very much as in the acid-enzyme process.

Isomerization Processes

The success of the corn sweetener industry was enormous. Their products displaced sucrose in many applications, primarily because corn sweeteners were cheaper on a weight basis. There were two reasons for this price advantage: (1) the raw material, maize, was produced in vast quantities in the U.S. and was about the cheapest agricultural raw material it was possible to find, and (2) the sugar beet and sugar cane political lobbiers, and the influence of U. S. sugar refineries, kept the price of sucrose artificially high by causing the U.S. congress to enact subsidies which elevated the domesic prices of cane and beet sugars far above their prices on the world market and, in fact, far above their cost sof production even in the U.S. Nonetheless, cane and beet sugars have retained a very large presence in the food ingredient sector. The reasons for this were partly traditional, but a more basic reason was that dextrose is not as sweet as sucrose, so it took more of a corn sweetener to equal the flavor impact of a given amount of sucrose. Also, it is not convenient to use a liquid material in many foods (a prepared cake mix, for example), and the powdered form of corn sweeteners is not only more expensive than an equal amount of sweetener in syrup form, but it has solubility and hygroscopicity features which are often undesirable. The corn sweetener industry constantly sought for ways to improve their cornpetitive position, and they made a major advance by developing high fructose corn syrups.

It had been known for more than a hundred years that acid Gater, enzyme) treatment of sucrose solutions yielded a product ("invert syrup") that was sweeter than the original material. This is due to the hydrolysis of the disaccharide (Sucrose) molecule into the two monosaccharides fructose and glucose. Although these two hexoses have the same chemical formula, their molecular conformation is different (one is an aldehyde and the other a ketone form) and they have distinctly different organoleptic, chemical, and physical properties. Glucose is less sweet than sucrose on an equal weight basis but fructose is substantially sweeter than sucrose. It is hardly possible to give sweetness ratios that are applicable in all cases, in spite of the many seemingly authoritative statements in the literature that fructose is "twice as sweet as sugar," etc. Some rather simple tests will show that the perceived sweetness of fructose, glucose, and sucrose will vary depending upon concentration, pH, temperature, personal idiosyncrasies, certain metallic ions, etc. Furthermore, the three saccharides often respond differently to these factors, so that two systems showing equal sweetness to an "average" consumer under one set of conditions might give quite a different impression under a different set. Nonetheless, it is certainly clear that isomerizing glucose into fructose will yield a finished product with much improved sweetness.

There are other advantages to changing glucose to fructose. There is a tendency for glucose to crystallize in the concentrated high DE syrups and this can be very troublesome, especially in bulk handling systems where "freezing" of the syrup in a pump or pipe can be disastrous. Consequently, these syrups are usually stored at elevated temperatures in bulk systems and this leads to another problem, browning, which is accornpanied by development of off-flavors and unwanted color. Low DE syrups are less subject to the crystallization phenomenon, but they exhibit very high viscosities when concentrated to high solids levels, at room temperature or colder becorning somewhat like tar in consistency. This, of course, causes handling problems and difficulties in mixing with other liquids or solids.

Fructose is much more soluble and much less subject to crystallization than glucose, which means the syrups can be stored, pumped, and mixed with greater facility than regular corn sweeteners. Fructose is somewhat less stable than glucose, and will undergo Maillard reactions more readiiy.

Microbiologists have known for many years that there are microorganisms which elaborate enzymes capable of isomerizing glucose solutions to yield a mixture of glucose and fructose. By dint of inspired direction and shrewd technological effort, a corn sweetener manufacturer was able to develop a practical method for producing from ordinary corn syrup of high DE a simulated invert sugar syrup, that is, a syrup containing a mixture of about equal proportions of glucose and fructose. The initial products offered cornmercially had a somewhat lower level of fructose than regular invert syrup, but they were certainly much sweeter than glucose syrups. Continued improvements in the process led to the production of syrups with much higher contents of invert.

In the manufacture of high fructose corn syrup, dextrose solutions or high DE substrates produced by acid-enzyme or dual enzyme processes are refined by carbon adsorbent and ion exchange systems, then further treated enzymatically with a purified isomerase. This enzyme converts glucose to fructose. Isomerase reactors utilize an immobilized enzyme system which is capable of continuously isomerizing a stream of glucose solution. Isomerization is usually carried out to the point where the substrate contains 42% fructose. Following this step, the product is again refined through carbon and ion exchange systems before it is finally evaporated to a viscous syrup containing about 71% dry substance.

Published reports indicate that a large amount of the isomerized syrup produced today depends on the use of *Streptomyces rubiginosus* immobilized on DEAE-cellulose in multi-layered shallow-bed reactors. Other isomerization schemes use *Bacillus coagulans* cell homogenate cross-linked with glutaraldehyde and *Actinoplanes missouriensis* cells entrapped in gelatin gel beads and cross.linked with glutaraldehyde. In a recent development, crude soluble isomerase from a *Streptomyces rubiginosus* culture is purified and crystallized, then adsorbed from solution on to a carrier (an extruded cornposite of 30% DEAE-cellulose, 20% titanium dioxide, and 50% food grade polystyrene). The carrier can be easily regenerated.

If the manufacturer desires to produce a syrup having a fructose concentration above 42%, the feedstock corning from the isomerase reactors and purification system is passed through separation columns which retain fructose while allowing glucose to pass through. This is possible because of the greater affinity of fructose for divalent calcium and other cationic groups which are present in the column's packing. The fructose retained in the column can be flushed from the system with deionized water, while the glucose is recirculated for further isomerization. Both batch and continuous systems are used for this separation process, with the continuous systems being based on a simulated moving bed design. Fructose fractions are generally recovered at an 80 to 90% concentration. This fraction and the 42% fructose feedstock are/mixed to produce the cornmercial product with 55% fructose content. Blended syrups are refined with both carbon and ion exchange systems before they are evaporated to a dry substance level of 77%.

The high level fructose feedstock may itself be refined and evaporated for users who demand a very high fructose product. There is currently available a high fructose corn syrup with a solids content of 71%, of which solids 43% is fructose, 52% is glucose, and 5% is other sugars. The syrup's color is water white and the pH is 4.0. Another version is 77% solids, of which 55% is fructose, 42% is dextrose, and 3% is other sugars. These ingredients cornmand premium prices as cornpared to corn syrups with lesser amounts of fructose, but, presumably, they will be priced below inverted sucrose syrups. A specialty syrup available in limited quantities has specifications of 77% solids, of which 90% is fructose, 7% is glucose, and 3% is other sugars. The pH of this product is 3.5, and the ash (sulfated) is a maximum of 0.03%. It has a density of 11.53 pounds per gallon and a viscosity of752 cps at 80°F.

Crystalline fructose is also available. This material, which is prepared by processes, will have some appeal for specialty applications although its price is considerably above that of sucrose, on a dry weight basis. Crystalline, maltose derived from plant starch has also becorne available.

Further Processing and Products

Dextrose.-Dextrose is the cornmercial name given to dry preparations of substantially pure D-glucose, principally because the name "glucose" had earlier been used (and is still sometimes used) for corn syrups. In the following discussion, "dextrose" can be taken to mean a dry, powdered, corn sweetener consisting principally of D-glucose. Dextrose is given a special place in this discussion because of its large usage. The manufacturing information given above indicates that, when it is desired to produce sugars by hydrolyzing starch, lower concentrations of starch should be used in the slurry. It is also customary to use slightly higher acid concentrations and higher temperatures for longer times. The secondary reactions are not as important because the precipitated saccharides go through crystallization and washing steps which remove most of the undesirable flavor and color constituents. Nearly all cornmercial dextrose is now produced by the enzymatic hydrolysis of starch, although acid hydrolysis may be used as an initial step.

Newkirk (1936) described the manufacturing conditions and problems encountered in the preparation of dextrose. The procedure involves introducing the starch hydrolyzate, which has been concentrated by evaporation, into large vessels which are equipped with agitators. The solution is "seeded" with dextrose crystals and held at a temperature just above ambient for several days. After the dextrose has crystallized, the mother liquor is removed by centrifugation. The practical details for obtaining the final product (crystalline dextrose), reworking the mother liquor, and controlling the crystallization can be found in the several publications and patents of Newkirk. Perhaps the most important discovery described in this literature was the finding that, if the crystallization was allowed to take place while the system was being agitated, and if the concentration of the sugar was high enough, dextrose would crystallize in the form of a nearly chemically pure product.

As this work was continued, conditions were worked out which favored the production of ß-dextrose. This particular crystalline form of dextrose has the property of dissolving easily and rapidly in water. Its use in beverages and other products requiring ease of solution followed immediately.

Maltodextrins.-Maltodextrins are not really "sweeteners," since they have little or no sweet taste. They are produced in a manner very similar to that used for making corn syrup, however, thus justifying a discussion of their properties at this point. Both acid and enzyme processes are used in their manufacture. When making maltodextrins, the starch conversion process is stopped at an early stage to keep ilie DE below 20. Refining of the syrup is conducted as with corn syrups, then the reaction mixture is dried. Maltodextrins are usually spray-dried to provide white free-flowing powders which are only slightly hygroscopic. They are used mainly as viscosity inducers in liquids or as bulking agents in dry foods where sweetness would be objectionable. They can be used in savory/salty fat spreads, such as the peanut filling in cracker sandwich "cookies."

PROCESSING CORN OIL

Oils derived from cereal grains constitute important food ingredients in cornmerce, but their total world production is considerably below levels of output for many other vegetable, marine, and animal fats and oils. Oils from corn, rice, and wheat are produced in many countries throughout the world, but the U.S. produces the largest quantity of corn oil. Of the edible oils from vegetable sources produced in the U.S., those from soybeans and cottonseed each greatly exceed the total output of cereal oils.

If it were not for the fact that during the preparation of cornstarch the germ is almost completely separated from the rest of the products, corn oil would not have become an important food ingredient. Wheat germ oil has practically no significance as a food oil. Although of greater significance in other parts of the world, particularly the orient, rice oil has not yet reached a level of commercial importance in the U.S.

Extracting the Oil

The separation of lipids from vegetable materials comprises a distinct and specialized branch of fat and oil technology. All extraction processes have certain objects in common which may be mentioned briefly here: (1) to obtain the oil undamaged and as free of undesirable impurities as is practical, (2) to obtain the oil in as high a yield as possible, consistent with the economic realities of the process, and (3) to produce an oil cake or residue of the greatest possible value as a by-product.

The raw material for corn oil extraction is the germ after it has been separated from the corn kernel. The kernel of corn contains as an average about 3 to 6% oil. The germ, though but a small part of the kernel, is so high in oil content that it contains about a third to a half of the total oil in the entire grain. There has never been a commercial effort to extract a food ingredient oil from the endosperm or other parts of the corn kernel. When the germs have been collected, they are washed and dried. They are then heated prior to their introduction into the oil extraction presses. Oil may be extracted in hydraulic presses, but the usual practice in the U.S. is to use semi-continuous or continuous screw-type presses of the design called Anderson expellers.

When Anderson expellers are to be used, the germs are first passed through flaking rolls until they are ground into a coarse meal. This material is passed into steam-heated temperers and then into the expeller press. Here, the germs are forced under high pressure through a slotted barrel made up of steel sections in the form of a rotating screen called the "oil reel." During this stage of processing, most of the oil is pressed out through the slots, while the fibrous portions, called the "foots," are discharged at the end of the barrel. This rejected material is usually returned through the expeller unit for repressing, but ultimately the residue will retain about 5 to 8% of its original oil content.

After it leaves the expeller units, the crude oil is usually pumped through a filter press or clarifying press. This filtration constitutes only the first of several such steps which will be encountered throughout the entire refining process.

Some refiners employ a combination of mechanical presses and solvent extraction for removing oil from the grain germs. Solvent extraction is a highly efficient means of recovering the oil for it is capable of reducing the oil content of the residue to about 0.5% as compared with at least 5% retained in the mechanically-expressed residues. Although solvent extraction is mostly used in the processing of raw materials of extremely low fat content, it has been found to be advantageous in the processing of corn germs.

It is common practice to "pre-press" seeds of high oil content in low pressure screw presses to obtain a residue containing about 10% oil, and then solvent extract the residue. Solvents commonly employed in this process are the so-called extraction naphthas such as light petroleum fractions consisting chiefly of n-hexane.

The solvent-oil mixture from the extractor is filtered to remove any solid matter, then the solvent is separated from the oil in an evaporator or stripping column. Here the solvent boils off, and the vapor is condensed and collected for re-use. The germ flake from the extractor contains a certain amount of solvent and this is usually recovered by a steaming and heating process. The extracted flake; now stripped of almost its entire oil content, may be used in livestock feeds. Sometimes, instead of filtering the oil coming from the solvent extractor, it is simply run into large tanks where the solids settle to the bottom and are subsequently drawn off. These solids, known collectively as "foots," are utilized mainly in soap manufacture.

Some Characteristics of Corn Oil

It is difficult to conceive of a system or a plan which would take into account all of the many factors affecting the suitability of vegetable oils and fats for food use. Corn, rice, and wheat oils fall into the Hilditch Classification Group IVa, mono- and di-ethylenic and saturated fatty acids (containing principally oleic, linoleic, and palmitic acid components). Chemical group or type would be oleic-linoleic acid for corn and rice, and linoleic acid for wheat. What does all this mean to the practical scientist or technologist? Not much.

Crude corn oil has a dark reddish amber color. Even after refining, it is considerably darker than many other vegetable oils. By applying strong bleaching treatments, however, it can be lightened to a golden yellow color. This oil, unless subjected to stringent deodorization action, retains the strong taste and odor characteristic of the original corn kernel. The unrefined oil contains relatively large amounts of phosphatides and other nonoil substances (often in excess of 2%) and its free fatty acid content (usually above 1.5%) is higher than that found in most vegetable oils.

The refined oil contains small amounts of waxes which cause a precipitate or "cloud" to form in oil held at refrigerator temperatures unless the wax is selectively removed by a process called winterization. This process will be described in a later section of this chapter. The keeping quality of refined corn oil is fairly good. The crude oil, however, is rapidly hydrolyzed unless processing proceeds without delay. Such degradation is hastened when the oil remains in the presence of corn meal impurities.

Refining of Oil

Further refining of the extracted oil must be undertaken to remove fatty acids, phosphatides, and other gummy or mucilaginous materials. The first step in fatty acid removal is to expose the oil to a strong aqueous solution of alkali. This process involves three steps: (1) emulsification of the oil with a considerable excess of alkali, (2) heating to break the emulsion, and (3) separating the refined oil from the precipitated soapy substances and miscellaneous associated impurities. The precipitated material is still another substance termed "foots," or sometimes "soapstock," and has commercial value, for it contains about 20 to 50% free and combined fatty acids. Separation of the refined oil from the impurities is accomplished by

centrifugation. The impurities are collected and separated for the value of some of the components. By means of the alkali treatment for removal of fatty acids, crude oils which would seldom contain less than 0.5% free fatty acids are reduced to a free fatty acid content of about 0.01 ato 0.03%. Significant improvements in production efficiency have been achieved in recent years through the introduction of a continuous method of caustic soda refining to replace the more conventional batch method. This technique prevents, to a large extent, the so-called neutral losses which are common in the batch technique. These losses are reduced about 25 to 30% by decreasing the time of contact between the corn Oil and the caustic material and through efficient separation of the oil and the soap stock in very high-speed centrifuges.

Bleaching.-A bleaching treatment of corn oil is usually required, since the alkali-refining process does not produce a sufficiently light-colored oil for marketing purposes. Bleaching is usually accomplished by treating the refined oil with an absorbent material in powdered form. Both natural and acid-activated bleaching earths (e.g., fuller's earth or clay) are used as adsorbents. The acid-treated powders are more expensive, but they have a greater adsorptive power for the colored cornpounds, particularly for chlorophyll or related pigments. Bleaching is usually conducted at a temperature between 220. to 240. F and at atmospheric pressure. Slightly lower temperatules may be utilized when the process is done under vacuum. When a good activated adsorbent earth is employed, only about 1% is required to bleach an oil of good quality. Considerably larger amounts of earth material may be required, however, if a natural earth oflower activity is used or if the oil is of poor grade and highly colored. Equilibrium between unadsorbed pigments in the oil and adsorbed pigments in the earth is usually established within a five minute period if the two phases are vigorously mixed.

In the cornmon practice of bleaching on a batch basis, the oil and adsorbent are mixed together in a kettle or vat of about 30,000 lb capacity. To avoid oxidation of the oil and improve bleaching efficiency, this procedure is most often performed under reduced pressure, although the use of open kettles for the operation is well known. The mixed and reacted batch is pumped from the kettle through a filter press. The press cake of spent adsorbent is blown with air, or with a mixture of steam and air, to reduce its entrained oil content to a level of 30 to 35%. Following this effort to recover oil, in some cornmercial operations solvent extraction is carried out on the press cake to recover more oil. Ultimately, the press cake of adsorbent earth material is discarded.

Winterization.-The bleaching step is usually followed in the oil refining process by a chilling treatment called "winterization." Winterization, or destearination as it is also called, are term~ applied to the method of removing from the oil certain substances which, though soluble at medium or higher storage temperatures, crystallize out and make the oil turbid in appearance under colder conditions. Particularly when edible oils are used as salad oils, li small fraction of solid glycerides must be removed, as their presence makes the oil appear cloudy, an appearance which many consumers interpret as indicating spoilage or contamination. In corn oil, however, it is not so much the high-melting glycerides as a very small portion of waxes that causes the undesirable turbidity.

The first step in the process of winterizing consists in cooling the oil some degrees below the temperature at which it is required to remain clear and holding at this temperature until the troublesome constituents solidify. The oil is cooled by contading the outer shell of the storage container with refrigerated brine or cold water or by cooling the air in a storage room where the oil is maintained. The rate of cooling must be slow er.ough to enable the higher melting cornponents to form large solid crystals. Small crystals resulting from cooling that is too rapid make filtration difficult. Frequently, a suitable filter aid is added to the oil before cooling, so that the particles can act as crystallization centers. To ensure continuance of the low temperatures during filtration, the filters are often placed in the cooling room or else the filter presses are provided with internal channels for cooling.

Deodorization.-The final step in the refining process is usually the deodorization of the oil. Practically all of the vegetable oiis used as edible fats in the U.S., as well as in most other western nations, are subjected to a deodorizing treatment. Deodorization is a process of steam distillation, in which the relatively nonvolatile oil is held at a high temperature, under reduced pressures, while it is stripped of the relatively volatile constituents responsible for flavors and odors in the crude or partially refined oil. Another result of the deodorization process is that free fatty acids in the oil are usually reduced to about 0.01 to 0.03%. Bleaching or loss of color of the oil will also occur.

Modem deodorization equipment operates in the temperature range of about 4250 to 475°F and at very high vacuum levels. Many processors deodorize salad and cooking oils at somewhat lower temperatures than they do hydrogenated oils. The rigorous exclusion of oxygen during this process may be regarded as essential to the effectiveness of the operation. The steam jets which produce the vacuum are attached to the top of a typical deodorizer vat.

The stability of vegetable oils of good quality is usually improved considerably by the deodorization process. Deodorization destroys any peroxides in the oil and removes aldehydes or other volatile products which may have developed through atmospheric oxidation, but it should be noted that strongly rancid oils cannot be cornpletely reclaimed by deodorization.

Batch-type processes are giving way to newer continuous processes for deodorization. In the former, the steps of heating, deodorizing, cooling,

and filtering may take from 5 to 8 hr depending on the actual conditions of the operation and on the size and quality of the equipment. Development of continuous or semi-continuous units with automatic controls have resulted in cornplete deodorization being effected in 2.5 hr. If deodorization has been properly conducted, removal of odoriferous contaminants from the oil will be substantially cornplete. Well-deodorized oils from different sources, when fresh, cannot be easily distinguished from one another by odor or taste. They are quite bland and merely give the consumer a sensation of oiliness in the mouth.

Hydrogenation

Following deodorization and cooling, corn oil is usually packaged. A substantial portion of the total edible oil produced in the U.S. is subjected to hydrogenation, which is not considered a refining process. Primarily, hydrogenation is a means of converting liquid oils to semi-solid plastic fats suitable for use in margarine or as shortening. By means of this process, enhancement of the oil's stability and lightening of its color is achieved. In the hydrogenation process, hydrogen is added at the double-bonds in the fatty acid chains. Hydrogenation as a process is more than just a means of producing substitute products, for hydrogenated fats may be tailor-made to produce ingredients superior in some important characteristics to any of the natural plastic fats.

9

Products and their Uses

Fractions resulting from the normal corn wet-milling operation are: (1) steepwater, (2) starch, (3) gluten, (4) germ, and (5) hulls. There can be various combinations of these fractions. For example, steepwater is evaporated to yield concentrates, but it can be added to hull and gluten and dried to give an important feed ingredient. The germ is pressed and extracted to yield crode oil and corn oil meal. Much of the starch is, sold-mostly to the paper and textile industries-in substantially unchanged form. Some of the starch goes into building materials, and food usage is also very substantial. Cornstarch is normally one of the cheapest food ingredients available, and it is used as a filler -wherever possible. Whenever a gel structure is need, as in gum drops or puddings, cornstarch (natural or modified) is used, if possible. It is also indispensable in some special uses, such as molds for candy pieces (e.g., Mogul shaping of cream centers). Starch is modified in several ways to produce derivatives which have special advantages for certain food uses.

The corn syrups described in an earlier section are widely used as sweeteners and texturizers. Corn syrups are sold at retail for use as sweeteners in home cooking, especially as a candy ingredient, as a component of baby formulas, and (when flavored) for use on pancakes, waffles, etc. There is no economic advantage over sugar for home use, however, since the relatively expensive container required for the syrup, and the extra cost of transporting the water in the syrup, offset any saving due to the cost of the basic material. Syrups are also less convenient to measure and mix than sugar when used as an ingredient in home cooking.

The applications of cornstarch, corn syrups, and corn sugars in the food industry are so numerous that only a few of the most important ones will be mentioned. Satisfactory jams, jellies, and preserves can be made when some of the sugar solids are replaced with corn sugar. The extent of the substitution is limited by Federal Standards. The same situation applies to canned fruits. Manufacturers of carbonated beverages utilize vast quantities of corn syrup, especially high fructose corn syrup, although it is still not universally agreed that cornplete replacement of sugar is feasible in these products. Dessert sauces such as ice cream toppings nearly always contain substantial percentages of corn syrup; these ingredients are useful as viscosity modifiers and "cling" agents in toppings. Corn syrup is a valuable ingredient in ice creams, sherbets, and the like; it modifies the initial texture and also retards the development of crystals of ice, lactose, and sucrose. .The baking industry uses corn syrup to make icings and frostings, fruit fillings for pies and sweet rolls, jelly rolls, etc. It is used to a minor extent in cookies. Most producers of caramel color use corn syrup as a raw material; treatment of the syrup with alkali or acid under rigidly controlled temperature conditions can yield colors having widely different properties.

Dried corn syrups and dextrose are used mainly by bread bakers and cereal manufacturers. They are also used in canned, bottled, frozen, and preserved foods, candy, ice cream, "cream" fillings for cookies, mayonnaise, salad dressings, catsup, cheese spread, mustard, pickles, and prepared meats.

Almost all corn oil is made into specialty margarines and salad or cooking oils. Cooking oil is not winterized, salad oil is. The reason for the popularity of corn oil for these purposes is that the oil has a reputation for being more healthful, as a result of its content of some unsaturated fatty acids. Corn oil apparently has a relatively high resistance to the development of rancidity, which makes it especially valuable as an ingredient in products like mayonnaise or semisolid salad dressings. Corn oil is at an economic disadvantage in these uses, however, since it cornpetes directly with cottonseed and soybean oil, and now canola, which are almost always significantly cheaper than corn oil. In applications where the health superiority (real or not) of corn oil can be presented directly to the consumer, the economic disadvantage is probably of little importance.

A high smoke point makes corn oil a good candidate for use in deep fat frying. The relatively high temperatures that it can tolerate, coupled with other favorable characteristics make this oil particularly good for frying potato chips and doughnuts. It is said that corn oil does not absorb flavors from the cooked food as rapidly as some other food oils do.

The extensive use of the by-product of corn oil manufacture called soap stock in the manufacture of soap and allied products, represents the most important nonfood application of corn oil. Smaller quantities of either crude or refined corn oil are used in ammunition, chemicals and insecticides, paint and varnish substitutes, rust preventive cornpounds, and textiles. Sulfonated corn oil has important applications in tanning and processing of leather. Refined corn oil has found wide usage as a carrier for vitamins and in other medicinal preparations.

As previously mentioned, steepwater is usually dried in cornbination with one or more of the other by-products of starch manufacture, and the solids used as a feed cornpoonent. On a dry-solids basis, the steepwater corning from a modem plant contains about 48% protein, 26% lactic acid,

Table 9.1. AMINO ACID CONTENT OF CORN AND WET MILLING BY-PRODUCTS[1]

Amino acid	Corn	Corn gluten feed	Gluten meal	Germ meal	Steep liquor
	%*	%*	%*	%*	%*
Lysine	0.22	0.65	1.1	1.0	1.6
Methionine	0.15	0.55	2.1	0.7	1.0
Cystine	0.19	0.55	1.2	0.44	1.6
Tryptophan	0.07	0.11	0.33	0.22	0.1
Threonine	0.31	1.0	2.2	1.2	1.8
Isoleucine	0.34	0.7	2.6	0.8	1.4
Leucine	1. 05	2.1	11.1	2.0	4.0
Phenylalanine	0.42	0.9	4.2	1.0	1.6
Tyrosine	0.33	0.7	3.2	0.8	1.0
Valine	0.38	1.1	3.0	1.3	2.4
Histidine	0.25	0.8	1.3	0.8	1.4
Arginine	0.42	1.1	2.1	1.4	2.2
Glycine	0.37	1.1	1.8	1.22	2.2
Serine	Q.44	1.1	3.4	1.1	2.0
Alanine	0.78	1.7	5.8	1.6	3.6
Aspartic acid	0.68	1.3	4.0	1.6	2.8
Glutamic acid	1. 77	3.7	15.3	3.6	7.0
Proline	0.84	1.9	6.1	1.4	4.0

1 Anon. 1982. * Dry weight basis.

18% ash, and much smaller amounts of other substances. The amino acids of steepwater are not well-balanced from a nutritional standpoint, making it inadequate as the sole source of protein for animal feeding. It contains nine vitamins; those present in the largest amounts are inositol, choline, niacin, and pantothenic acid. It was originally used for yeast culture, and then in the World War II period it became important in the penicillin production method. It has also been used as a nutrient in the production of chloramphenicol, chlortetracycline, erythromycin, polymixins, tetracyclines, streptomycins, and doubtless other antibiotics and the like prepared from microbiological cultures. It can be used in the fermentative production of vitamins, and inositol (a member of the B-cornplex) can be produced from steepwater.

Gluten can be mixed with steepwater, corn oil meal, hulls, or any cornbination of these fractions to give corn gluten feed. Usually, these high protein supplements are mixed with carbohydrate sources or fibrous materials. A sweetened corn gluten feed is made by adding hydrol or corn sugar molasses, a by-product derived from the corn sugar refining process which cannot be used as human food. Zein can be extracted from the gluten as a more or less pure protein and used for certain specialty applications, such as a coating and antioxidant carrier for nut pieces.

The amino acid cornposition of wet milling byproducts is an important co~sideration to feed formulators; typical contents are shown in Table 9.1.

QUALITY CONTROL TESTS

There are bench-scale methods for determining the yield of products to be expected from wet-milling a given lot of corn. Most of the steps followed in modern plants are followed in these procedures. Although the results of the small-scale processing tests do not correspond exactly to the results obtained in cornmercial milling of grain from the same batch, the differences are, in general, constant, predictable, and relatively minor.

The standard tests listed in Table 9.2 were approved by an analytical cornmittee of the wet-milling industry and are run on the materials indicated. In addition to the tests listed in this table, many other evaluation procedures applying only to corn syrup have industry-wide standard methods. Some of these are: Baume, calcium, chloride, color, copper, dextrose equivalent, heavy metals, iron, fermentables, refractive index, specific rotation, and sulfate. There have been several published procedures for automating the determination of dextrose equivalents of corn starch hydrolysates. In the following discussion, very brief descriptions will be given of the most important test methods applied to cornstarch and oil. More detailed descriptions can be found in the cited texts.

Table 9.2. TESTS COMMONLY APPLIED IN WET MILLING[1]

Test	Corn	Corn starch	Corn syrups	Feed-stuffs
Ash	x	x	x	x
Moisture	x	x	x	x
Protein	x	x	x	x
Insect infestation	x	-	-	-
"Starch	x	-	-	x
Acidity	-	x	x	x
Crude fat	-	x	-	x
Total	fat	-	x	-
pH	-	x	x	x
Solubles	-	x	-	x
Sulfur dioxide	-	x	x	-

1 Matz (1970)

Moisture is cornmonly determined on grains and starches by drying to constant weight in a vacuum oven held at 212° to 248°F. Azeotropic distillation is the basis of the referee procedure of the corn wet-milling, industry, but it is probably too time-consuming for routine analyses. The Karl Fischer titration method is sometimes applied to starch products suspected of containing substantial amounts of volatiles other than water. Nuclear magnetic resonance (NMR) techniques for determining moisture in cornstarch were developed by the Corn Industries Research Foundation, and resulted in the manufacture of a cornmercial instrument which can determine water in cornstarch, flour, and similar materials in one minute with better precision than is obtained with standard methods requiring much longer to perform.

Inorganic materials are customarily determined as the residue (ash) remaining after the sample has been burned at a specified temperature. The initial incineration may be over an open flame, but the final heating is usually in a furnace at 525°F for about two hours, or until the residue is free of carbon. The amount of ash in most cornmercial starch batches is quite small. To determine calcium, the sample is ashed and the residue dissolved in dilute hydrochloric acid before titrating with a standard solution of EDTA. The indicator is hydroxynaphthol blue.

Sulfur dioxide, as well as sulfites, may be carried over in free or cornbined form from the steeping operation or other steps in which it has been added as a preservative or conditioner. The Monier-Williams procedure can be used to estimate the amount of this substance after it has' been stripped from an acidified suspension of the sample by carbon dioxide. Alternatively, an extract can be colorimetrically titrated with iodine.

Acids present in the sample are determined by titration of a slurry or extract with standard alkali solutions. The pH is usually determined on a slurry. Most unmodified starches are adjusted to a pH of about 5.0 during the final stages of processing.

The well-known Kjeldahl procedure, or some modification of it, is used to determine the nitrogen in grains and starches. The factor 6.25 is applied to convert nitrogen to protein.

Measurements of the physical properties of starches are highly important to the buyer, often being much more indicative of their quality for a given use than chemical tests would be. Determining the viscosity of a suspension cooked in a given way is a valuable test of utility for many applications. Several different instruments have been developed over the years to give empirical results which are useful for certain purposes. Among the most successful of these have been the Brabender Amylograph and the Corn Industries Viscorneter. These devices record the change in apparent viscosity of a starch suspension as it is taken through a heating and cooling program. The Brookfield Synchro-Lectric Viscorneter and many other "viscosity"-measuring instruments have been applied to control or research testing of starch gels.

Business transactions in crude and refined oils in the United States are conducted with the aid of uniform standards, specifications, and trading rules established by various trade organizations, government agencies, and associated scientific or technical societies. Trading rules generally set forth specifications for different grades of each oil and in some cases include systems for the establishment of premiums or penalties based on the contract price for oil which is better or poorer in quality than the standard for a basis grade.

Although it is not directly concerned with cornmerce in oil, the American Oil Chemists' Society has for many years been active in the development of analytical methods which are generally the basis for trading rules utilized by the industry. Official and tentative test methods (AOCS) cornmonly used in examining and evaluating the various properties of corn oil or other vegetable oils include free fatty acids and acid value, color, cold test, peroxide value, and smoke point. These critical tests will be described briefly.

Free fatty acids and acid'value are quantitative measurements of the amount of uncornbined free fatty acids present in the oil. Determinations of the residual free fatty acids and acid value serve as a measure of the effectiveness of the total refining procedure. The acid value is defined as the number of milligrams of potassium hydroxide required to neutralize one gram of the oil.

Color is important not only as an aspect of the appearance of the oil itself, but also as it affects the color of the product to which the oil may be added. The bleaching step in the refining process is varied according to the color in the oil which is actually desired. Although there are many methods for measuring color, it has been customary to report color in edible oils in terms of Lovibond units. This method expresses the color in a sample by cornparing the oil with red and yellow Lovibond glasses of known optical characteristics.

The cold test measures the ability of an oil to remain sparkling cle~r at refrigeration temperatures. It is a check on the effectiveness of the removal of solid glycerides and wax during the winterization process. The test is made by holding a sample of the oil at 32°F for 5.5 hr and then visually examining it for any evidence of cloudiness or turbidity.

Peroxide value is a measure of the degree of oxidation that has taken place in the oil. Oxidation is related to rancidity and the test is indicative of the status of the oil in terms of probable handling conditions that the oil has undergone, including temperature and exposure to light and air.

Smoke point represents the temperature at which the oil first gives off a continuous stream of smoke. This value is fairly constant for each particular type of oil and is indicative of one aspect of the oil's suitability for deep fat frying.

10

Processing Ready-to Eat Breakfast Cereals

Flakes

General considerations.-Flaking is a relatively simple process, consisting in its most elemental form of cooking fragments of cereal grains (or in some cases whole grains) with water, flattening the soft particles between large steel rollers, and toasting the resultant flake at high temperatures. Apparently, the first cornmercial production of such a food occurred around the turn of the century 'when J. H. Kellogg and W. H. Kellogg made whole wheat flakes in a barn behind the B{lttle Creek Sanitorium. Since that time, many cornplications have been introduced into the process in attempts to improve the flavor of the product and the efficiency of operations, and to gain the uniformity of flake size and appearance which is so desirable to the manufacturer and perhaps even to the consumer.

Flakes owe their popularity with consumers to their crisp but friable texture, to their sweet but rather bland flavor, and to the ease with which they can be readied for consumption.

In the basic processing steps, the raw material undergoes the following changes: (1) the starch is gelatinized and probably slightly hydrolyzed; (2) the particle undergoes a browning reaction due probably to interaction of protein: and sugars; (3) enzymatic processes are stopped, rendering the final product more stable; (4) dextrinization and caramelization of the sugars occur as a result of the high temperatures in the roasting oven; and (5) the flake becornes crisper as a result of reduction ofits moisture content to a very low level.

Early methods for making flaked cereals, e.g., wheat or corn flakes, were based on the use of a fairly large chunk of the grain, which retained its integrity throughout the entire process. Conventional corn flakes are still made this way. The technique has some disadvantages, such as the restrictions it places on the size, shape, and cornposition of the particle. One of the early patents describing a method of circumventing these restrictions was that of Clausi *et al.* In essence, this invention required the extrusion of a dough piece by a pelletingg mill, and the subsequent puffing or flaking of the piece. In the world of the patent, the process involved "gelatinizing hydrated, ungelatinized cereal dough pieces having a major proportion of at least one highly nutritious cereal flour [and at a moisture content of about 22% to about 36%] at temperatures from about 215° to about 265°F at steam pressures of from about 1 to about 23 psig, cooling the gelatinzed cereal dough pieces to a temperature whereat they are less plastic and their stiffness is increased, by cooling temperatures from above about 150° to about 205°F, pelletizing the cereal dough pieces, partially drying the gelatinized dough pieces to from about 5% to about 21% moisture, mechanically modifying the shape of the dough piece {as by flaking], and drying the. . .[flakes] to a moisture content of from about 1% to about 3.5% moisture under conditions such that the temperature of the cereal dough pieces does not exceed about 250°F." The patent indicates that pelletizing was to be done by a conventional, cornmercial pelletizing machine, which is a much simpler device than the cooking extruders to be discussed later in this chapter.

The Clausi *et al.* patent disclosed several formulas which could be used for cornpounded doughs suitable for processing by the invention. Two of these are shown in Table 10.1.

In the subsequent paragraphs of this section, a fairly straightforward

Table 10.1. FORMULAS FOR PELLETIZED AND FLAKED CEREALS

Formula A		Formula B	
Ingredient	Percent by weight	Ingredient	Percent by weight
Oat flour	60-70	Soy flour	80.4
Rice flour.	7-12	Sucrose	8.
Soy flour	5-10	Casein	5.
Sucrose	5-15	Malt syrup	4.
Lecithin	0.05-0.15,	Salt	2.5
Salt	2-4	Vanilla flavor	0.1
Milk casein	1.5-10.0		

corn flake operation will be described first, followed by a discussion of a wheat flake process which is considerably more cornplex. Bran flakes, 40% bran flakes, and rice flakes are also marketed. They are manufactured by methods having much similarity to the corn flake process.

Corn flakes.-Hybrid yellow corn is most often used as the raw material for corn flakes, although white corn provides an equally satisfactory ingredient. The corn is broken (milled) so as to yield a No.4 to No.5 grit free of germ and bran. These large pieces represent about half of a corn kernel and they retain their identity throughout the process, each particle eventually emerging as a corn flake. The hulls resulting from the milling operation are used in animal feeds, and the germs are pressed in expellers to yield the corn oil of cornmerce and a meal or cake which can serve as a protein enrichment in animal feeds.

Into a cylindrical pressure cooker or retort are placed about 1,700 lb of grits and 36 gal of a flavoring syrup made from sugar, nondiastatic malt, salt, and water. Occasionally, niacin will be added at this point. During cooking, the charge accumulates additional water from the steam which is introduced into the retort, and its moisture content rises to about 33%,

The contents of the slowly rotating retort are cooked at 15 to 23 (typically 18) pounds steam pressure for 1 to 2 hr. Different lots of corn can vary appreciably in their cooking time requirements. The end point can be judged by examining a small sample which is blown out through a gate valve. A uniform transparency in the kernels indicates an adequate cook. At the expiration of the cooking time, pressure in the vessel is reduced to atmospheric level, the retort is opened, and its contents are dumped onto a moving belt.

After the lumps from the cooker are broken down to individual particles by a revolving reel, they are distributed to a set of driers. The latter devices are essentially large tubes or tanks extending vertically for several stories. Wet kernels enter the top and are dried by a countercurrent of hot (150°F) air as they travel to the bottom. Another type of drying equipment consists of horizontal rotating cylinders having numerous steamheated pipes passing longitudinally through them. Louver driers may also be used.

As they exit the driers, the corn particles contain 19 to 23% mnisture, but the water is unevenly distributed, so the material is transferred to tempering bins for several hours (as many as 24) so that the moisture can equilibrate. After tempering, the hard dark brown grits are ready for flaking.

Fig. 10.2 A set of flaking rolls

The flaking rolls are steel cylinders weighing over a ton. They revolve at a speed of about 180 to 200 rpm, and are cooled by internal circulation of water. Hydraulic controls maintain a pressure of over 40 tons at the nip of the rollers. According to Fast *et ai.* (1990) the most popular sizes of rolls are 20 inches in diameter x 30 inches wide and 26x40, with other standards being 32x40, 24x40, and 20x24.5 for ready-to-eat cereals. The cooked dried grits are pressed into thin flakes as they pass between the rolls. The flake is rather flexible at this time, and lacks the desired crispness and toasted flavor of the finished corn flake. Figure 10.2 shows a pair of flaking rolls, such as are used to make corn flakes.

From the rolls, flakes pass directly to a rotating toasting oven which is usually gas-fired. The moist flakes tumble through the perforated drums and pass within a few inches of gas flames. Treatment may be, for example, 50 sec at 575°F or 2 to 3 min at 550°F. In addition to being thoroughly dehydrated by this process, the flakes are toasted and blistered. They contain less than 3% moisture when they emerge from the oven.

From the ovens, flakes are carried by belts to expansion bins where they are permitted to cool to room temperature. During transfer, the corn flakes are cooled by circulating air and they are usually sprayed with a solution of thiamin and perhaps other B-vitamins.

Corn flakes can also be made by cooking the corn in an extruder, cooling the cooked mass to perhaps 25°C (to eliminate post-extrusion expansion) then passing it through a die to form strands which are cut into short lengths (e.g., 5 mm), A finer grind of corn may be used in this method, as cornpared to the raw material required in the traditional method described previously, since the size of the flake is not dependent on the dimensions of the corn grit. The cooked pellets are then flaked and toasted in equipment very similar to that used for "old-fashioned" corn flakes. Flaking is done by pairs of large steel cylinders operating at a speed differential that shapes the strands into thin flakes. Adjustments of the rollers can be used to control the thickness, texture, and surface characteristics of the finished flake. Final drying and toasting can be conducted in any convenient type of hot air unit which does not subject the flake to excessive attrition. Belt dryers or fluid bed units are possible choices. In any case, the moisture content of the flake must be reduced from about 20% to about 3 or 4%. Applying the hottest air to the entry point causes blistering of the flake, which is generally considered desirable. It is said that extruded flakes can be cornpletely processed in 30 minutes, or even less, as cornpared to an 8 hour cycle time for conventional processing. Midden says there is an 11% savings in costs when corn flakes are made by the extrusion method.

Briefly, this involves extruding pelleted half-products made principally of corn or some other cereal flour, drying these to a moisture content of 9.5 to 17.0%, conditioning the dried half-products to a moisture content of between 17 and 23%, treating the conditioned half-products with a moisture-absorbing cornpound to reduce the stickiness of their outer surfaces, flaking the half-products by the usual method, reducing the moisture content of the flakes to about 15 to 18%, and toasting the flakes to a final moisture content of 2 to 5%. The method of these inventors for producing cereal flakes from pellets of half products is shown in Figure 10.3.

Wheat flakes.-Plump kernels of soft wheat ate frequently used as the raw material for wheat flakes. After cleaning and sorting according to size, the kernels are tempered in steel bins of small diameter by adding moisture and holding at about 80°F for about 24 hr. The wheat may be transferred one or more times during this period if such a procedure is necessary in order to

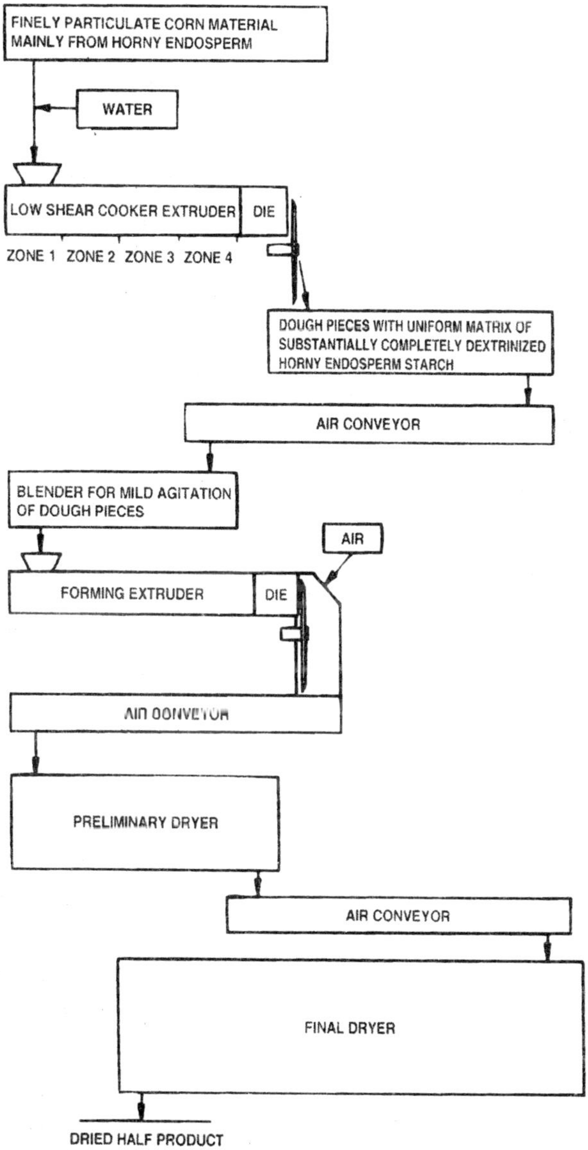

Fig. 10.3 Method for preparing cereal flakes from pelleted half products.

keep the temperature within reasonable limits. After tempering, the wheat is steamed at atmospheric pressure until it reaches 203°F and 21% moisture.

The steamed wheat is bumped between smooth steel rollers set considerably farther apart than are flaking rollers. This treatment flattens the grain slightly, and ruptures the bran coat in several places making the kernel more permeable to the moisture which will be added during the cooking step. Next, the flattened kernels are transferred to pressure cookers, which are similar to those used for corn flakes, and the other ingredients are added. These ingredients normally include sugars, salt, malt, and sometimes a coloring substance such as caramel.

The retort contents are cooked at 20 psi steam pressure for 90 min while the vessel is slowly rotating. After cooking, the grains are soft, translucent, and brown. They contain about 45 to 50% moisture. Their starch has been cornpletely gelatinized, of course. The retort is now opened and rotated so that its contents fall onto a moving belt which transfers the cooked mass to a chute leading to a "wiggler."

The wiggler consists of a horizontal perforated disc and a rotating arm carrying vertically-oriented rigid fingers around its upper surface. The clumps of slightly adhering grains are dropped onto the center of the perforated disc, through which warm air is being blown in an upward direction. The moving fingers break up the lumps and move individual grains outwardly until they fall from the edge of the disc into a pneumatic conveyor and are transferred to a horizontal rotating cylinder fitted with internal louvres. In this drier, air at 250° to 300°F is passed over the grain, eventually reducing it to 28 to 31% moisture content. At this point the grains are still intact and are rather tough and chewy in texture. Holding bins are used to store this material until it can be transferred to the presses.

Additional processing is needed to secure the desired crispness and flavor. First, the equilibrated or tempered wheat pieces travel through a drier. This could be a Proctor and Schwarz drier cornposed of three sections, the first at 280°F, the second at 290°F, and the third unheated. Rate of movement of the material is adjusted so as to yield an emerging product of about 21% moisture content. A spray of B-cornplex vitamins is applied at this stage.

Screw conveyors or drag chain conveyors transport the partially dried pellets to the flaking rollers. Just before they fall into the flaking rolls, the pellets are heated to about 180. to 190.F, making them more plastic in consistency. The large steel flaking rollers are practically identical with those used for making corn flakes. The pressure they apply to the pellets increases the latter's diameter several times and decreases their thickness proportionately.

After they pass through the rolls, the flakes contain 10 to 15% moisture and are still slightly flexible. To obtain the necessary crispness, the flakes are toasted and dehydrated to less than 3% moisture content in a drier provided with a perforated metal conveyor belt. There are typically four temperature zones in the oven; these may include, for example, heated sections at 310°,300°, and 280°F, and an unheated section to partially cool the flakes. The decreasing temperature pattern is said to promote the development of desirable curling and blistering.

A process patented by Benson and Merboth describes the production of breakfast cereal flakes from a continuous sheet of dough, with the improvement of gaining greater control over size and shape of the finished product. The thickness of the dough is reduced by running the conveyor belt faster than the extruded sheet, and tempering is accomplished by cooling the outer surface of the dough sheet with currents of air.

Like most breakfast cereals, wheat flakes are susceptible to the development of rancidity after extended storage. Addition of the common antioxidants BHA and BHT increases shelf life somewhat. For extruded wheat flakes, they are less satisfactory when added to the pre-mix because the high temperatures of processing tend to destroy or vaporize the antioxidants. Megremis reveals that mixed tocopherols will survive' the conditions of extrusion and substantially extend the storage life of wheat flakes made by this method.

Bran flakes.-Bran flakes constituted a rather minor part of the breakfast cereal market until the recent fiber craze, when they began to assume a much more important role. Old-fashioned bran flakes were manufactured by combining a dried portion containing wheat and sufficient amounts of bran to yield flakes containing about four grams of fiber per ounce of cereal. Use of larger amounts of bran, with the aim of providing consumers with a product having greater fiber content, leads to grave difficulties in flaking and soft (not crisp) products. Most cereals of very high bran content are extruded so as to yield, typically, the shreds sold as "All Bran."

To make bran flakes, the dry wheat and bran are combined with a flavoring syrup containing sugar, corn syrup, malt, and salt, then cooked until the starch is completely gelatinized. The cooked particles are partially dried, tempered, flaked by previously described methods, and finally, toasted to give finished flakes having a thickness of 0.005 to 0.040 inch.

Bolles *et al.* (1989) described a method said to give bran flakes containing up to eight grams of fiber per ounce of cereal. Their process involves mixing a grain, such as wheat or rice, with a fiber source, such as wheat bran or oat bran, in a ratio of about 6 to 4, then reacting the mixture with an a-amylase. The enzymes suggested in the patent are bacterial and fungal in origin. It is important that there be limited or partial digestion of the starch, so the amount of enzym an the reaction conditions are critical. Generally, the cornbination of bran cracked wheat, and enzyme are mixed thoroughly and heated to a temperature within the range of 115° to 130"F. Processing times ranging between 2 and 4 minutes are suggested.

The digested mixturo is then -. cooked in a pressurized vessel under conditions which inactlvate the enzyme, say, at about 300°F for 35 minutes. The moisture content of the material corning out of the cooking vessel should be about 30%. This is lowered to about 19% by any convenient method, and the agglomerates are tempered and cooled for about 30 to 60 minutes. Subsequently, the lumps are flaked by passing them between rollers in the manner which has already been described for wheat flakes. A flake thickness in the range of 0.005 to 0.040 inch is said to be satisfactory. The flakes are toasted in improve flavor.

Additional cornment on extruded bran shreds may be appropriate at this point, although they are not "flakes" by any normal definition. It is characteristic of these products that they contain more fiber than the usual bran flake, as indicated by the trade-names of "40% Bran Flakes" for the former and "All Bran" buds for the latter. In batch production of the shreds, the first step might involve mixing 100 lb wheat bran, 5 lb wheat flour, 7.5 lb of another kind of flour, water, and flavorings. This mixture is pressure cooked at about 260°F for a half hour, then extruded under low shear conditions to form nuggets or buds which are dried and perhaps sprayed with a vitamin solution. Cereals produced by this method generally stay crisp in milk for about 2 to 3 minutes before they start to disintegrate.

A continuous process for mixing, heat processing, and forming a bran cereal cornposition in a cornbination cooker-extruder has been described by Calandro *et al.* Dry ingredients (including at least one cereal bran cornponent) are mixed with a syrup containing at least one sugar cornponent in the blending zone of a twin screw extruder. The wetted bran mixture is then cooked in another zone before it is passed through a headspace zone adjacent to the extrusion die. Extrusion takes place through narrow orifices, and the strands of cereal spontaneously break into pieces which fall onto a moving belt. Note that the strands are not cut into predetermined lengths.

The cooked and fragmented strands are then dried and toasted in an oven. The cereal pieces are described as having a visibly roughened surface and an unplasticized appearance with discrete bran particles. Pressure drop across the die, pressures within the extruder barrel and temperatures within the extruder are kept low so as to prevent plasticization of the extrudate, since it is desired to avoid producing smooth, continuous, spaghetti-like strands or overexpansion. Pressure within the extruder should be less than 400 psig and the temperature should be 270°F or less. Pressure drop across the die should preferably be 140 to 275 psig.

As it exits the die, the cooked bran will contain about 26% moisture, sugar solids of about 18%, and about 56% bran. There may be a few percent of minor texturizing and flavoring ingredients. This moist material is dried to a water content of 6% or less. It is said the dried and toasted strands, with their uncut ends, remain crisp in milk for at least four minutes. Flavoring and texturizing ingredients mentioned in the patent include fruit juices, malt, and flavors such as maple. A formula is 55.5% raw wheat bran, 1.4% malt, 23% sucrose syrup (67% solids), 16.2% water, 1.1% salt, 1.3% fig juice concentrate, 1.3% prune juice concentrate, and 0.2% vitamin premix of fat.

Flakes from other grains.-Because of the cornparatively high level in oats, flakes made from this grain in the conventional way have a unacceptably short storage life. Lilly and Reinhart describe a process said to give oat products of satisfactory stability. Oat groats are pressure-cooked until the starch is gelatinized, and then kneaded while being held at a temperature of 150° to 212°F until a plastic dough is formed. The dough is shaped into flakes about 0.011 inch in thickness and these are flash dried to 2 to 10% moisture content by contact with air having a temperature in the range of 400° to 800°F.

Although the author does not know of any cornmercial breakfast cereal flakes made entirely or mostly, from barley, it has been suggested that this grain would be suitable for the purpose. According to one authority, "When extruded, barley will yield a harder, nore crispy flake than corn or wheat.The stronger texture contributed by barley helps minimize breakage to the cereal flakes during transport or consumer handling" Anon. (1989A).

There does not appear to have ever been a rye flake which gained wide cornmercial distribution, but the patent of Gulstad (1971) describes a method for making such a product. In one example, clean dry rye kernels having a moisture content of about 8.3% were fed into a continuous puffing gun at a feed rate of about 10 lb/min. The following gun conditions were used: Steam pressure 100 psig, steam temperature 385°F, barrel angle of 3 degrees below the horizontal, barrel rotation of 45 rpm, puffing orifice diameter of 0.5 inch, barrel diameter 10 inches. and barrel length 12 ft. The puffed rye was milled into flour on a pin mill. A dough was formed by mixing 388 parts of the rye flour with 54.5 parts sucrose, 11.3 parts salt, and 169 parts water, so as to give a mixture having a moisture content of about 32.5%. The resulting dough was processed in a piston type extruder at a pressure of about 2200 psig, and cut into pellets about 0.25 inch in diameter. After the pellets were surface dried to about 23% moisture, they were passed between a pair of flaking rolls spaced about 0.020 inch apart, then dried in a belt oven to a moisture content of about 1%.

No reference can be found to flakes made from grain sorghum, although these seeds would be likely to respond much like the other grains when subjected to the same type of process. Of course, sorghum grains are much smaller than other cereal kernels, and conditions would have to be adjusted to take this difference into account.

Shreds

Shredded wheat biscuits.-The most popular representative of this class is the pillow-shaped shredded wheat biscuit manufactured by Nabisco. It differs from most other ready-to-eat breakfast cereals in that it is made from whole grain without the addition of any flavor and without removal of the germ or bran. Cooking is typically done at atmospheric pressure in boiling water. After one hour or more of cooking, moisture content of the wheat kernels will have reached 50 to 60% and the grain will be very soft. Some preliminary drying in louvred ovens may follow, but the whole wheat is not brought much below 45 to 50% moisture content. The cooked and slightly dried wheat is transferred to stainless steel bins and tempered for many hours before it goes to the shredding rolls.

The shredding rolls are from 6 to 8 inches in diameter and as wide as the finished biscuit is to be, thus much smaller than flaking rolls. One of the pair of rolls has a series of 20 shallow corrugations or ridges running around its periphery. In cross section, these corrugations may be rectangular, triangular, or a cornbination of these shapes. The other roll of the pair is smooth-surfaced. Moist, softened wheat is drawn between these rollers as they rotate, and it issues as continuous strands of dough. By cutting grooves perpendicular to the circumferential corrugations, shred layers having a net-like effect can be obtained. Hall and Carpenter described the preparation of a biscuit having a lattice-like network of shreds. Their product may also be puffed, giving an additional variation in texture and appearance.

Fig. 10.4 Separated shreded wheat into individual biscuits

Biscuits are built up by layering strands on a moving belt which passes under sets of rolls positioned in tandem. Ten to 18 rolls may be used for circular biscuits, while 22 rolls is a cornmon number for rectangular biscuits. In the latter case, layered strands are separated into biscuits by passing them below blunt "knives" which press a thin line of the dough into a solid mass at regular intervals. Figure 10.4 shows the layered strands being separated into biscuits.

Circular biscuits, which are probably not being made anymore in the U.S., were formed quite differently. One end of the sheet formed from layered strands of whole wheat dough is caught up by a smooth roll which rotates just above the belt. This roller turns the layer of strands back upon itself, arid the forward motion of the belt cornbined with the reverse and upward motion of the cylinder surface, causes the layer to roll up into a circular biscuit. As the biscuit reaches a predetermined diameter, a knife chops down on the belt, severing the strands so that the formed biscuit can be released. Automatic controls vary the speed of the belt as the diameter of the biscuit increases. The cornpleted disc falls into a cup from which it is transferred to a belt leading to the ovens.

Since the biscuits are formed from dough of relatively high moisture content, they are quite tender and fragile, and must be handled very carefully to prevent distortion. In practice, this means that the transfer steps must proceed more slowly than is necessary with flakes or puffed products.

The wet biscuits are placed on a metal belt moving through a high temperature gas-fired oven. After 10 to 15 minutes, the outside of the product is dry and toasted but the interior is still wet. Then, the biscuits are transferred to another hot air oven (or to a different section of the same oven) where they are dried at 250°F for 30 to 60 minutes through-time, depending on the size of the biscuit and the rate of air flow. Finished moisture content should be about 11%. The cornbination of heat treatments causes the biscuit to assume the familiar oval cross section (pillow shape) as a result of differential shrinkage of the layers.

A triple shredding mill is used for producing bite-size breakfast cereals. Dough made from wheat, corn, or rice is fed to long, water-cooled shredding rolls. These rolls deposit a shredded dough sheet onto a constant speed conveyor to form a wide, three-layer ribbon. The rolls on the first and third shredding mills extrude dough sheets with a laced pattern, due to the use of cornbinations of smooth and grooved rolls. The middle set of rolls revolves at higher speed than the other two pairs. As a result, the dough sheet in the middle folds as it falls onto the relatively slow moving conveyor belt which has been covered by the first dough sheet. Sugar is sprinkled over the middle dough sheet, and the top sheet is then added. The cornbined structure passes between scoring rolls, and the baked cereal is finally broken along scored lines to form individual bite-size pieces.

It can be seen that the process described in the immediately preceding paragraph can be varied to give many different kinds of products; for example, biscuits containing layers of different kinds of grain.

The flavor of shredded wheat differs significantly from that of whole wheat flakes because the latter includes added condiments and is subjected to much more heat in both the cooking and toasting steps. The more rigorous heat treatment applied to flakes results in considerably more caramelization and other browning reactions in the finished product.

Since shredded wheat is made from the whole kernel, it contains all of the relatively unstable oils from the germ. As a result, rancid odors tend to accumulate in the container if shredded wheat is stored in sealed packages. It is for this reason that the product is normally sold in "breather" boxes without outer or inner linings. When so packaged, the odors of incipient rancidity diffuse from the container, and the product has satisfactory storage stability. Of course, such packages also allow moisture absorption to occur in atmospheres of high relative humidity, with a consequent loss of crispriess, but it appears that consumers of this product are not as demanding, in terms of their texture requirements, as are consumers of, say, corn flakes or crisped rice.

A method of making a breakfast type cereal by forming corrugated flakes of non-uniform thickness on a pair of rolls, one of which is grooved. The flakes are said to have thin connecting membranes that dissolve in milk to leave the remainder in the form of shreds. The non-dissolving shreds essentially duplicate in eating qualities a shredded biscuit-type cereal product.

11

Popcorn

Popcorn is unique among grains in that a high degree of expansion can be achieved when it is heated at atmospheric pressure. Other grains must be superheated in pressurized vessels and then suddenly transferred to a region of lower pressure if much expansion is to be obtained. Popcorn evidently behaves as it does because of the physical structure of the entire kernel and the microscopic structure of the endosperm; characteristics of the starch undoubtedly have an effect.

It should not be necessary to emphasize the commercial importance of popcorn and the snacks derived from it. What may not be so obvious to the casual observer is the firm bases on which the popularity of these snacks rests. The crisp texture, fluffy white appearance, and convenient piece size of popped com provide an almost unique combination of properties that can be utilized to advantage in many different types of snack products. When the ease of processing and the relative cheapness of the raw material are also considered, the widespread use and acceptance of popcorn snacks can be readily understood. Popcorn does have a number of disadvantages, however. Among them are its fragility, its nonuniformity, and its unfavorable response to adverse environmental influences such as high humidity.

Several other kinds of grain, including field corn, can be popped or puffed under certain conditions, but good quality popcorn can be prepared under simple conditions with minimal equipment, and the finished product holds up comparatively well under handling and further preparation such as the application of melted butter or candy-coating. As will be explained later, specialized equipment can be used to puff corn meal and other starchy materials.

Some specialized terms used in the popcorn trade should be defined in order to avoid misunderstandings. Popped corn with a highly irregular pronged appearance is know as the "buttefly" type, while kernels that are predominantly spheroidal with relatively few projections are called "mushroom" or "ball" varieties. Sometimes the popped kernels are called "flakes. "

Four Types of Popcorn

Trade buyers "recognize four major types of popcorn: (1) white hullless, primarily used for home popping; (2) yellow hull-less, which is also sold in kernel form to consumers for home popping, but is used in large amounts by concessionaires, especially in hot and humid regions, because it retains better texture at higher moisture contents than other hybrids do; (3) large kernel yellow, which is popular for factory popping and the theater trade because it pops into large flakes with good visual appeal and is resistant to rough handling-it requires more oil than the other types and becomes tough in the presence of moisture; and (4) medium yellow, a compromise having good appearance when popped and reasonably good texture. It should be understood that there is considerable overlapping of characteristics between the types. Further details on some of the types will be given in the following paragraphs.

White popcorn is rarely used for commercial production of snacks. This category includes varieties ranging in size from small kernels up to the size normally associated with the large yellow varieties. Small kernel size generally leads to the highest-volume popped corn, but fragility of these kernels leads to excessive crumbling when they are processed on a large scale.

Large kernel yellow hybrids pop out large in size-they have a creamy yellow appearance. Under the usual popping conditions, a ratio of about 25% mushroom or ball kernels to 75% butterfly kernels will be observed. Large kernel hybrids are popular with the confectionery industry and for factory popping because the popped com resists breaking better than any of the other kinds of hybrids. They do, however, require more oil and humidity-resistant packaging because they get tough and elastic when they absorb even a small amount of moisture.

Small yellow hull-less popcorn is preferred for consumer preparation because it pops at a relatively low temperature and has superior eating quality. It has also been widely used in low-volume on-premises outlets in the South and Southeast, where the consumer requires corn that is tender and palatable under a wide variety of atmospheric conditions. This type of corn will remain acceptable at a higher moisture content than any of the other hybrids. Its main disadvantages are small size of the popped kernels and its high degree of fragility.

Medium-kernel yellow was developed as a compromise between the yellow hull-less and the large yellow hybrids. In appearance and response to moisture uptake it occupies an intermediate level between the last two types mentioned above. It will form a reasonably high percentage of mushrooms when popped-not as many as a good large-kernel hybrid, but enough to make good caramel corn and cheese corn with only moderate breakage.

Mechanism of Popping

The endosperms of different types of grains show different degrees of starch granule gelatinization when the kernels are expanded by popping. In barley and wheat, which do not expand much, some starch granules undergo complete gelatinization without apparent expansion while other gelatinized granules expand and fuse. Localized cell-wall rupturing occurs. when these kernels split open, and a few intracellular voids or enlarged bubbles can be seen in the gelatinized starch granules as a result of the explosion. Ungelatinized and partly gelatinized. starch granules predominate immediately below the aleurone layer and near the scutellum.

Localized cell-wall rupturing also occurs in the expanded endosperms of popped grain sorghum, popcorn, and dent corn, but the spongy expanded endosperms consist of intact cells within which the gelatinized starch granules form a characteristic structure of "soap bubble" appearance, each bubble representing a starch granule. The cell walls are not destroyed and remain clearly identifiable except where wall rupturing contributes to both expansion and formation of voids. The starch granules are not exploded but are gelatinized and dried into a three-dimensional network or reticulum surrounding empty spaces.

Expansion is much less pronounced in dent corn than in popcorn and sorghum, in which more cell rupturing occurs to form voids. The soap bubble type of structure is less intensively developed in all poorly popped kernels. Some unaltered and partly gelatinized starch granules are also present immediately below the aleurone and near the scutellum even in fully popped kernels.

Quality factors

Consumers may choose between several brands of popcorn sold in polyethylene bags of one pound or multiples thereof, and from smaller quantities packed with oil and (usually) salt in packages adapted to stovetop

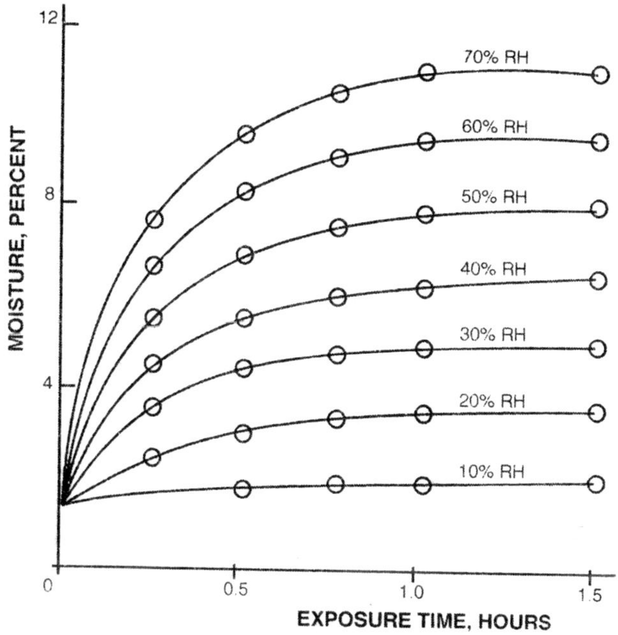

Fig. 11.1 Moisture absoption by popped corn held at various relative humidities.

popping or microwave popping. The packages intended for microwave popping may contain seasonings of various kinds. The consumers' choice must be largely guided by previous experience with the brands, since there is little or no quality information available on the label, and there are no specific Federal regulations or standards which restrict the contents or claims for popcorn. If the package is transparent, some decisions can be made on the basis of appearance-the color of the corn, the' kernel size, any broken kernels which are present, the amount of loose debris. There is no guide to the moisture content of the corn, which is a strong determinant of popping performance and which must be. highly variable considering the kind of packaging used for the retail packs. No doubt a great deal of consumer dissatisfaction exists with respect to the results obtained from retail packed popcorn.

Large purchasers can establish specifications and make at least some simple tests to insure a minimal level of quality. It takes very little time and labor to conduct a pilot plant test of representative samples presented by prospective suppliers and to verify the quality of deliveries by the same means.

The consumer is primarily interested in price, flavor, appearance, and texture. Flavor is strongly influenced by the butter or oil used as a topping, and by the salt. In discussions of popcorn quality in the literature, flavor is rarely mentioned. Yet, freshly popped corn does have a distinctive and appealing flavor. This soon dissipates, and most prepared commercial products provide a very bland base for the oil and salt. So, in home-popped com which is consumed soon after preparation, favor is a major quality factor, while it is much less important in commercial popcorn where texture and appearance are the main quality factors arising from the corn itself.

Texture is strongly related to the intrinsic specific volume of the popped kernel, which may be quite different from the apparent specific volume, the latter being much affected by the shape of the kernel. Texture also reflects in part the presence of hard particles, i.e., the parts of the hulls which remain attached to the puffed grain. In addition, the moisture content of the popped corn at the moment of consumption has a direct effect on the texture. Popped corn continues to evolve moisture untii it cools down, but its low water activity causes it to absorb moisture from air of moderate relative humidity. Even a small rise in the moisture content causes the kernel to become tough and flexible, and so the popped corn loses much of its appeal. Figure 11.1 represents some unpublished data (about 1970) obtained by R. Fosnot showing the uptake of moisture by popped corn corn stored at various relative humidities.

Although commercial distributors of popcorn claim that they consider the kernel texture, flavor, and other subjective characteristics in evaluating the quality of lots offered to them, the chief basis for judging popcorn desirability has always been the relative amount of kernel expansion that is obtained when the com is popped. The percentage of non-popping kernel is a factor in this test. This is an understandable tendency, since expansion is closely related to the price received by the processor. Popped com is usually sold and bought by the consumer (in convenience stores, amusement parks, theaters, etc.) on the basis of volume rather than weight. The concessionaire must fill a bag or box of given volume with popped com, regardless of whether the raw popcorn is of high or low expansion. Naturally, the concessionaire prefers a com of higher expansion since fewer pounds of raw material will fill the required number of containers. Furthermore, com of higher expansion potential generally has a more tender texture than does com oflower expansion.

Vendors of popcorn must also be concerned with "eatability." This factor is related to expansion to some extent. The eatability, which could be roughly defined as the taste satisfaction experienced by the consumer, is dependent on such qualities as flavor, tenderness, and uniformity of the popped kernels as well as on the proportion of oil, salt, and other adjuncts applied to the product.

The trade measures expansion by popping a given weight or volume of com under controlled conditions, dumping the popped kernels into a graduated plastic cylinder of standard diameter, and reading the height of the column of product. Formerly, a standard volume of grain was used for test popping, but measurement in this manner did-not always express the contribution of kernel weight to the results, so a change was made in the procedure, and currently a. standard weight of grain is used in the test. Results are expressed as cubic centimeters of popped kernels per gram of raw kernels. It is also common to express expansion as the ratio of the volume of popped com to the volume of the unpopped kernels. Most commercial com gives an expansion ratio of between 30 and 35 fold, although a few hybrids give expansion ratios as high as 40 fold.

Other factors that have some effect on popping expansion are weight per bushel and mechanical injury to the kernel. Heavier weight per bushel usually leads to greater expansion, probably because the starch is more dense and there are more starch grains per kernel (this would not apply when ,the weight:volume test is used). Rough handling during shelling or processing and damage ,to the kernel by disease. rodents, or insects may lower popping expansion.

It has been suggested that pericarp thickness should be used as another indicator of popcorn quality. In this test. the pericarp 'Sections are mounted on edge in modeling clay and observed under :a compound microscope equipped with an ocular micrometer. Hull sections .are more easily obtained from popped samples than from unpopped kemels. The pericarp thickness is expressed in micrometers. and in a large series of hybrid popcorn samples varied between 41 and 65. The measurement is thought to give an indication of quality because it is related to the amount of tough, horny material remaining on the popped corn and thus is related to the acceptability of the product. Pericarp thickness is largely influenced by genetic factors, although growing conditions have some effect.

The moisture content of kernels can have a strong effect on expansion. The optimum moisture content has been stated as 13.5%, on average. In working with hybrids, Huelsen and Bemis (1954) found that increasing the moisture, at least to about 14.0%, increased expansion. However, the response to increased moisture was related to maturity at harvest and to popping temperatures. Com harvested at more advanced maturity (as shown by moisture contents of, e.g., 15.65%) gave higher popping expansion than com harvested at 31% moisture content. The temperature required to give optimum expansion in the popper varied with different hybrids. Reducing the moisture content at popping likewise reduced the required popping time. There was an inverse relationshiop between popping expansion and time required to pop. The temperature at " which popping began decreased with increasing moisture content.

Differences in the distribution of horny and floury endosperm, and differences in the protein content of these structures, influence the capacity to expand. A major difference between popcorn and other types of corn is that popcorn has a denser and harder endosperm throughout. Apparently, under certain conditions of heating this structure causes steam pressure to build up until a sudden rupture of the pericarp allows the endosperm to expand to form a porous starch network. This foamy or puffy formation is then firmed up or solidified as it cools and dries. The temperature just before the explosion must be sufficient to create the necessary water vapor pressure without burning the pericarp, and the rate of temperature increase must be fast enough to build up the required pressure before too much of the moisture diffuses from the kernel. Damaged kernels may pop poorly or not at all because the water tends to boil away without developing sufficient internal pressure.

Moisture content of the kernel has a pronounced effect on popping behavior. Kernels that are too dry pop feebly, giving off a somewhat mumed sound; the kernel often splits partly open and the unpopped area appears rather dark or scorched. Corn that is too moist pops with a loud explosion but the expanded kernels are small, rough, jagged, and tough. The effect of moisture content on volume attained by popped corn prepared by both of the common methods, oil popping and air popping, was examined by Metzger *et al.* (1989). They found that oil popped kernels achieved maximum volume (cubic cm per g dry matter) when the raw corn was at a moisture content of 13.54%, while air popped corn achieved maximum volume at 14.03%. Air popping produced a maximum specific volume of 55.3 cu cm per g, 27% more than the highest specific volume (43.6 cu cm per g) of the oil popped samples. All tests were conducted with a single popcorn variety. Volume, refers to apparent (bulk) specific volume while dry matter refers to the weight of the unpopped corn calculated as moisture-free substance. It would be interesting to compare microwave popping volume with volume achieved with the other two methods.

The hull is the outer covering or pericarp of the corn kernel. It varies considerably in thickness among the different varieties, but no varietv is completely free of hull, even though some types have been described as hull-less. Generally, the larger the kernel, the thicker the pericarp. The hull is torn and fragmented when the kernel violently expands, and some of it is dislodged from the corn, but most of it remains. In addition to the undesirable appearance contributed by clinging hull fragments, the texture of the popped kernel is adversely affected-the hulls "get between the teeth" is a common complaint. Light-colored pericarp is much less noticeable and, if it is also very thin, the hull-less condition may appear on cursory inspection to have been achieved.

Shape of the popped kernel is affected by variety, moisture content, and popping conditions. Corn yielding a round or ball shape is called the mushroom type, whereas kernels yielding a highly irregular pronged shape are known as butterfly type. All, or nearly all, types will yield kernels which have some of both characteristics. Kernels having the mushroom configuration are preferred by manufacturers of coated or flavored popcorn because they break up less during the mixing operation and accept a more even coating of syrup. The same resistance to rough handling makes it more acceptable to vending machine operators and to wholesale distributors of popped corn. On the other hand, buttefly corn has a lower apparent bulk density and retains salt well. In most cases, its texture is also considered superior to that of mushroom-type corn. For these reasons, it is procured by the majority of on-site poppers, such as theater concessionaires.

Processing

Popcorn is commercially popped by either the dry method or the wet method. Home popping can also be performed by either of these two methods and by microwave heating.

Home popping usually is wet popping, a method in which some sort of vegetable oil is used as a heat transfer medium, but perforated baskets for dry popping over an open fire have been in use ever since colonial times. Commercial poppers were originally wet poppers, too, but there are inefficiencies connected with this process that led to the development of dry popping equipment. Commercial popping units have developed through a series of evolutionary changes from the skillet or kettle used in home popping to very efficient continuous units that can deliver several hundred pounds per hour of extremely uniform product.

Commercial poppers.-Although dry poppers predominate in continuous production factories today, there is still some use of wet-popping equipment.

The nature of the wet-popping process requires that it be a batch-type procedure. A fully automated wet-popping line called the Pop-O Matic controls loading, popping, and dumping automatically in accordance with the temperature sequence. The complete plant includes a seasoning mixer kettle, a conveyor assembly for moving the popped kernels to a tumbler where small pieces, unpopped corn, etc., are removed, a blower conveyor, and a remote-control panel. It accepts a 5-lb charge of corn about every three minutes from a hopper holding 400 lb or more. Seasoning oil and salt are dispensed in measured amounts for each batch, and the quantities may be changed to suit different formulations.

Another commercial line of straight-line wet-method popping plants consists of conveying systems, mechanical oil feeder, poppers, and a sifter. The popped corn storage bin is fabricated on-site to fit the space limitations of the producer's plant. The basic module contains three gas popping units, and any number of the units can be assembled to give the needed output. The framework of this plant is reinforced 2-inch tubing covered with baked white enamel. The conveyor is 10-inch wide sanitary coated belting that travels inside a stainless steel trough attached to the frame, and it is driven by a one-third horsepower gearhead motor. This system has a positive displacement pump that constantly recirculates the oil at low pressure past the discharge points. the popping units. The oil charge is measured automatically in a volumetric tube at each discharge point. A turn of the valve releases a measured oil charge directly into the kettle. Returning the valve to its original position allows the volumetric tube to refill in preparation for the next batch.

A third type of wet popping or "French fry" plant consists of poppers that can be assembled in a series over a conveyor belt to give semicon tinuous operation. The heavy, cast-aluminum kettles can pop about 3 lb of corn per cycle. Gas is supplied through a ball joint coupling which allows the kettle to be rotated for dumping the charge. A motorized stirrer is mounted in the cover. Figure 11.2 illustrates a complete small factory for oil popping of corn. Visible in-the photo, in addition to four poppers, are conveyors, rotary sifting reels, a coating pan, and equipment for making coating syrup (Source: Krispy Kist Korn Machine Co.)

There are two kinds of dry poppers: the batch style, which may be automated and assembled in groups to give essentially continuous operation, and the truly continuous style. Batch poppers consist of a rotating perforated drum mounted inside an insulated cylindrical housing which is heated with

Fig. 11.2 A small factory or pilot plant for oil popped corn.

gas flames. A typical commercial model can deliver approximately 150 lb per hr of popped corn, equivalent to 10-12 lb per cycle. The poppers are manually loaded with weighed amounts of corn.

Havighorst described a large popcorn plant built to supply popped corn to concessions in a chain of 287 theaters. The corn is received in 100-lb bags and stored in a cool area to reduce moisture loss. When needed, the corn is dumped into a conveyor, which delivers it to a series of hoppers, each hopper supplying two batch-type popping machines. As directed by the automated system, a hopper will deliver eight pounds of corn through a flexible metal pipe to the popper. This popper has no direct temperature controls, but the temperature at the stack where the air exits is about 650°F. Popping time is adjustable, but in this facility it is claimed to be about 4.5 min. Automatic controls reverse the perforated drum to allow removal of any unpopped kernels through a slot made by overlapping part of the drum surface.

A typical fully automated dry-popping line might include cleaning devices for the grain, a continuous dry popper, a sifter to separate popped from unpopped kernels, a coating reel to apply oil and seasonings, and the conveyors (mechanical and pneumatic) needed to get the ingredients from one processing unit to the next. If caramel corn is being made, the additional equipment required would be a caramel mixing kettle with automatic controls and a metering pump, a film-type caramel concentrator, a corn coater, a cooling separator tunnel, and a continuous belt-type cooling conveyor that delivers finished product to the packaging equipment.

The Cretors "Flo Thru 200" automatic and continuous popper processes approximately 200 lb per hr of raw corn. An immersion-type gas burner consumes about 100 ft3 per hr of 1,000 Btu natural gas fed at 6 to 8 inches water pressure. Major elements within the oven are a supply fan, gas burner, and popping drum. The enclosure is insulated with two inches of fiberglass.

The Manley continuous flow automatic dry popper is made in two sizes- a large unit having a capacity of 350 to 600 lb per hr and a smaller machine with a capacity of 200 to 250 lb per hr. An adjustable speed feeding device automatically delivers the raw kernels into the popping tumbler. Forced hot air at controlled temperature is directed against the tumbling kernels. As the kernels pop, they are immediately moved to the exit end of the drum, leaving only unpopped corn in the heated zone. The machine has a recirculating airflow system with an Eclipse fresh-air burner. Gas controls are fully automatic and include safety devices. Controls include a Partlow indicating temperature controller, a Honeywell modulating controller, a pilot pressure regulator, and a Partlow high temperature cut-off.

Microwave heating is an excellent method of preparing popcorn in the home. According to legend, popcorn was the first food to be cooked in the microwave. The inventor of radar, knowing that some wavelengths used in that technology were absorbed by water molecules with, of course, the evolution of heat, was moved by curiosity to put some popcorn in a chamber where these waves were present at a high concentration. This crude experiment was a success, but the commercial importance of microwave cooking took a few decades to be fully appreciated.

Microwaves are apparently not used commercially to pop com in large quantities. Hot air poppers do as good a job, they are easier to control and are probably safer, and the equipment cost is much lower. In the home, however, consumers appreciate. the greater convenience of microwave popping, which permits preparation of the snack in the container in which it will be served, and which eliminates the need for flame or electric heating of a cooking utensil as well as the requirement for constant shaking. As a result, the sale of portion and multi-portion packs of popcorn in paperplastic bags specially designed for microwave heating has been a huge success in the U.S. These bags may also contain flavored oils and salt, or sometimes, ingredients alleged to produce caramel com. Most, if not all, of the more recent designs include susceptor panels (usually made of some kind of metal foil or powder designed to heat up rapidly) which increase the speed of popping by accelerating temperature buildup at the bottom of the bag. There are some drawbacks to the method. Steam accumulates within the bag as water is driven from the kernels, and this must be vented quickly after popping is complete or it will be re-absorbed into the popped kernels, making them soft and elastic. In addition, venting the steam usually involves some risk of the consumer experiencing burned fingers, which tends to take the edge of this enjoyment of the product.

A recent patent describes an improvement in microwave popping speed which occurs when the com kernels are encased in a thin film of (for example) solidified oil or beeswax and then coated with another thin film of (for example) gelatin or polyvinyl alcohol. The oil or wax can be flavored, though this is not necessary. The inventors claim the com pops more rapidly and completely when heated in a microwave oven.

Sifters.-After the com is popped, it should be sifted to remove unpopped kernels, small fragments of popped com, charred debris, etc. Most firms which manufacture poppers also offer sifters to round out their line. All popped com sifters consist of a rotating inclined drum made of wire screen or perforated metal. Unwanted scrap pieces fall through the screen and are collected in a pan or on a conveyor underneath the drum. The pattern of the mesh weave and the. size of the openings are critical in reducing clogging of the sieve by lodged kernels, and they also have an effect on the percentage of kernels broken down by the tumbling and abrading action of the sifter. A helical metal ribbon is affixed to the inside of the cylinder to ensure movement of the kernels toward the exit end. Usually, the rate ofrotation is fixed. The steel mesh cylinder may be totally enclosed by a metal housing, or the top half may be left exposed. Typical throughput is 750 lb per hr.

Coaters.-Most popped corn sold through retail outlets is coated with butter-flavored oil and salt. A considerable amount is sold with cheese flavored coating. Although it is possible to purchase butter-flavoured oil in drums and spray it on the popcorn without further treatment, the better procedure is to bring the oil within a temperature range that is optimum for spraying. Not only does this improve coverage, but it facilitates pumping and metering. Powdered cheese flavors can be mixed with the oil and the mixture pumped to the coating reel, where it is sprayed on the popped corn. Alternatively, the cheese-flavored powder can be dispersed into coating reels by various types of feeders. There it adheres to the liquid oil which has been sprayed on the corn.

Various methods have been developed for coating popcorn with flavors in oily media. The patent of Cooley and Douglas (1989) is fairly typical of the approaches used. They prepare an oil-based flavoring system by dry-blending solid particles of fat with a flavoring. The fat has a melting point of no less than about 95°F so that the combined flavoring material is free-flowing at room temperature. The fat-flavor system is sprinkled onto hot popped corn so that the fat melts and the flavoring component is adhered to the popcorn. This is said to produce a popcorn product having an even flavor distribution but no waxy mouthfeel. A typical formula is about 50% fat (a beaded fat comprising a mixture of partially hydrogenated vegetable oils) and 50% flavor (such as sour cream and onion seasoning blend).

Coating popcorn with flavors suspended in oil or by coating first with oil and then with powder are relatively simple processing methods as compared with the application of crisp coatings made principally of sugar. These coatings can be variously flavored and colored, but by far the majority of sugar glazed popcorn is of the so-called caramel corn variety, which implies a heat treated mixture of sugar and butter. Cracker Jack is a variant of this type with a strong molasses component in the flavor.

Caramel corn factories.-A fairly large percentage of commercially popped corn is further processed into caramel corn of various types. The range in size of these operations is extremely wide, varying from small retail operations that may produce a few tens of pounds per hour in hand stirred kettles to fully automated lines putting out thousands of pounds per hour of nationally distributed caramel corn confections.

Caramel corn can be produced, as it originally was, in gas-heated copper or tinned pans of the Savage type, in which the operator stirs the contents of the kettle with a wooden or plastic paddle and adjusts the temperature by manually turning a gas valve until the results meet some subjective standard. Equipment of this general type is actually in current use, producing some widely distributed gourmet confections. The drawbacks of such an operation are too obvious to require comment. It is possible, nonetheless, to produce good-quality caramel corn if the operator is sufficiently skilled and conscientious.

The next step up in plant size would require equipment such as the hydraulic candy com mixer made by Krispy Kist. This machinery is said to be capable of producing up to 1,200 lb per hr of finished product. A cylindrical stainless steel kettle or mixing can fits on a rotating turntable that can be raised and lowered hydraulically. An auger-shaped agitator is mounted near one side of the turntable to give a compound mixing action. Popped com and molten candy are manually scaled into the mixing can in the desired proportions.

Large-scale batch-type caramel com plants are relatively efficient and can produce good quality, relatively uniform product. Integrated systems for cooking and mixing, with capacities of 100 to 1,000 lb per hr and requiring only one person in attendance, are commercially available. They can be combined with product bins, a soda dispenser (for peanut brittle types of products), ingredient vats, dispensing devices, and a two-stage heat control to give completely automated plants. Operation should proceed as follows: (1) An air conveying system loads the popcorn hopper; (2) a level. control in the hopper shuts off the popcorn supply and starts a pump, allowing a pre-measured amount of syrup to be delivered to the kettle; (3) the heat is then turned on and agitation begins; (4) at a first determined temperature level, butter and nuts are fed into the kettle; (5) when a second temperatur~ stage is reached, soda is added and the heat is shut off; (6) finally, popcorn is added and blending continued for a selected length of time; (7) after which the kettle is rotated to dump its contents and complete the cycle. The hot, coated product must be passed through separating tumblers and cooling conveyors.

Completely automatic systems for producing caramel corn will include as a minimum metering and mixing equipment for blending the candy ingredients, a film-type concentrator to reduce the moisture content of the syrup and bring it to a molten condition, a com coater for distributing the molten syrup onto the popped kernels, a cooling-separating tumbler that allows the candy to harden while preventing excessive agglomeration of the individual pieces, and a cooling/spreading conveyor on which the final product size is established and the temperature is reduced to a level suitable for packing.

Most of the concentrators used in the caramel com industry resemble vertical metal cylinders and are based on falling film evaporation. A typical caramel coating would consist of liquid sugar, com syrup, coloring and flavor. These ingredients would be continuously mixed and heated to between 150. and 180.F in a steam-jacketed kettle equipped with automatic temperature controls. The blended ingredients would be continuously pumped at a controlled rate into the concentrator where high-pressure steam heats a thin film, evaporating nearly all the water content to produce an effluent material having a boiling point of about 290.F. Average residence time of the syrup in the concentrator will be between 4 and 10 seconds.

Dwell time can be varied to cause different extents of caramelization-color and flavor development. Salt and/or soda can be metered into the syrup as it emerges from the concentrator and falls into the collecting receptacle. Typical hourly output is 430 lb per hr per tube.

Continuous coaters for caramel com generally take the form of heated screw conveyors that thoroughly mix the com, nuts, and syrup. In some cases, large rotating drums with helical flights are used to perform this function. Gentle action is needed in order to avoid excessive breakdown of the com, and this dictates slow speeds, a minimum of tumbling, and no compaction. The action of the continuous units is generally more severe than that of the batch mixers. A typical commercial unit is a mixing screw conveyor that is steam-jacketed and has a hollow, steam-heated screw, and has a capacity of 700 lb per hr. Popped com is dropped through a chute at one end of the jacket and the molten candy is fed in at an opening a short distance downstream. If product is to contain nuts, the roasted nuts are added some distance downstream from the syrup. Total length of this unit is 6 ft, and the inside diameter is 8 in. It is driven by a 0.5 hp motor having a variable speed drive.

Whether the com is coated in batch- or continuous-type mixers, it must subsequently be cooled and separated to produce clusters of the desired size. Several firms distribute equipment for this purpose. In one example, the hot confection first enters a conveyor consisting of a stainless steel woven-wire belt traveling between upper and lower plenum chambers through which air is circulated by two fans. Ambient air is used, i.e., there is no refrigeration. The conveyor speed is variable. From the slightly elevated exit end of the conveyor, the still warm confection drops into a separator. The latter is a horizontally disposed drum with stainless steel ends and paddles, the circumference being made of 0.25 inch diameter steel rods. The drum is rotated by a 0.5 hp motor operating through a variable speed drive. In a modified design, the drum has square mesh openings rather than slots.

The Cretors cooling and separating tumbler consists of a large cylinder of perforated metal with helical flights inside. Its axis is slightly inclined to the horizontal plane. Power for rotation is applied by motorized variable speed wheels to two tracks running around the exterior of the drum. Ambient air is forced by a fan into the drum from a plenum applied to the bottom of the cylinder.

In still another system, the plastic mass of coated popcorn is passed between metal rollers as it leaves the coating conveyor. The rolls are separated a considerable distance and turn slowly so that individual kernels are not crushed; the large lumps are pressed into layers a little more than one kernel thick. These large lumps pass under teflon wheels which spread them horizontally, creating fairly small agglomerates. All of this must be done promptly as the candy sets up into a rigid framework very quickly, and when this happens the agglomerates cannot be reduced in size without breaking the pieces.

After separating the product into clusters of the required size, it is desirable to chill it still further so that the coating will be nonsticky and the clusters completely firm before the product is packaged. This is generally accomplished by equipment consisting of conveyor belts passing through chambers in which ambient air is circulated. The belts must be wide enough so there is essential no contact between clusters. In a few operations, refrigerated air is used to speed cooling and increase the throughput. In a typical ambient air unit, the warm clusters are fed onto a wire-mesh conveyor belt that passes through the cooling chamber in three tiers. Fanforced air is filtered before it contacts the product.

Candy coatings of types other than caramel make up only a small proportion of the total category sales. These processes are all based on the preparation of at kind of hard candy (boiled sweets) and applying it at a temperature and moisture content such that a relatively uniform coating can be applied to the popped kernels. Fruit flavours, butter flavours, and spice flavours are among the varieties which have been offered.

12

Formulated Puffed Snacks

It is characteristic of popcorn that the whole kernel is used. Fractured or partial kernels do not expand well, if at all. As mentioned before, other grains can be puffed by special methods, and sorghum can be popped fairly well using the simple procedure which is effective for popcorn, but there is obviously a need for techniques which can make puffed snacks of different shapes, sizes, colors, flavors, and textures, and can use a variety of flours and meals. This has been achieved, and it is the purpose of this section to review the technology of the extrusion puffing of meals and doughs.

Ingredients

Other grain products.-Large quantities of corn meal are used in puffed, extruded snack products and in many brands of fried corn chip snacks. The production of corn flour and corn meal by dry milling operations is discussed in another chapter. Field (dent variety) corn is sometimes processed directly into alkaline-treated masa for use in corn chips based on the traditional tortilla preparation method (such as "Fritos"). These production methods will be discussed below.

Flour and other derivatives of the wheat kernel are used in many baked, fried, and extruded snack products, some examples being pretzels, flavored crackers (cheese, etc.), and cookies. Flour, bran, farina, and other fractions of the wheat kernel are obtained by means of the milling process, which is a combination of conditioning, grinding, and particle-classification operations.

The type of wheat has an important influence on the characteristics of flour milled from it. These differences result, at least in part, from the percentage of protein in the endosperm (white starchy interior) of the wheat. Hard wheat, which can be further subdivided into spring and winter wheats, generally has a relatively high protein content. It yields flour which can absorb large amounts of water and can be processed into doughs which are tough and extensible. Flours from hard wheat are used as ingredients for such products as bread, rolls, pretzels, English muffins, etc. Doughs made from soft wheat flours tend to require smaller quantities of water in their preparation and to be soft and less elastic. Soft wheat flour is used mainly for cakes, cookies, and quick breads such as baking powder biscuits and cake-type muffins.

Milling by-products (e.g" bran) have been combined with soy protein and other adjuncts to produce expanded snack foods having special nutritional characteristics by Seyam *et ai.* (1976). Bran and some other millfeeds are good sources of fiber for snack foods.

Oats, rice, and barley (and fractions derived from these grains) have been used as components in different kinds of snacks, primarily to provide some real or imagined nutritional benefit. Extrusion-expanded rice snacks tend to be somewhat crisper or shorter in texture than similar products made from cornmeal, and they have a blander flavor and lighter color. Explosion-puffed and oven=puffed rice, such as is sold for breakfast cereals, can serve as bases for snack foods, either by adding flavors to them or fflrming them into aggregates or cakes. In fact, sugar-coated puffed rice breakfast cereal is frequently used as a sweet snack by children. Details of manufacture can be found in an article by Brockington and Kelly (1972) and elsewhere.

Rye has not been much used in snack foods except as an ingredient in the toasted and flavored bread or bagel chips that are sold as specialty items. Flour from this grain has also been used as a component in crackers, with added caraway seeds to give the typical rye bread flavor. Use of rye in snack foods is not even mentioned as one of the grain's applications in the monograph by Bushuk (1974).

Meal made from grain sorghum has been used to replace part of the com in masa. The results were said to be satisfactory, except for a discoloration which resulted from the reaction of polyphenols in the sorghum cortex with the alkaline ingredients of masa (Bedolla and Rooney 1982). Sorghum meal has also been suggested as a partial replacement for wheat flour in cookies, crackers, and some other snack foods. Since the sorghum ingredient adds nothing positive to the physical characteristics of the dough, or to the flavor, texture, or nutritional content of the finished product, it must be regarded solely as a filler in these applications.

Following the lead provided by popcorn, food manufacturers made efforts to puff other whole kernels. Consistent expansion to low densities could not be achieved with other cereal grains when the simple processing methods used for popcorn were applied. Good results were obtained, however, when moistened grain was superheated (Le., brought to a temperature above the boiling point of water at atmospheric pressure) and then suddenly transferred to a space of substantially lower pressure. These methods became commercially successful, and breakfast cereals "shot from guns" resulted.

It was recognized that variations in shape, size, and composition of the finished products were severely limited as long as VII01e kernels had to be used for the raw material. The desire for greater freedom in product design led to the development of methods for puffing pellets made from corn meal.

The breakfast cereal industry was the first to make use of methods for puffing cornmeal products. The puffing equipment was the same as had been used for puffing kernels of wheat, rice, etc. Pellets were prepared by adding water to a farinaceous material containing a substantial proportion of dried corn particles (such as cornmeal, corn flour, or corn cones), drying the pellets to a moisture content suitable for puffing, expanding the dried pellets in a puffing gun, and driving off additional moisture from the puffed pellets.

Similar techniques have been used in the snack industry. "Halfproducts" are pieces formed from doughs that have been cooked and extruded, but not puffed, in continuous mixers. They have the approximate shape and weight of the finished product, although, of course, the expansion process which is later applied to them will much increase the size and somewhat alter their shape, while loss of moisture will decrease their weight. When they are to be finished, these half-products can be expanded by baking or frying without using complex high-extrusion apparatus.

Certain kinds of modified starches can be mixed in ordinary bakery mixers to form doughs which, when cut into shapes, can be expanded in standard ovens and friers. This development has blurred the dividing line between extrusion-puffed snacks, since the mixing and forming methods closely resemble those used in cookie and cracker baking. In this book, however. baked snacks will be defined as those products leavened (Le., expanded) primarily by carbon dioxide originating from yeast or sodium bicarbonate and heat processed at ambinent pressures.

The logical next step was puffing extruded material directly. Enough heat and mechanical energy must be applied to the cereal-based raw materials to thoroughly gelatinize the starch. All extruder-puffers perform this func~ion.

Extrusion puffers are designed to compress the dough, mix and shear it, and heat it to more than 212°F so that the water in the extrudate rapidly bursts into vapor as the material emerges from the die. The dough then expands from the intemal steam pressure, becoming cellular and porous, and finally sets up (becomes firm) due to cooling and drying. The shape and size of the product are determined by the die design and the speed of the knife that cuts the strands. Temperature, extrusion rate, pressure, moisture content, and composition of the dough also affect the appearance of the piece.

Expandable ingredients.-Many types of starchy flours and meals obtained from grains, tubers, etc., have been found to be suitable ingredients for puffed snacks. Rice flour expands readily into a low-density, white, and bland tasting product of crisp but rather fragile texture. Corn meals can be expanded with little difficulty into crisp pieces having the typical corn flavor and a color that is white or light yellow according to the type of corn. Due to its relatively high fat content, oat flour requires high levels of moisture and a high temperature for moderate expansion into fairly soft and frangible masses. Relatively high moisture and high temperature are required to satisfactorily puff wheat flour; it does not expand as well as corn and rice. Potato flour also requires high moisture and high temperature, but extrudes well under these conditions and forms collets of excellent texture. Tapioca flour gives bland tasting puffs when processed at high temperatures and a moderate moisture content. Soy flour can be used as an auxiliary ingredient to improve the protein content and protein quality of the finished cereal product but generally has adverse effects on color, flavor and texture.

The preferred ingredient for most extrusion processes is number two grade dry-milled corneal with hull and germ removed. The fat content of this material is normally less than 1%. Cost is generally favorable compared to likely alternatives. Particle size is important. Combinations of rice and corn are sOpletimes used. Rice, if present in sufficient quantity, provides a crisper and blander product.. Milled second-head rice is suitable for this purpose. Purified starches, and modified starches, can also be extruded into puffed snacks.

Fats, Oils, Emulsifiers, and Antioxidants

The ingredients described in this section are included here because they are used in the preparation of snack products. Other materials of the same type are discussed in the chapter on bakery products.

Frying fat is both a processing agent (heat transfer medium) and an ingredient in many important snack products, such as potato chips. In other snacks, it may function only as an ingredient. In any case, it has significant effecta on the appearance, flavor, and texture of the product and is often the ingredient which limits shelf-life. It may also be the most expensive ingredient in the product.

Fats and oils are triglycerides of fatty acids, that is, they contain three fatty acid molecules which have combined with one glycerol molecule to yield one molecule of oil or fat. Fatty acids are straight chain compounds bearing a single carboxyl group at one end. Naturally occurring fatty acids almost always have an even number (between 4 and 26) of carbon atoms. Their melting point increases with chain length, and fatty acids with twelve or more carbon atoms are solid at room temperature.

If a fatty acid contains double-bond linkages, it is classified as unsaturated. Such compounds tend to be considerably more reactive than saturated fatty acids, and they melt at lower temperatures than saturated fatty acids with the same number of carbon atoms. Polyunsaturated (more than one unsaturation point) fatty acids are regarded as beneficial in the diet.

Major sources of food lipids are annual field crops of soybeans, peanuts, cottonseed, rapeseed ("canota"), com, and sunflower seed. Of course, some of these crops, such as cotton, are not grown primarily for their oil content. Animal fats, including butter, lard, tallow, and grease, are very important snack ingredients. Palm, palm kernel, coconut, and olive oils are food oils originating from trees grown almost entirely in the tropics. Cocoa butter is an expensive but highly important fat in confectionery manufacture. Marine lipids are of very little importance in food manufacture, although menhaden oil processed in specific ways has clearance for use in some products.

Shortenings.-The shortenings used in some snacks include animal fats and oils and vegetable fats and oils. The animal products include butter, beef fats, and a few other minor items. Vegetable shortenings are based on many different kinds of fats and oils from seeds, fruits, and nuts. Space limitations preclude extensive discussions of these materials in this book. Readers interested in more deta,ils should consult "The Technology of Materials of Baking" (Matz 1989).

Butter contains over 80% butterfat, about 16% water, 0.5% lactose, and 0.1 to 3.0% ash (mostly from added salt). The structure of butter consists of a continuous phase of solid butterfat inclosing globules of liquid fatty material and drops of aqueous solution. Crystals or agglomerates of solid fatty'substance may also be present in forms sufficiently large to be detected microscopically. Some authorities believe that a second continuous phase composed of aqueous solution exists in butter.

Since butter is quite expensive relative to most other fats, its use is restricted to those products in which its flavor makes a significant contribution to acceptability or in which its use permits advertising claims having marketing value. Popcorn is traditionally seasoned with butter, but virtually all commercially popped com of the "buttered" variety will contain vegetable oil materials with added artificial or natural butter flavors. If some of the natural product is to be included for labeling and marketing purposes, low-score butter is often preferred to the blander high-score products.

Specially "ripened" butter of extremely intense flavor can be used to reduce cost. Commercial butter is classified in the following U.S. grades: AA or 93 score, A or 92 score, B or 90 score, and C or 89 score.

Lard has a distinctive natural flavor that is thought to be desirable in some foods, although it is not a common ingredient in snacks because of its limited stability. Lard is classified on the basis of the rendering method used as either prime-steam, dry-rendered, open kettle-rendered, or continuous process lard. Lard sold to bakers and other food processors is called "relined pure lard" and may be made by any of these methods. Lard was the traditional frying fat used'in tortilla chip manufacture, but it has been replaced by vegetable oils in all national brands. Under most marketing conditions, lard is an economical frying fat.

Characteristics of lard are governed by composition of the hog fat from which it is made, by the method of rendering, and by the refining processes applied to the extracted fat. Variations in hardness of the lard depend mostly on the body location of the fats. For example, internal fats such as leaf fats, are always higher in melting point than fat from the external part of the hog carcase. Refiners control and standardize the product by selecting and blending different fats. Special grades are produced by segregating certain fats and by using special rendering methods. Pure leaf lard, which has the highest melting point of any commercial type, is made only from leaf fat. If an even firmer shortening is required, hydrogenated lard flakes can be added to the natural (ats. By varying the amount of hydrogenated material, a wide range of melting points can be obtained.

Beef tallow is obtained from edible fatty tissues of cattle. As with lard, its Pllysical properties can vary considerably, depending on the history of the cattle from which the fat is taken. It is normally a hard but plastic fat having a melting point of about 110' to 120'F. Because of its hardness, it is often subjected to further processing rather than used in its native form.

Beef fats rendered by special methods are separated by fractional crystallization into oleo oil (low melting fraction) and oleo stearin (high melting fraction). Its short plastic range (from about 70° to 80°F) and relatively low melting point make oleo oil a fairly good substitute for coconut oil in some applications. Use of oleo oil, or a blend of oleo oil and some other fat, as a frying medium was one of the "secrets" to the unique flavor of McDonald's french fries.

Soybean oil and cottonseed oil are corl1mon frying fats and are the principal raw materials for hydrogenated vegetable oil shortenings. Where bland flavors or vegetable origins are important to the consumer, hydrogenated fats prepared from soybean oil or cottonseed oil are the shortenings of choice. Coconut oil is widely used as a spray fat, and in fillings and coatings. Cocoa butter is an essential part of pure chocolate coatings and is used in a few other special formulas. Peanut, corn, and palm oils are less frequently used in snacks. Olive oil, though an important item of commerce, is probably never used in snacks.

Vegetable oils are either presed or solvent extracted from the seeds, and in their original form contain many nonglyceride components or impurities. Among these may be found free fatty acids, amino acid polymers, phospholipids, resins, pigments, mucilaginous substances, and carbohydrates. Crude oils are not usable directly in snack products because of these impurities and must be processed to remove the more objectionable substances. Some of the impurities may be natural antioxidants, so it is possible for crude or partially purified oils to be more resistant than refined oils to the development of rancidity.

All vegetable oils offered to snack manufacturers have been refined and deodorized. The refining process involves mixing the oil with alkali and then washing it. Deodorizing by steam or vacuum stripping follows. The oils are usually bleached. Cottonseed oil and partially hydrogenated soybean oil may also be treated by methods which remove the higher melting fraction to give a "winterized" or salad oil which does not separate into a solid fraction and a liquid fraction when it is stored in the cold. Although for many purposes soybean oil and cottonseed oil may be used interchangeably, the latter has a reputation for being more resistant to oxidation or flavor reversion.

Refined soy and cottonseed oils are usually further treated by blending, hydrogenation, addition of emulsifiers and antioxidations, and other processes.

Frying fats.-Fats used for frying snack products must have different properties from the fats intended for use as shortenings or as coatings. A high smoke point and excellent stability to hydrolysis and oxidation at elevated temperatures are essential characteristics. In most markets, the frying fat is expected to contribute little flavor of its own to the finished product, although some regions of the country have become accustomed to the flavor of lard. Hydrogenated cottonseed oil is a common frying fat, and it is essentially flavorless.

Fresh fat, as it is received, may not be completely satisfactory for frying because the heat transfer characteristics-partly a function of, vicosity-are not optimal for this purpose. If the frying kettle is replenished from time to time with small additions of fresh fat, an equilibrium state can be maintained in which the finished product always has satisfactory properties. When the frying equipment contains only fresh fat, it must be 'broken in" by heating the fat at frying temperatures and in contact with product until a free fatty acid content of about 0.4% is reached, or until the product is being cooked as desired.

Fat is broken down to free fatty acids and glycerine by steam from the product, by oxygen from the air, and by heat. Excessive deterioration is evidenced by smoking, darkening, and foaming. Methyl silicone is often effective in reducing foaming. Filtration is effective in removing particles that can char and discolor the products, but it does not retard oxidation and it does not affect the free fatty acid composition or the viscosity of shortening.

Copper ions greatly accelerate the development of oxidative rancidity, so fats should be prevented from contacting copper, brass, or bronze utensils or fitments at any time.

Antioxidants.-Although there is a great diversity in the composition of snack foods, they all contain some fat, either added as such or present as a component of another ingredient. All of these fat~ are subject to oxidative and hydrolytic rancidity, which can cause the development of objectionable odors and flavors.

Antioxidants are substances capable of retarding the development of rancidity in foods. Natural antioxidants can be found in many nonpurified fats, such as cocoa butter, while certain synthetic chemical compounds can be added to fats for the same purpose.

From a chemical standpoint, rancidity is of two types: (1) hydrolytic rancidity, which can lead to the occurrence of 'soapy flavors, and (2) oxidative rancidity, which causes the pungent or acrid odor characteristic of badly deteriorated fat. When hydrolytic rancidity occurs, oxidative rancidity development is facilitated. Oxidative rancidity is unquestionably the most important of these two mechanisms so far as effects on food acceptability are concerned. The susceptibility of a fat to oxidation depends to a considerable extent on the number of unsaturated bonds in the fatty acid moiety. Polyunsaturated fats are very prone to oxidation, whereas fully saturated fats and oils are much more stable.

In hydrolytic rancidity, moisture and enzymes cause splitting of the triglyceride molecule into glycerol and free fatty acids. The rate of lipolysis of the fat is strongly influenced by temperature. Optimum temperatures for such reactions are usually near 100.F. Hydrolytic rancidity can be controlled by bringing the product to a low moisture content, storing the product at a low temperature, and inactivating the enzymes by heat treatplent. The high processing temperatures to which most snacks are subjected are usually sufficient to destroy the enzymes which would otherwise lead to hydrolysis offats.

A great amount of reseach activity has been directed toward finding substances that will retard the development of oxidative rancidity in foods and at the same time be acceptable as food additives by federal regulatory agencies. At the present time, only four chemical compounds are commercially important as antioxidants for foods. They are butylated hydroxyanisole (BHA), butylated hydroxytoluene (BHT), tertiary butylhydroquinone (TBHQ), and propyl gallate (PG). According to data released by its manufacturer, TBHQ seems to be somewhat more effective than BRA in retarding the development of rancidity in dry cereals, which products can be reasonably assumed to react like many snack foods. The FDA says that the concentration of antioxidants must be such that the combined total of BRA, BHT, TBHQ, and propyl gallate does not exceed 0.02% of the weight of the fat and oil (including essential oils) in the product. Regulations concerning antioxidants in animal fats, as promulgated by the USDA, are slightly different.

Citric or phosphoric acid improve the effectiveness of antioxidants by chelating ions of copper or iron, but they do not themselves function directly to prevent fat oxidation. These relatively innocuous substances are very frequently added as part of the antioxidant mixture. It should be noted that citric acid is not very resistant to high temperatures, as in frying.

In the antioxidant treatment of nuts, tortilla chips, or any other foodstuff subject to oxidative rancidity, it is important to add the preservative before oxidation begins in the oil phase of the snack. When added to fresh nuts, the antioxidant is available to terminate the free' radicals as they form. The antioxidant cannot reverse or mask fat oxidation that has already occurred.

Antioxidants can be applied by spraying a more or less dilute solution on the nuts, popcorn, chips, etc., although they are more commonly added to the frying or roasting oil. Sodium chloride to which antioxidants have been added by the salt manufacturer can be used as a simple means of applying the fat preservatives to snacks. Packaging materials are frequently treated with antioxidants so that the oils that contact and penetrate into the boards or films will not undergo the rapid rancidification that would otherwise occur. There is also reason for believing that the antioxidant-treated packaging material gives off vapors that can have some effect (probably minor) on the noncontacting product.

Sweeteners

Sweeteners are used in large quantities for glazed popcorn ("caramel com" and the like) and some other snacks. Various kinds of formulated snack foods depend on sugar and com syrup as both texturizing and flavoring ingredients. The powdery coatings for savory/salty snacks may also contain sweeteners.

Commercial sucrose-refined cane or beet sugar-is one of the purest ingredients available to the food manufacturer. It is truly "natural" in that the chemical form in which it reaches the consumer is exactly the same chemical form found in the juice of the cane or beet. The composition of the fractional percentage of nonsucrose material in beet sugar differs slightly from that of cane sugar, but in practice the two sugars can be used interchangeably.

Cane or beet sugars from various manufacturers do not differ significantly in composition, although the physical properties (granulation) may vary. Brown sugars and other non-white types can vary substantially from manufacturer to manufacturer. Nearly all commercially available white sugars contain in excess of 99.8% sucrose, with less than 0.5% moisture, about 0.05% invert sugar and other carbohydrates besides sucrose, and a trace of ash.

The obvious advantages, in many applications, of handling sugar in dissolved form have led to the extensive distribution of sucrose as syrups. Sucrose syrup is available at solids contents of 66.5 to 68%, which is the limit of solubility of sucrose in water at ordinary temperatures. Refinery syrups or liquid brown sugars are also available in some localities. Refiners' syrups are obtained by special processing of material drawn off from the intermediate steps in the manufacturing of cane sugar. They have a relatively strong flavor and a dark color that can be advantageous in certain food uses and tolerated in some others. Since they are usually lower-priced than pure granulated sugar, substitution is desirable wherever it is feasible. These syrups contain a total of 50 to 75% sucrose and invert solids combined, and other soluble substances to make a total of 70 to 80& solids.

Com syrups, which consist of cornstarch hydrolyzed to varying degrees have the outstanding advantage of being cheaper, on a solids basis, than refined cane or beet sugar. Sugar and corn syrup are not interchangeable on an ad lib basis, but substitution of the cheaper material is often successful if minor adjustments can be made in formulas and slight differences in the finished products can be accepted. Too, there are instances in which corn syrup has functional advantages compared to sugar.

Two specifications of prime importance in corn syrup procurement are dextrose equivalent (DE) and degrees Baume. The former figure indicates the exent to which the starch has been converted to sugar and thus is related to sweetness, viscosity, and preservative quality of the material, whereas degrees Baume is related to the solids content of the syrup. For some special syrups, additional information is required, since the distribution of molecular species is not always the same for syrups having the same DE; this is true in the case of fructose-containing syrups, which will be discussed later (also, high maltose syrups).

Corn syrup solids and dextrose are available for those users who desire a higher concentration of solids or who do not want to handle the liquid form. As the name suggests, corn syrup solids are prepared by drying corn syrups. The normal moisture contents of these products lies between 3.0 and 3.5%. Corn syrup solids are offered at several dextrose equivalents, but the common type is 42 DE. The usual dextrose powder is a monohydrate of glucose, but at least one manufacturer offers anhydrous dextrose.

Other Ingredients

Snack food manufacturers procure large quantities of many ingredients not described in the preceding discussion. To avoid duplication with the Bakery Products sections on ingredients, and similar discussions elsewhere, these ingredients will not be described here but will be covered by references to the appropriate article, when necessary.

FACTORS AFFECTING QUALITY OF PUFFED SNACKS

The use of cereal flours and meals as the major ingredients in puffed snacks has been a natural result of the low cost and excellent expansion potential of such materials as cornmeal. Snacks made with cornmeal have a typical flavor which, though not objectionable in itself, may not be entirely compatible with other flavors which may be needed to characterize a new type of snack. The demand for blander ingredients, or ingredients which could give structures and textures not obtainable with cereal or root flours, has led to extensive experimentation with purified or modified starches.

Unmodified cereal starches can be puffed at medium to high temperatures using either steam or water as moisturizers; they can serve as bland-tasting bases for formulated products such as nutritional snacks.

Uncooked granular Starches are suitable bases for half-products. A simple formula would include .It and monoglycerides, color, flavor, and 16% water. The ingredients would be preblended and processed through a continuous cooker-extruder at 250° to 350°F.

Conditions in the extruder must be sufficiently rigorous to rupture the starch granules. After cooking, the dough is formed into desired shapes and sizes by any convenient method. As with most half-products, the dough pieces can be either baked immediately or dried to some lower moisture content and then deep-fat fried. Depending on the conditions of cooking and expansion and the amount and type of ingredients, the structure of the collet will vary from a low-density, large-cell foam to a brittle, dense network.

The extent of volume expansion and the texture of the finished snack are influenced by the amylose:amylopection ratio. Available cornstarches range from high (50-70%) amylose through regular dent (25-27% amylose) to the waxy maize varieties that are virtually 100% amylopectin. Sorghum starches with amylopectin contents from 17% to almost 100% are also being offered. Starches having high amylopectin contents tend to give fragile products of low density.

Some amylose must be present to give adequate resistance to breakage and textures that are acceptable to the consumer. On the other hand, products containing only corn, red milo, and tapioca starches will be hard in texture and too high in density. The texture can be softened somewhat by the addition of plasticizers such as sucrose, dextrose, or sorbitol, but normally 50% or more amylopectin is needed for a good quality product. A starch system containing 5-20% amylose was suggested as most suitable by Feldberg (1969). In baked-type puffed snacks, pre-extrusion moisture contents in the range of 20-35% and a starch having 80-100% amylopectin content are necessary to yield acceptable products.

Certain pregelatinized and chemically treated starches have been offered to snack manufacturers specifically as bases for half-products. Chemical modification processes include cross-bonding, pregelatinizing, and the forming of phosphate, acetate, and hydroxypropyl derivatives. Many of . these raw materials can be satisfactorily formed by conventional laboratory, pilot plant, or commercial sheeting and cutting equipment after the dough has been mixed in conventional vertical blenders.

The starch is first mixed with the other ingredients, such as flour, color, flavor, and spices, then about 20% (15-25%) water is added and the mixture fed into an extruder, from which the desired shapes are obtained. The formed piece can be baked either in microwave ovens or in standard ovens at 375°-425°F. When they are dried to 10-15% moisture, the dough pieces can be deep-fat fried. This method is very suitable for addition of flavours in the dough because of the blandness of the starch base and the relatively low processing temperatures, which drive off less of the volatile aromatics.

Effect of Moisture Content

Moisture content of the meal is a critical factor affecting the extrusion temperature, pressure, and product texture. Moisture contents of 13 to 14% are generally recommended. As feed moisture increases, extrusion temperature drops and less expansion occurs in the extrudate. Pores in the product become larger and walls of the pores become thicker. After it is baked, the- product is crisper or crunchier in texture. Low moisture results in '1 dense and hard product due to incomplete gelatinization of the starch. Such products are suitable for frying under some conditions.

As feed moisture is reduced, extrusion temperature rises, the extrudate expands more, and the pores get smaller-with thinner walls. After baking (i.e., drying), the collet is softer and has less crunch. The collets start to darken and scorch as the moisture content approaches a low level. Production rate is also affected by the moisture content of the meal. Throughput can be increased by decreasing the moisture content of the feed, but this generally has an adverse effect on product quality.

Moisture should be evenly distributed throughout the" meal. Gross non-uniformity can lead to stratified areas in the collets, to scorched particles, and other product defects. Ideally, any moisture added as water or aqueous solutions should be allowed to equilibrate throughout the bulk material before it is fed into the extruder, even though acceptable results can sometimes be obtained by dripping moisture into the extrusion. chamber, particularly if only very small amounts are required.

The product collected from the extruder normally reaches an overall moisture content of about 8%, and this is further reduced to 4% or less in hot air dryers (ovens) or deep-fat fryers.

Effect of pH

Variations in pH of the ingredient mixture that can be expected to result from the usual combination of cereal flours and tap water seem to have little effect on the extrusion~peration or quality of the finished product. When Cabrera extruded wheat starch at pH levels between 4.4 aDd 9.0, the expansion ration remained substantially constant. Below pH 4.4, expansion decreased, a phenomenon attributed to acid hydrolysis of starch in the extruder barrel. When the pH was between 3.0 and 3.4, extruder throughput and power consumption were reduced. At alkaline pH levels, the extrudate became darker. Most food producers will not be dealing with ingredient mixtures containing strongly acidic or alkaline components, so they can expect to avoid the complicating effects of very high or very low pH. Water, in the amounts usually added, should not have a marked effect on the pH of the total mixture, especially since the cereal ingredients have a fairly good buffering capacity. If alkalized com dough (masa) is being" processed, the situation may be different.

Added Flavours and Colours

Flavoring materials added to extruder feed stock undergo significant changes during puffing, and most of the changes are undesirable. Volatile flavor components flash off. Interactions and decomposition Occur as a result of the high temperatures. Even when flavor quality does not change, there is nearly always a need to include much larger quantities of flavor than would be required for ordinary cooked products. There are some indications that improved results are obtained when encapsulated flavors are used. In a few cases, the flavoring materials interfere with texture development, this being particularly true if they introduce fatty substances. For these reasons, the usual practice is to add flavors to the puffed and dried collet. A popular combination is oil, salt, and cheese powder, and the ingredients are often mixed together in stainless steel kettles before being dribbled or sprayed onto the collets in a tumbling-type coater. The vegetable oil is generally coconut oil or a combination of coconut with soybean or cottonseed oil.

Half-products made with integral flavoring ingredients may retain them reasonably well through the "'even-puffing or frying process. The chemical stability and volatility of the flavor components are the chief determinants of success in this approach. Natural flavoring materials such as cheese powder have noticeable effects on the texture and amount of expansion.

Extrusion-puffed snacks can be satisfactorily colored with food dyes, in some cases. Between 30 and 600 ppm of FD&C pigments may be required to achieve the desired results. Higher levels often lead to products that are gaudy and unnatural looking. Colors can be added by a dry-blending process prior to extrusion. Dye solutions are sometimes metered at the feed screw ahead of the pressure chamber. If added moisture cannot be tolerated, it may be possible to use other polar solvents, such as propylene glycol or alcohol. Titanium dioxide, FD&C lakes, and iron oxides, being insoluble, cannot be metered into batches in the form gf solutions.

Fading of colors in extruded and expanded snacks is frequently observed and can be related to four key factors: (1) excessive heat, (2) reaction with various proteins, (3) reaction with reducing ions such as iron and aluminum, and (4) reactions with reducing sugars. There is also a physical cause of fading. The foam structure of puffed snacks causes a refraction of light, which whitens or lightens the basic color of the material. The smaller the bubbles (or cells), the lighter the color.

EXTRUDERS AND EXTRUDING

Types of Extruders

Many kinds of extruders are used in the food industry: sausages, pet foods, pasta, surimi, and several kinds of bakery products are processed by extrusion processes. These machines may differ in several respects from the equipment used to make puffed snack foods, but breakfast cereals of certain types, crispbreads, and croutons are often manufactured by equipment not much different from that used for some snacks. In this section, however, only equipment having specific applications to snack food production will be discussed.

Extruders used in processing snack foods can have four functions: mixing, cooking, shaping, and puffing. Various combinations of these functions can be performed simultaneously by a single piece of equipment.

Mixing occurs in most extruders except those designed to receive a premixed plug or cylinder of dough, such as those used to shape corn chips. Even though a plunger is intended primarily to force a plug of dough through a die, some mixing will occur as the dough slides along the side wall and flows toward the die orifice.

To achieve good mixing of these extremely viscous materials, however, special agitator designs are required. If cooking is to be performed, jackets are ordinarily provided to supplement the heat originating from the

work performed on the dough. Shaping or forming is a result of the. configuration of the orifice through which the material is extruded and the relative speeds of the cutoff knife and the dough strand. The equipment will function as a puffer if the dough temperature is substantially in excess of the boiling point of water when the dough leaves the pressurized chamber. In most extruder designs, two or more of these functions will be performed simultaneously.

Extruders for snack foods accept either doughs or 'an ,unblended mixture of ingredients at one end of a generally cylindrical casing, and, while forcing the mass to the opposite end with a generally helical rotating screw, mix, shear, and pressurize the contents before pushing the mass through one or more relatively small orifices. The casing (and the screw) mayor may not be heated or cooled by circulating fluids.

Extruders can be classified in several different ways-according to the geometry of the extruder screws, for example. For our purposes, in this discussion of snack food manufacturing, it is useful to consider the two types of extruder systems as low pressure with low or moderate heating

Table 12.1 Different Shear Classifications of Single Screw Extruders[1]

	Class of extruder		
Characteristic	Low shear	Medium shear	High shear
Product moisture, &	25-75	15-30	5-8
Product density, g/L	320-380	160-510	32-200
Max. Barrel temp., °C	20-65	21-42	42-84
Max. Barrel pressure*	6-63	21-42	42-84
Screw diameter	3-5.3	5.0-8.5	8.0-18.
Parallel flow chanels, #	1	2	2 or3
Screw speed, rpm	<100	.200	>200
Energy conversion **	0.01-0.04	0.02-0.08	0.10-0.16
Typical products	Pasta, 3rd generation, snaks, gums, meat products	Textured soy, expanded pet food, breading	Snacks, breakfast cereals, croutons, starches

capabilities and high pressure with high heat generating capabilities. Hauck and Huber (1989) published a useful table summarizing some of the characteristics oflow shear, medium shear, and high shear extruders of the single screw type. Table 12.1 reproduces this information in a modified form.

Low-pressure forming.-The simplest type of extruder used in snack manufacturing is the low-pressure equipment used to force pre-mixed doughs or masa through simple dies. Many of these presses are employed in com chip (tortilla chip) plants. They are effective with doughs of low to moderate apparent viscosity and do not lead to any expansion or puffing in the extruded dough. If the orifices are of reasonable size (or if there are many of them) or the extrusion rates are low, pressure buildup is avoided, shear is nominal, and temperatures can be held close to ambient. Instead of screws, simple pistons, hydraulically activated, are often the sources of power which force the dough through the dies.

Macaroni presses, modified sausage stuffers, and cookie depositors have been used to form snack-type pieces that are later cooked. Onionflavored rings and similar ring-shaped products have been commercially manufactured from seasoned cereal mixes by modified Bock (Haskon) fillers. These rings are generally breaded in a separate operation before they are fried. Another typical low-pressure extruder is the Autoprod. One company extrudes a dough containing diced onions from specially designed low pressure equipment. Some of these extruders have many similarities to equipment used for years by the cookie industry in which rotating metal cylinders draw batter from a hopper and force it through a number Of relatively large orifices, while extruders based on the macaroni press use auger-type pressurizing methods and can develop moderate .pressures. Certain kinds of doughnut depositors use an air-pressurized hopper to drive batter through portioning orifices which are intermittently closed by pistons; some low pressure snack extruders may have been based on these machines.

High-pressure cooker-extruders.-Engineering principles behind the design and selection of high pressure extrusion presses are too complex to be reviewed in detail in the present article. Readers interested in these topics may consult the articles of Fichtall and van de V oort (1989), Hauck and Huber (1989), Padmanabhan and Bhattacharya (1989), and Camire *et ai.* (1990) or the book edited by Jowitt (1984). A very brief summary of the technology is given below.

One scheme categorizes extruders as (1) single screw extruders and (2) twin screw extruders, with the latter class divided into counter-rotating twin screw extruders and co-rotating twin screw extruders. Each of the latter two types can be divided into intermeshing or non-intermeshing types. According to Hauck and Huber, the intensity with which the extrudate is sheared is perhaps the most practical basis for classifying cooking extruders. It was reported by Fichtall and van de Voort that nonintermeshing twin screw extruders are rarely used in the food industry.

Twin screw extruders with fully intermeshing screws have the screws contained in C-shaped chambers surrounding the screws. In counter- rotating systems, these chambers have a relatively small volume, so there is little leakage of material from one screw to the other. Co-rotating screws have more open channels and allow material interchange from one chamber to the other.

Extrusion cookers are composed of several components: (1) A live bin which provides a buff~ stock of raw material at the extruder inlet, (2) a variable speed feeding screw which meters raw material into the extruder barrel at a predetermined rate, (3) an optional preconditioning cylinder which injects steam and/or water into the powdered ingredients and allows the mixture to at least partially equilibrate, and (4) the extruder barrel. The extruder barrel consists of the chamber walls, which inclose the screws and, . the material as it is being processed, jacketed heads, and rotating screws. The extruder heads have jackets containing circulating steam, water, or other heat transfer mediums which permit adjustment of the temperature along the length of the barrel.

The diameter of the extruder cavity may be uniform throughout its length, or it may be tapered (decreasing in diameter) from front to back; some of the sections may be tapered while others are not. The barrel is capped with a die plate containing one or several orifices through which the extrudate is forced.

The openings are shaped to furnish the cross-sectional design of the finished product, and 'a knife rotating against the die face (or a remotely positioned cutting device) establishes the final product length. It is important to remember that the finished product may resemble only slightly the appearance of the orifice as it is viewed from outside the machine. Different speeds of extrusion at different parts of the orifice, non-uniform expansion, coalescing of parts of the extrudate past the barrel, and other phenomena can radically change the shape of the extrudate.

The screw of the extruder can be continuous from front to back, or it can be composed of segments allowing different types of processing to occur as the dough proceeds along the barrel. Single screw extruders are satisfactory for many applications, but they do not efficiently transport sticky or gummy doughs. The barrel wall may cause inadequate resistance, leading to slippage of the extrudate,ko that it simply rotates rather than being pushed forward by the screw. To remedy this problem, the inside of the barrel is often provided with grooves, which may either be longitudinal or helical. There are several types of design for single screw systems. The simplest design is the screw with constant pitch and depth throughout the length, but most are formed so as to have the screw pitch and flight depth decrease from inlet to discharge. This takes into account the densification of the dough as it progresses from front to discharge.

Co-rotating twin screw cooking extruders reduce fluctuation of pressure at the die because the intermeshing screws lead to a more positive transport mechanism. They rely not only on friction with the wall, but also on the interaction of the two screw flights within the same flow channel to force the dough forward. This positive pumping action does, however, reduce the heat input due to friction, and to obtain sufficient heat for cooking It is necessary to Introduce reverse-directed screw elements or lobeshaped kneading elements onto the shaft. Either of these elements increase compression, heating, and shearing. The final section of the screw, as it approaches the inner face of the die plate, can be either uniform in diameter or somewhat conical. The conical design results in a rapid compression of the extrudate and increaed barrel pressure, leading to a high degree of stability and control.

Example of a Twin-screw Extruder

The most complex type of extruder used in snack food manufacture, as well as in some other cereal processing such as the producing of certain types of breakfast cereals, is the twin screw extruder. A few of the distinguishing features of these devices have been described above. Since the most advanced designs of these extruders embody all the principles used in any other type of extruder, it is worthwhile to examine them in more detail. The description which will be given is based on Calandro *et al* (1989), and is related to Fig. 12.3. In this figure, which is modified from the Calandro *et al.* patent, is shown the compound screw and the enclosing chamber of one-half of a twin screw extruder. The other screw will be lying alongside this chamber and partly intermeshing with the elements of it. Both screws are enclosed in cylindrical chambers, open at the contiguous sides where they join to form a "double-barreled" arrangement. The function and design of the different elements of the extruder are described as follows.

Dry ingredients enter the chamber through an upper inlet port near one end of the jacket. Generally, there would be no need here for a valve or other closure mechanism to prevent the escape of material which is being. processed in the chamber. A short distance downstream, another port on the top of the chamber -g:llows the introduction of liquid int .-edients into the blending or feed section. In a few specialized cases, it might be necessary to have a second liquid port a short distance from the first one.

A driving shaft, to be seen at the left side of the diagram, carries a gear which coordinates the motion of the second shaft, so that the intermeshing action, which is such an important part of the twin-screw process, can occur in an efficient manner and without damage to either screw. In an alternative arrangement, each shaft can be driven by a separate motor operating in synchronous relationship to its counterpart. The conveying screw to be seen in the feed section of the diagram meshes with its counterpart on the other shaft to ensure positive movement of the ingredients along the barrel, so there can be no possibility of backflow at this point.

In the first mixing region, a series of so-called "paddles," which actually have more the appearance of cams, are oriented at, typically, a 45' angle to one another in a circular progression along the length of the shaft. They interact with a similar series of paddles on the second shaft. The two sets of paddles are so oriented that the paddles of shaft #1 wipe the paddles of shaft #2, causing positive material displacement through the extruder. Different numbers of paddles may be required to obtain the desired mixing action for different products.

As they leave the first mixing zone, the dry and liquid ingredients have been mixed together. The blended material then enters a cooking zone where starches can be gelatinized, sugars caramelized, proteins denatured, and flavors developed. In the cooking zone temperatures are raised by friction and fluid shear to within the range of, say, 190° to 270°F. To obtain the temperature necessary for a specific process, external heating or cooling may be applied here, or anywhere in the extruder, by jackets containing a circulating heat exchange medium. Pressure in the cooking zone may be in the range of 50 psig to 120 psig.

A shearing screw can be seen in the shearing region of the cooking zone. It is made with a narrow lead and pitch. The screws on the two shafts intermesh in this section to cause positive displacement of the material, and pressure increases here. Typically, the shearing action will be intense enough to maintain cooking temperatures with little or no need for external heating. Following the shearing region is another mixing section, identified as "Mix

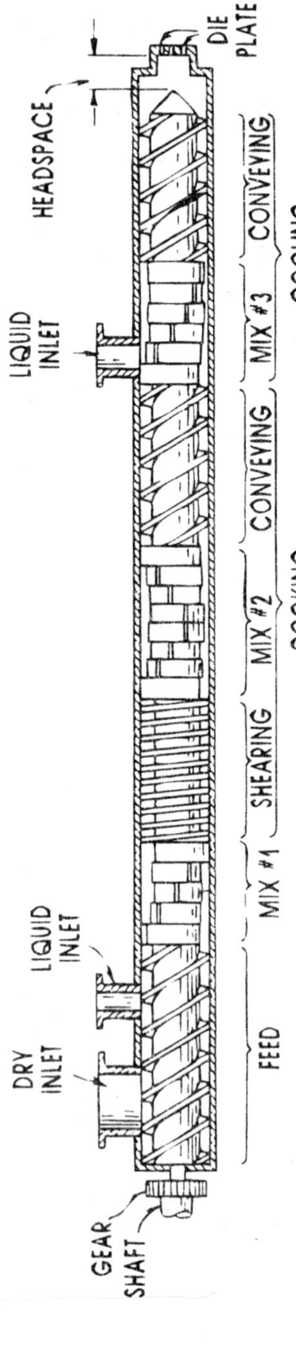

Fig. 12.3 Compound screw or auger for an extruder press.

#2" in the drawing. At this point, the shaft carries an arrangement of paddles similar in many respects to that found in the first mixing section. Pressure increases in this region as a result of the action of the intermeshing paddles.

Following the second mixing section is a conveying screw which forces the cooked material into the cooling zone. In the first part of this zone, another set of paddles provides further mixing. At the end of this set is a pair of paddles oriented at 90' angles to One another; they cause intensified' blending of the material. At the end of the cooling zone, and near the end of the shaft, is a conveying screw which forces material to the tip of the screw. An unobstructed headspace exists between the tip and the inner die face which forms the end of the chamber.

The headspace will amount to perhaps 10% of the length of the screw and is designed to be sufficient to maintain the presssure of the cooked mixture at a level suitable for extrusion. If the volume of the headspace is decreased, the material tends to compact and the pressure will increase. Temperature in the cooling zone will usually have to be adjusted by circulating water through a jacket built around the chamber at this point; For a specific case, the temperature may need to be lowered to within the range 1700 to 195°F if a non-puffed extruded product is desired. Puffed products must be raised to substantially higher temperatures so as to cause steam evolution when the product strands leave the die. In the diagram, an inlet port is shown near the beginning of the cooling section, so that water, or some other fluid, may be injected into the mass to 1;:001 it. Such an arrangement may ,not be suitable for many products, apd fluid injected at this point must enter the chamber through pressure' cpntrol valves and inlets which substantially increase the complexity of the process.

The ratio of the length to the diameter of the extruder shaft, from its beginning to its end, may be in the range of 5:1 to 100:1, but typically will be 15:1 for the process described in the patent of Calandro *et at.* The barrel, or inside of the extruder chamber, closely fits the periphery of the screw elements. The residence time of the material within the extruder barrel can be highly variable, depending upon the product and process.

The die, which forms the exit end of the extruder chamber, is a relatively thick piece of metal penetrated by a number of orifices through which the cooked material will be forced by the pressure existing within the headspace. Die thickness, headspace, and extrusion pressure are related in that thicker dies tend to produce higher back pressure in the extruder and more expansion in the emerging product strand. After a thickness which will withstand the stress of continuous extrusion is selected, the headspace can be specified at a figure suitable for controlling the pressure of the material which accumulates upstream of the die. The head space may be modified by using die holders which provide a hollow space upstream of the internal die face.

13

Manufacturing Corn Chips

Extrusion processes are used extensively to make such baked or fried snaks as corn ("tortilla") chips, which do not require puffing and which are cooked in a separate operation. Corn chips undergo essentially no expansion or puffing when they leae the extruder. The first step in producing conventional corn chips is the cooking of dried corn kernels (often a mixture of white and yellow dent corn) in lime water so as to develop the characteristics flavor of tortillas and to put the kernels in a condition better suited to the grinding process. Usually, the corn is first cooked for a short period in the lime solution and then allowed to steep for several hours. The extended steep period can be eliminated and the process made continuous by cooking the corn kernels under pressure with sufficient lime or other alkali. The minimum amount of lime required in this process is 1.5% by weight of the dry corn. Because the kernels are completely cooked and the starch gelatinized before the dough is placed in the extruder, further heat treatment is not required and puffing does not occur when the dough strip emerges from the extruder. Some puffing or blistering does occur, however, after the raw piece is placed in the frying fat.

Various pieces of equipment are available for washing the corn kernels to remove hulls, excess lime, etc. A typical corn washer uses a magetic plate to remove metal particles from the incoming cooked corn. The kernels then enter the submerged end of a perforated drum in the washer's sloped tank-the'" water level is adjustable to vary the degree of washing. Inside the drum, a metering helix advances the corn through a series of high-pressure freshwater sprays. Continuous overflow drainage flushes loose hulls and other foreign particles from the washer.

Table 13.1 Formulas using shredded or chopped corn gel

Ingredient	Percent*
Shredded corn gel	51.9
Amioca	7.8
Pregelatinized corn flour	2.6
Pregelatinized rice flour	7.8
Corn starch	5.4
Soy oil	2.8
Durem GMO emulsifier	0.1
Water	21.6

Willard (1989) patented an unusual variation on the corn chip process, which he says produces a snack with more uniform texture, is less expensive to produce, and does not have the characteristic limed flavor of nixtamal-type products. First, he forms a thoroughly gelatinized ingredient by cooking a grain and water slurry, cooling the material, then shredding or chopping it. Dry flavoring and characterizing ingredients are added to the gel, which is then formed into individual snack food pieces. The pieces may be fried immediately or stored for further use. A formula utilizing the shredded corn gel of this invention is given in Table 13.1.

Corn chips can be shaped on equipment which uses cylindrical rollers to prepare a sheet of dough, and dies to form circular, triangular, or rectangular pieces from the sheet. A typical tortilla sheeter includes two cylindrical one-piece stainless steel rollers to form the dough sheet, hoppers to hold the masa, a stripping wire pulled tight by pneumatic cylinders to separate the sheet from the front roller, a dial-indicator handwheel to adjust the separation of the rollers, brass dies to form the pieces, a rigid quickrelease doctor blade to remove dough from the rear roller, a variable-speed drive system, a stainless steel mesh conveyor belt to transfer product to the oven or fryer, and emergency stop switches. Although this is a somewhat older method and is more labor intensive than the hydraulic or pneumatic press system, it has worked effectively in many factories.

Some presses for corn chips employ hydraulically or pneumatically activated pistons to force cornmeal through the shaping orifices. They are generally batch presses, that is, the piston must be completely withdrawn and a charge of dough inserted into the chamber at the start of each cycle. These machines have a number of obvious similarities to the old-style macaroni (and noodle) extruders and to sausage stuffers. Pressures reached in the chamber are much lower than pressures generated in the continuous extrusion chambers used for mixing, cooking, and puffing snack products such as corn curls.

As a result of the low pressure and minimal shear, little or no steam evolution occurs within the dough and it does not expand as it exits from the die. Chip size or strip length can be controlled by varying the speed of rotation of the cutoff knife, or continuous sheets can be led from the orifice to auxiliary shaping or forming equipment. The variety of shapes that can be generated in this manner is relatively limited, since the threedimensional effect obtainable in puffed snacks is lacking.

Semi-automatic hydraulic presses of modern designs have pistons that can develop 1,500 psi of force using fluid supplied by a separate pump unit that can be located at some distance from the processing line. Extrusion begins automatically when the food-holding cylinder is manually locked into operating position. When the cylinder is empty, the extruder piston automatically retracts, allowing the operator to swing the cylinder 90. to one side for quick refilling, cleaning, or die changing. Interchangeable stainless steel, brass, or Teflon dies are available in many shapes and sizes. These extruders can be ordered in single- or double-cylinder models. The extrusion cylinder can be vertically oriented, an arrangement that is said to give better control of product length, or horizontally disposed, which is somewhat more convenient for loading.

Snacks That Are Cooked and Formed

Some snacks are cooked and formed by low-pressure (i.e., operating near atmospheric pressure) extruders which are based on screw-shaped mixing elements. The chamber wall may be jacketed so as to provide heating and cooling at appropriate times. The screws may be of complex design with interrupted flights or other means to secure better dough circulation and increase the hold time. Doughs usually increase in temperature during their travel through the extruder as a result of the . mechanical work exerted by the screw and heat transferred from low pressure steam or other fluid circulating through the jacket. After it has been thoroughly mixed, gelatinized, developed, etc., the dough passes through a cooling section maintained at less than 212°F and is finally forced through a die at the exit end of the extruder barrel. Expansion or puffing of the dough does not occur to any marked extent at this point. The dough may exit in the form of a strip or sheet that is cut and shaped by other equipment, but a more modern practice is to do as much as possible of the shaping at the die face. Additional processing steps, such as drying, frying, or toasting (baking) are necessary in order to produce a finished snack item. Also, the bulk product of these presses may be treated as an intermediate and transferred to another press maintained at higher pressure and temperature and there puffed by steam expansion

In a typical low-pressure cooking and forming operation, the dry ingredients are mixed with water and fed to a cooking extruder. Hightemperature fluid is circulated through the jacket and, in some designs, through the screw, and additional heat is generated as a result of the work performed on the dough. Temperature and time are controlled to get the necessary degree of starch gelatinization in the dough. The dough is cooled, usually by a refrigerated die, before it emerges into the atmosphere, so that the water in it does not flash into steam. As a result, the extruded dough remains dense and is substantially free of bubbles instead of being expanded and foam-like.

High-pressure cooking and forming procedures require raising the starchy dough to temperatures substantially above 212°F. Energy input is from the heated jacket and internal friction. Compression of the plastic mass within the chamber by the tapered screw prevents vaporization of the water. Pressure results from a resistance to flow of the extrudate. The meal or dough is held in the extruder for a longer time so that more mechanical energy is absorbed and the temperature rises, i.e., higher pressure results in higher product temperatures, other factors remaining the same. As a result the extrudate expands more and has smaller pores and a softer texture. Lower viscosity leads to lower back pressure and lower extrusion temperature, other conditions being equal, and the extrudate expands less and has larger vesicles, coarser walls, and a harder texture.

There are a number of ways to adjust the pressure in an extruder. As the number of die openings (or their size) is increased, the pressure falls. Increasing the rpm of the extruder will increase pressure. A secondary or backup die through which the dough is forced before it reaches the extrusion orifices will increase the temperature.

Half-product Processing

Half-products have been defined as special food formulations that, upon immersion in hot frying oil, rapidly expand into a low-density product. These items, sometimes called "intermediates," are often produced by gelatinization of a starchy dough that is then shaped into chip form and dried to a horny consistency. A representative process was disclosed in the patent of Campfield (1964). A raw starchy material such as com, potato, tapioca, wheat, rice, sorghum, or oatmeal undergoes a simultaneous cooking and kneading operation so that the starch granules are swollen. A typical dough would consist of 81.5% com flour, 16.5% water, and 2% salto The dough is directly transferred to an extrusion chamber under pressure sufficient to cause the rupture of some starch granules. The pressures are of a magnitude sufficiently great to cause the extrudate to expand upon emergence to normal atmospheric conditions, but expansion is avoided by cooling the dough. An extrudate having a moisture content of about 15 to 35% issues in a compact, densified condition. It is usually cut or otherwise formed into desired shapes before further processing. The strand of dense, gelatinized dough is dried to a moisture content of less than 12%, typically 9%. Equilibration of the moisture content may be introduced at this point. If conditions are satisfactory, the horny-textured chips will puff upon immersion in hot (e.g., 400°F) frying oil for 5 to 10 seconds. The resultant snack base has a light, vesicular, crisp consistency and ~ pleasant flavor.

Popel (1974) patented a method for producing a puffed snack food from starch-containing materials in a continuous process without the need for expensive high-pressure extrusion equipment. Also, there is no need for a holding or refrigerating step prior to forming the product and drying it. He also claimed that an improved flavor resulted from the use of his process. A, unique feature is the inclusion in the starting mixture of a rather high proportion of starch having a high setback or congealing power. The presence of 20% or more of amylose in the starch is recommended. Specifically, in selecting the starch to be used. com wheat, or sago starches are found to give the desired characteristics when mixed with the foodstuffs in the amount of about 25% solids. For operating in the higher solids range, where the viscosity of the extruded gel may tend to be too high, acid modified or "thin boiling" starches from any source may be substituted. Some details of the process include the use of a relatively dilute mixture of starchy material, water, and flavor; this is heated sufficiently to gelatinize a substantial part of the starch. After a thin sheet of this dough has been formed, its surface is partially dried and it is subdivided into pieces of convelrient size before completion of drying. The pieces are french fried to puff them. Workable ingredient ranges described in the patent are 60 to 90% water, and 10 to 40% starch. The inventor claims particulate substances such as grains and potato pieces can be added to the gel to give interesting flavor and texture combinations in the finished puff.

Although it is probably most common to finish off half-products in deep fat fryers, they can also be cooked in air ovens and microwave ovens. They can also be puffed in hot airstreams. Clausi (1969) described a method for puffing cereal pellets to 1.5 to 3 times their original size by heating them in a high-velocity current of hot air. A cereal dough containing from 22 to 27% moisture is prepared by mixing corn, wheat, barley, or flour with flavoring syrup. The dough is cooked, as in a closed pressure vessel, at approximately 20 psig for 6 to 30 min. The cooked mixture is formed into pellets, which are case-hardened by blowing ambient air through a bed of them until the critical moisture range of 16 to 21% is reached. Drier pellets will be hard and will not puff, whereas pellets having a moisture content above about 21% will expand into very fragile hollow spheres. The casehardened pellets are reduced in thickness by passing them through flaking rolls adjusted in separation distance to give pellets thicker than conventional corn flakes, since thinner pellets cannot be puffed. The bumped pellets are then heated at temperatures of from about 350. to about 750.F for 8 to 35 seconds while being conveyed by air having a velocity of at least 500 it per min. The moisture content of the cereal immediately after puffing is usually in the range 3 to 7%. The moisture may be further reduced and the product toasted at 225. to 500.F for about 2 to 10 min. Although the patent indicates the application is intended for the manufacture of breakfast cereals, it is obviously suitable for making certain kinds of snacks.

Various publications and patents have presented detailed methods for microwave puffing of half-products. In a series of unpublished experiments performed during the 1970s, the author developed prototypes of half-products and packages for them that were suitable for oven baking or microwave heating so that hot puffed snacks could be prepared in the home. These included pellets which were essentially fat-free, to improve expansion, but were cooked in a shallow bed of fat to improve flavor and texture. None of these items were marketed. A recent article (Anon. 1990) described a half-product designed to be popped under the same conditions used for home popping of corn in paper bags in microwave ovens. The negative effect of low-fat formulations is noted, and a method of offsetting it by use of specially developed flavors is revealed.

Half-products can also be finished in the gun-puffing apparatus used for many breakfast cereal products. In fact, many popular breakfast cereals were first made in this way. Sticking or clustering of the dough pellets is often encountered in gun puffing. Chilling of the pellets prior to puffing somewhat reduces these tendencies. Coating the pellets with edible oil is also effective if the oil can be retained on the pellets during the heating process. Using a small amount, say 1.5% of a fatty acid monoglyceride as an ingredient will reduce or eliminate the sticking problem but apparently causes some uneveness of color in the finished product.

Fig. 13.2 Simple extruder for making one type of puffed corn curls.

The term "third generation products" has been applied by some writers to snacks made by a two-stage extrusion process. This could be regarded as a modification of half-product manufacture. In a typical process, the ingredient mixture is heated by mechanical shear and steam injection in an extruder so as to form a cooked, expanded material having an open cell structure. This extrudate is fed to a second extruder that compresses the gelatinous mass. The redensified dough then passes through a finishing die where the length is established by a cutoff knife. The resulting pieces pass through a dryer-cooler that reduces their moisture content to about 7%. The finished pellets may be bagged and sold for frying at wholesale or retail outlets near the points of sale, or they may be deep-fat fried, possibly coated with salt or other flavoring materials, and packaged at the central plant (Matson 1982). In examining the value of this two-stage extrusion, as compared to a single-stage preparation of half-products, it would appear that an advantage is obtained by forming minute bubbles or voids during the first extrusion step, so as to provide foci for the eventual evolution of steam when the final cooking step is applied.

Direct or One-stage Puffing

The use of pressurized extrusion systems for making puffed or expanded snacks directly from raw com meal in one pass through an extruder was a later development, though now four or more decades old. This invention was immediately recognized as a significant improvement on prior processes, however, and the technology progressed rapidly. Machines designed for this type of processing must have strong barrel walls, sturdy screws, and powerful drives. They are often, but not always, substantially more expensive than most of the units previously described.

In one of the earliest and simplest types of unit for puffing corn curls, the problem of reducing equipment cost was approached by making the chamber small, but this also meant that the output was low. These units consist of a short tapered spiral feed element rotating inside a strong, closely fitting chamber. The space available for the feed material becomes increasingly restricted as it moves toward the outlet. This leads to a great increase in pressure. Temperature also increases from the absorption of kinetic energy and may be further heightened by heat applied to the jacket or die--some of these units are not jacketed, however, and rely on the mechanical energy input to raise the contents to an appropriate temperature. Particles of the feed material form a plastic mass, essentially free of undissolved gas, under these conditions. As the compressed dough is released from the extruder orifice, the lower pressure it encounters allows some of the water to flash into steam, expanding the mass into a lowdensity cellular structure. Maximum expansion of the dough is not achieved under these conditions, and the corn curl that is obtained is of a firmer, crisper, and more uneven texture than those yielded by large extruders. Some consumers prefer this firmer texture, however. After the puffed pieces are dried in ovens or fried in hot oil baths, flavoring materials such as salt, cheese, and oil are applied. The machine shown in Figure 3.1 is an example of such an extruder (Source: Richeim)

In high pressure extruders, the strand of dough passing through the die channel contains water at a temperature far above its boiling point at atmospheric pressure, but the water is held in liquid form by the high pressures existing in the chamber. As the dough emerges from the orifice, excess pressure is released and the free liquid vaporizes almost instantaneously. The dough is elastic and llormally very viscous at this point so that large amounts of steam are temporarily trapped within its structure. The vaporizing water forces the dough piece to expand. At some point, the elastic limit of the structure is reached, vesicles burst, and the hot gas escapes; internal pressure drops precipitously. The walls of the vesicles contract or collapse as the internal pressure is relieved, and the piece shrinks somewhat. This process normally stops far ,short of a complete return to the original density, however, because the entire structure sets up, or becomes relatively firm and rigid as a result both of water loss and cooling. Retention of maximum specific volume of the pieces is encouraged by factors that accelerate the setting up process, including the following, among others: Keeping the dough moisture content at the minimum consistent with attainment of desired expansion, keeping the exit temperature at a minimum consistent with desired expansion, and keeping the piece size as small as possible (or, at least, keeping one of its dimensions small). The structure is often still under stress at the time it sets up, so that increasing the mobility of the intermolecular bonds, as by absorption of moisture, will permit additional shrinkage to occur. This is the reason puffed snacks become smaller and change their shape when they become wet.

Large differences in the physical characteristics of the product can be achieved by modifications in the conditions of the process. For example, there are two main types of corn curls, the fried type which is denser, crunchier, and more irregular in shape, and the baked type which is more uniform, more highly expanded, and softer in texture. The original corn curl was of the fried type, but it was largely replaced in the late 1940s and early 1950s by the baked collet. The feed stock is essentially the same for both products, with the usual exception of s slight variation in moisture content, and the very significant differences in organoleptic qualities are achieved solely by adjusting the extrusion conditions.

According to Smith (1979), steps that can be taken to affect texture, density, mouth feel, solubility, and form of extrusion-puffed snacks include the following:

(1) The method of feeding and preconditioning of ingredients and mixtures.

(2) The method and point of moisture application.

(3) Control of temperature and moisture contents of product entering. the extruder.

(4) Control of temperatures within each extruder section.

(5) Control of the point within the extruder where maximum dough viscosity is attained.

(6) Control of extrusion speeds.

(7) Control of time and temperature relationships within each section of the extruder.

(8) Control of the time during which product temperatures are elevated to maximum extrusion temperatures.

(9) Control offinal extrusion temperatures.

(10) Selection of the shaping and sizing devices.

(11) Selection of the type, dwell time, drying temperatures, and velocities within the drier and cooler and of the finished final product moisture.

(12) Point and method of flavor application.

The main steps in an extrusion-puffing operation, were described by Corbin *et ai.* (1972). The moisture content of a given lot of cornmeal in the particle size range of 40 to 60 mesh was adjusted to 12.5% moisture by the addition of a calculated amount of water. The moistened meal was stored in a closed container for 3 to 24 hr to allow equalization of the moisture content before it was fed to an extruder at the rate of about 400 lb per hr. Additional water was metered in to increase the total moisture content to about 25%. The extruder was preheated by means of a high pressure steam jacket. After operation started, the head of the extruder was cooled and the flow of steam adjusted to maintain a temperature of approximately 315°F. Product from the extruder was transferred to a hct-air dryer operating at 375°F and brought to a moisture level of less than 2%. The hot, dry collets were transferred to a flavoring reel, where a mixture of oil, salt, and cheese flavoring was added by a metering pump and spray nozzles so that the final product contained 15% fat, 9% cheese flavour, and 3.5% salt. The flavored coUets were then cooled and packaged.

Extrusion puffing can be used to produce from corn meal a very reasonable facsimile of popped corn. The product is denser than most popped corn and is missing the hulls, of course. The appearance is very satisfactory in some cases. One method was described as follows. Cornmeal having a moisture content between 10 and 12.3% is forced at high velocity (e.g., 950 to 1,300 inches per min) by means of a high pressure feeder through orifices in one or more extrusion plates. Both the size of the collecting pocket in the proximal die face and the extrusion rate must be closely controlled. The orifice size and cutoff length are obviously critical. The preferred particle size is no less than 20% on a No. 12 screen and 5% through a No. 40 screen. Temperature of the mass before it emerges from the die will be in the range of 250. to 400°F. The puffs formed under these conditions have smaller cells and are expanded more than corn curls. The small cells make the product whiter and provide eating qualities similar to those of popcorn.

Drying

Extrusion-puffed snacks usually reach a moisture content of about 8% as they set up, representing a loss of just a few percentage points as compared to the dough's moisture content. To gain the necessary crispness. it is necessary to dry the pieces to about 2 to 4% moisture content in a hotair oven or some equivalent type of heater. Lower moisture contents are not considered necessary and may lead to accelerated development of oxidative rancidity. In some cases, lower moisture contents may also cause a powdery mouth feel as the structure becomes excessively friable. The exact level to which the product must be dried depends to some extent on its composition and its surface area, but for most expanded snacks composed mostly of starch. 4% is a reasonable target. The 4% maximum is, of course, calculated on the basis of the collet itself, not the finished product with added oil, salt, and seasonings.

Many kinds of half-products are simultaneously dried and expanded by deep-fat frying, and most, if not all, tortilla chips and like products are dehydrated and cooked by the same means. Although it is technically possible to fry puffed pieces, such as corn curls, to lower their moisture content to acceptable levels and give them a fried flavor, this is not very practical in a commercial operation because the low density of the products makes it very difficult to submerge them, and the escape of hot gas from the air-filled products causes many problems with foaming. The original type of corn curl was fried after extruding and puffing, mainly for the flavor effects. Considerable quantities of these materials are. still being sold.

In the preface of "Extrusion Cooking Technology," edited by R. Howitt (1984), a list of guidelines is suggested for reporting conditions existing during experimental runs. Since these guidelines can be expected to comprise essentially all of the variables affecting the finished product (and some that don't), product development technologists may find the list a helpful first approximation in designing experiments and interpreting results. The following discussion is a modified, amplified, and paraphrased version of the original.

The make, type, model, size, and number of the extruder should be reported for exact identification. Non-standard modifications should be described. The following characteristics of the extruder barrel may affect the results: length, diameter (section in the case of a twin-screw extruder), specifications of grooves (if any), location and type of temperature adjustment systems, identification of heating or cooling zones, position openings such as input ports, and provisions for rapid opening of the barrel.

Also to be given, are detailed indications or dimensional drawings of the screws; number of screws; whether counter- or co-rotating, or selfwiping; length, diameter, dimensions of flights and number and angle of pitch for each successive screw segment (such as compression element, reverse flow element, mixing disc, steam lock, etc.); clearance between .screws, between screws and barrel, and between screws and dies; overall length/ diameter ratio of the screws; compression ratio; and wear which has affected screws.

Detailed information about die plates and inserts should be included. Dimensional drawings should indicate dimensions of dies and give the die's internal volume. The number and position of die inserts should be given.

Temperature probes are necessary for adequate process control. Make, type, and location of temperature probes, and their calibration history should be reported. Similar data should be given for the pressure transducers: location, type, and calibration history. Other instrumentation should be described, e.g., devices for measuring energy input, viscosity, torque, and on-line radioactivity detectors for residence time determination. Auxiliary equipment installed before and after the extruder should be described.

Full specifications of each ingredient, including minor additives and the water, should be reported. It is important to know if the dry mix has been checked for homogeneity, whether it was preconditioned for moisture and temperature, and how long it was held before extrusion. The feed rates and ratios of dry mix, water, oil, and any other ingredients must be reported. The aw and pH of the finished mix will sometimes be important.

For the extruded product the following data are useful: moisture content after cooling, variation of moisture content with time, moisture content after drying, and method of drying. Also, dimensions, bulk density, expansion coefficient (ratio of product dimensions to die dimensions or, preferably, ratio of product section area to die section area), and size and distribution of voids; product color and relationshiop to feed color, functinal properties of ground extruded product, texture of finished product, flavor and odor, and content of important nutrients.

Some of the extrusion conditions which should be considered as possibly affecting the product are:

(1) Process parameters. Sufficient time after start-up should be allowed *for* equilibration of the extruder before starting an experiment. This can be estimated by determining when constant torque or power use has been attained, or constant pressure at the die has been reached.

It should be indicated whether the extruder is starve-fed (with a screw feed, *for* instance, as is often done with twin-screw extruders) or fed "at will" by overflow (as is usually the case with single-screw. extruders). *For* reporting feed rates, determinations sh,ould be repeated several times with sample collection during appropriate time intervals. The true measured rate of rotation of the screw and the temperature of the barrel at different locations should be determined

(2) Some system parameters to be measured: Temperature of food during extrusion and location of measuring devices. Pressure within the extruder at different locations. Temperature and pressure profiles along the extruder. Mechanical and thermal energy inputs. Torque values. Residence times, with distribution curves and values *for* minimum, median, mean, maximum residence times and dispersion. Viscosity of extrudate in the die channel.

(3) Collection of extruded product and post-extrusion processing: Procedure *for* collecting and sampling of product; packaging and storage arrangements and post-extrusion processing, including, *for* example, cutting, stretching, flattening between rollers, drying, toasting, flavoring and packaging.

(4) Experimental design. of course, the above exhaustive list will be found impractical to follow in most experimental runs in the average pilot plant. In these cases, the following list of desirable minimum information *for* reporting extrusion cooking experiments was suggested:

(1) State make, type, and model of extruder. Supply dimensional drawings of barrel, screws, and dies.

(2) Describe equipment used *for* measuring temperature and pressure, and its location.

(3) List the exact composition of the food mix as percentage of each ingredient.

(4) Set down the process parameters including true rate of rotation of the screws, input feed rate, time allowed *for* equilibration, temperature of barrel at significant points, and any problems encountered during extrusion.

(5) Report the system parameters, such as temperature of food mix during extrusion, pressure within the extruder, and residence time distribution.

(6) Describe procedure for collecting and sampling extruded products and any post-extrusion processing.

14

Maize Products

Maize (Zea Mays) kernel is the largest of all the cereals. It also has a relatively larger germ than other cereals and contributes to 10-14 per cent of the kernel weight. Most of the oil (81-86%) is present in the germ which causes rancidity upon prolonged storage. Total carbohydrates accounts for as much as 60-70 per cent of the seed weight. Protein content ranges from 8-19 percent. Even though the protein content of cereal grains is only hafl that of various food legumes they still supplyover 70 percent of the total dietary intake of proteins. The amino acid composition of maize protein indicates lysine as the first and tyryptophan as the second liminating amino acids. The availability of proteins primarily depends upon their digestibility, incomplete digestion adversely effect the absorption and utilization of protein by the body. Utilizable protien is lowest (2.41%) in maize however, blending with 10 percent pulses enhances the protein utilization. Over 80 percent of the total minerals and vitamins are present in the outer layer usually removed during processing. Whole grain is more nutritious than their procssed counter part. Maize is used to produce corn starch, sweetners corn oil and various animal feed products. However, partly it is used for food products and alcoholic bevarages.

- Speed it round shallow fry
- Serve Hot

Nutritive value of tender dry maize

Nutrients	Tender Maize	Dry Maize
Protein (g)	4.7	11
Energy (Kcal)	125	342
Calcium (Kcal)	9	10
Phosphorous (mg)	121	348
Iron (Mg)	1.1	2.3
B-Carotene	32	90

Maize Rava Idly

Ingredients

Maize Soji	50 g
Parboiled Rice	25 g
Raw Rice	25 g
Curds	100 ml
Carrot (grated)	2 tsp
Coriander leaves	2 tsp
Water	as required
Salt	to taste

Method

- Soak maize soji, boiled rice and raw rice for 6 hours and drain out the water. Grind into fine paste.
- Ferment overnight. Add salt and mix it thoroughly with curds, carrot and coriander leaves.
- Apply a teaspoonful of oil to the idli making plates and pour idli paste.
- Steam in Idli Cooker
- Serve warm with chutney

Total yield 3 nos. (300 g)

Serving size 2 nos. (200 g.)

Maize Dosa

Ingredients

Maize Flour	20 g
Parboiled Rice	40 g
Raw Rice	40 g
Blackgram Dhal	25 g
Water	400 ml
Salt	to taste
Onion	100 g
Chilli	10 g
Coriander Leaves	10 g
Oil	150 ml

Method

- Soak blackgram dhal, raw rice and parboiled rice for 6 hours and drain out the water.

- Grind into find paste and add maize flavour.
- Ferment overnight, mix it and make it into a thin batter consistency by adding required quantity of water.
- Add chopped onion, chilli and coriander leaves to it along with salt to taste and mix it well.
- Apply little oil to the frying pan and put two tablespoon of butter.
- Spread it round, shallow fry
- Serve Hot.

15

Maize Starch

Maize Starch Powder : Starch are basically carbohydrates known as Polysaccharides i.e. multiple molecules of sugar. For commercial use, they are derived from a variety of cereals like rice, wheat, corn and tubers like potato, tapioca and mainly starches are mostly derived from corn and tapioca.

Starch is the most important source of carbohydrates in the human diet.

Structure : It is mixture of two polysaccharides, amylose, and amlyopectin. Corn starch consist of 10-20% amyloise and 80-90% amylopectin. Starch has number of commercial and industrial applications.

Industry Application

Textile	Sizing of yarns and finishing cotton and polyester fabric
Adhesives	Binding Capacity
Food	Thickening & bodying agent
Pharmaceutical	Binder for tablets and capsules

Paper Finishing and Touching

Liquid Glucose/Corn Syrup

- Liquid Glucose or Corn Syrup is colourless, viscous sweet syrup.
- Liquid Glucose/Corn Syrup is manufactured from refind starch. The starch is converted i.e. hydrolyzed by means of acids/ enzymes. Choice of Glucose syrup will depend upon the actual requirements.

Industry Application

Confectionary	Used in hard boiled candles, chewing gums & toffees etc.
Pharmaceutical	Cough syrup and antacid suspensions and other mixtures
Building	Used as a binder
Tobacco	Used in the curing of tobacco. Leather gives softness and weight gain to the leather. Used as a anticaking agent in shoe polish.

Malto Dextrin Powder

- Melto Dextrin is a white hygroscopic powder, moderately sweet in taste. It is produced by hydrolysis of glueten free starch by a typical total enzyme process.
- It is an essential ingredient of Baby foods and feed supplement.
- Flavouring, bodying and drying agent in chocolate drink, flavour powders, special diets, citrus powders and coffee powders.
- Bodying and bulking agent in puddings, soups and frozen deserts
- Moisture holding agent in Breads, Pastries and Meats.
- Soup powders, Concentrates and spices flavour blends. Powder, Cheese Sauces, Cream sauces, flavour enhancer, oxygen barrier, colour controller, stabilizing and viscosity builder and as a spray drying agent.
- Coffee whiteners, imitation sour creams, Imitation cheeses and whipped toppings.
- Candy coating and soft centre candies binding, plasticing and crystal inhibition.
- Malto dextrin is used in nutritional fluids, tableting and other medical application.

Dextrose Monohydrate

- Dextrose monohydrate is produced commercially by hydrolysis of starch and enzymatic process. It is a white crystallineor granular powder, odourless and sweet in taste. One gram of Dextrose Monohydrate supplies approximately 3.6 Calories of energy.

- Widely used in confectionary in marmalades and jellies. It increases the aroma and characteristics of fruit taste.
- Sweetening agent and an aroma enhancer in soft drink industry.
- Used in bakery industry because yeast acts more quickly on dextrose than on sucrose hence, less yeast is required to obtain a certain yeast action. Improves crispness, colour and flavour.
- Dextrose Monohydrate is used as a instant source of energy supplier Dextrose Monohydrate is also used in the manufacture of antibiotics like Pencillin, Ampicillin, also used in the manufacture of sorbitol. Calcium Gluconate and others.
- Dextrose Monohydrate is also used in the manufacture of adhesives boiler compounds, acids, dyes, enzymes explosives and in electro plating.

Maize Germ

Maize Germ is the endosperm of the Maize grain. It is yellow coloured germ free from harm full constituents and rancidity. Maize Germ has a minimum fat content of 40-44% with a low cholesterol level. It is used for extraction of Maize oil and feed supplements.

Maize Gluten

Maize Gluten is protein matter of Maize. Maize Gluten consists of about 50-55% protein, 5% fat, 35% starch together with fibre and little mineral matter.

Used in poultry feeds as maize glueten being rich source of proteins, amino acids, fat and minerals. Also used as a protein supplement in cattle feeds.

Corn steep liquor

Corn steep liquor is a by roduct of the wet milling of corn containing rich protein, carbohydrates and minerals. It is used in the manufacture of antibiotics like pencillin, auremycin, streptomycin etc. It is used in the manufacture of phytin. When dried and added to Gluten it adds nutrition in animal feeds.

16

Sweet Corn

Sweet corn *(Zea mays L saccharata*) is one of the most popular vegetables in countries like USA and it is becoming increasingly popular in India. It is consumed in the immature stage of the cob. Sweet corn varies from normal corn essentially for gene(s) that affect starch synthesis in the seed endosperm where in the recessive sugary (su) allele elevates the level of water soluble polysaccharides (sugars) and decreases starch. Thus the kernels of sweet corn taste sweet especially at 18 to 21 days after pollination. The total sugars in sweet corn ranges from 25-30 per cent. Sweet corn matures early and can be harvested in 75-80 days after planting. Thus it can fit easily in multiple or inter cropping systems. Due to the absence of starch in the kernels (seeds) the dried seed is shriveled in appearance.

Cultivation

Land selection: Sweet corn can be cultivated on all well drained soils and in frost free areas. There should be facility for 5-6 irrigations. Since all genes governing sweet corn are recessive, sweet corn is to be grown at a field isolation of 250 m from other corn or by a tassel date of 14 days difference.

Land preparation: It requires thorough disc ploughing followed by land levelling There after ridges and furrows are to be laid out with an inter row distance of 60 cm.Five-6 tons/ha of well rottened Farm yard manure is to be incorporated at the last ploughing.

Time of sowing: The planting time is June- July in *kharif* across the country and September-October in peninsular India in *rabi* season. It can also be grown in summer with assured irrigation (January - February).

Varieties: Both white and yellow grain types of sweet corn are grown. Some of the recommended sweet corn varieties released for cultivation are

- Madhuri
- Priya
- Almora sweet corn.

All these varieties mature in 80-90 days with 55,555 cobs ha^{-1}.

Seed rate: A seed rate of 15-20 kg/ha is recommended for composite variety while it is 20-25 kg/ha of certified seeds.

Seed treatment: Seed treatment with Imidacloprid 70WS @ 5g/Kg seed takes care of insect pests upto 30 days.

Method of sowing: Two seeds per hill are dibbled manually or mechanically one third from the top on the side of the ridge with an intra row spacing of 25 cm. Sowing on ridges serves the twin purpose of water conservation and protection from water logging in the initial stages to which sweet corn is highly susceptible. Plants are thinned to one plant per hill10-12 days after emergence. Studies conducted at the Main Research Station, Hebbal, Bangalore under red sandy loam soils indicated normal planting at 60 cm X 20 cm has given higher cob yield (20.07 t ha^{-1}) and green fodder yield (24.81 t ha^{-1}). But paired planting helps in reducing the cost on drip system (Table.16.1)

Nutrient management: Phosphorous and Potassium are incorporated basally@ 60 Kg/ha and 40 Kg /ha respectively. Nitrogen is applied@ 120 Kg/ ha in three equal splits - basally, at knee high stage (25 days after sowing) and at tasseling stages (45 days after sowing). Once in three crop seasons 10 kg/ha of Zinc sulphate is to be basally incorporated.

Weed management: After 1-2 days of the initial irrigation, weed control is achieved for 30- 35 days through a spray of the weedicide atrazine @ 1 Kg ai / ha.

Water management: Depending on the soil type the number of irrigations vary and range from 4 -5 irrigations in heavy soils and 7-8 irrigations in light soils. The water requirement is 300-350 mm. vegetative stage, tasseling and silking stage are critical stages for irrigation. Studies conducted by Viswanatha *et.al.,(2002)* revealed higher green cob (20.07 t ha^{-1}) and fodder yield (24.87 t ha^{-1}) of sweet corn with net returns of fsRs. 65117 ha^{-1} and Benefit: Cost ratio of 1 : 5.2 due to drip irrigation at 0.8 Epan. The water use efficiency was higher (40.04 kg ha^{-1} mm)with drip at 0.4 Epan with saving of187.36 mm of water.

Intercultivation: Top dressing of Urea is done 25 days after emergence after running a cultivator in between the rows that will help weed control and better root aeration apart from soil water conservation. Subsequently a ridger is run to prevent plant lodging and minimize volatalization losses of urea. Top dressing is followed by an irrigation.

Pest and disease management: A preventive spray of Endosulfan 35EC @ 2ml/l of water is given 10 days after thinning to take care of stalk borers *Chilo partellus* in *kharif* and *Sesamia inferens* in *rabi.* A spray with Bavistin @ 1 g/litre would take care of foliar diseases.

Plant growth picks up after the knee high stage rapidly as this is the grand growth stage. About 45 days after emergence, the tassel emerges and 2-3 days later the silks emerge. Top dressing with urea is done at tassel emergence. Sweet corn is an abundant pollen producer and seed set is usually very high. There should be no moisture stress at tasseling-silking stage as moisture stress reduces seed set and in extreme cases barren ears are also seen. Completion of pollination is indicated by the drying of the silks. 18-21 days after pollination is the right stage for harvest of sweet corn ears.

Harvesting and *Yield*

Delaying the harvest will progressively reduce the sugar content in the kernels. The ear husks are still green at this stage. The ears are harvested in 70-75 days during *kharifand* summer 80-85 days during *rabi* season. The kernels are lustrous and at milky stage the kernels taste very sweet, which is preferred by the consumers. Ears can be eaten raw as a dessert or ears can even be steam boiled, salted and eaten which is more relishing. Under good management, two ears are borne per plant especially in the *rabi* (winter) season. Staggered planting-of sweet corn at intervals of 7 -10 days will enable farmers to harvest sweet corn ears at intervals for continuous supply to the market and thereby get continuous and higher returns. The ears are graded according to the raw ear size and packed in polythene bags and sold in the market. Sweet corn can be preserved by canning in a 1 % brine solution and storing under refrigerated conditions (5-10°e). Under room temperatures sweet corn will lose 50 % or more of its sugars in 24 hours.

Sweet corn kernels possess a considerable amount of sugar which absorb water, making the cells turgid on drying these cells collapse, making the gains shriveled or wrinkled. It has sweeter taste than other corns.

Sweet com is growing in almost all the state of India. It is the important

Table 16.1 Response of sweet corn to method planting.

Spacing	Leaf area Index	LAD days	Dry matter accumulation g. plant^{-1}	50% teseling days	50% Silking days	No. of grains /row	No. of kernel /row	Cob yield	Fodder yeild
Normal	4.18	85.97	264.98	47.33	52.66	40.23	18.69	20.07	24.87
Paired	3.08	64.10	179.05	49.66	56.66	32.93	13.10	13.80	18.17

Table 16.2 Cost of sweet corn production and economic returns

Sl. No.	Particulars of Operation	Item/Quantity	Rate (Rs.)	Total Amount (Rs.)
1.	Pre-ploughing irritaion	Daily wage labours (6)	45/day	270.00
2.	Land preparation			
	(2 ploughing +passing	Bullock pair (5)	200/day	1000.00
	cultivator and leveling)	Men labours (8)	45/day	360.00
3.	Seed	25 kg	70/kg	1750.00
4.	Sowing	Bullock pair (3)	200/day	600.00
		Women labour (10)	42/day	420.00
5.	Manures and Fertilizers	FYM 10 tons	200/ton	2000.00
		Urea 260 kg	5.00 kg	1300.00
		SSP 375 kg	3.20/kg	1200.00
		MOP 67 kg	4.60/kg	308.00
		Men labour (6)	45/day	270.00
6.	Irrigation	Men labour (12)	45/day	540.00
7.	Weeding (twide)	Women labour (20)	42/day	840.00
8.	Hoeing (twice)	Bullock pairs (2)	200/day	400.00
9.	Harvesting (2-3 picking)	Women labour (30)	42/day	1260.00
10.	Harvesting of green fodder	Men labour (15)	45/day	675.00
		Total		**13193.00**

Out put and returns

	Seed yeild (q ha^{-1})	Green fodder yield (t ha^{-1})	Gross return (Rs)	Net return (Rs)
Sweet corn	17.00	21.50	77675.00	64482.00

@ Green cobs Rs. 4 kg^{-1} and green fodder Rs. 450t^{-1}

species of maize which has developed by crossing of different species of maize. This crop is having very good sugar content and carbohydrate which is useful for quality maintenance of sweet com.

Yield

Under best management practices sweet com can yield

Green cob yield of -13.0-17.0 t ha^{-1} and

Fodder yield of -17.7 -21.5 t ha^{-1}

Thrust Areas of Research

Strengthening post-harvest handling of sweet com for value addition

• Improve water, nutrition, weed management and tillage for crop establishment and develop resource conservation technology under rainfed conditions for higher yields.

• Popularization and diversification of sweet com in non traditional areas with emphasis on winter sweet com production.

Cost of production and returns

Sweet com hybrids on an average can yield 15-17 q ha^{-1} and 19 to 21.5t ha^{-1} of green fodder. The average cost of cultivation is Rs.12,500 to 13,500 ha^{-1} and the net returns could be Rs. 60,000 to 65,000 ha^{-1} (Table 16.2).

17

Baby Corn

Baby maize is latest addition to the maize type also called "Baby Corn" an offshoot of grain maize becoming popular among city elites and middle class people. It is grown for vegetable purpose, a venture that proved enormously successful in countries like Thailand, Taiwan, Srilanka and Myanmar. It is a widely accepted crop and habituated as a cereal vegetable in USA, Europe and in some Asian countries. Attention is now being paid to explore its potential in India for earning foreign exchange and economic returns to the farmers as is being attempted by Hong Kong, Singapore, Malaysia, the USA, Canada and Germany. In India, cultivation of baby corn is of recent development. It is an interesting development for diversification and value addition of maize as well as the growth of food processing industry. With the increasing concern for health, people have turned towards quality food in place of bulky items. In this context, baby corn has prime place as a safe and quality vegetable.

Baby corn is the ear of corn plant. Young, fresh, finger like green ears are harvested before or just at the time of silk emergence. The young ears, dehusked and desilked is served as a vegetable. Its delicate, sweet flavour and crisp nature contributes to its increasing popularity making as an indispensable ingredient in many fancy dishes of today.

Baby corn is a unique cereal with a difference of value addition in terms of the milky tender cob as a fresh natural food cum vegetable. The tender cobs are consumed as such as a natural food. It is very tasty, sweet and easy to consume because of its tenderness and sweetness with nutritive value addition. Added to this, it can be used as a vegetable in daily culinary preparations and for preparing delicacies for special occasions. Cultivation of baby corn generate employment for the rural poor since, 3-4 crops can be raised in a year. It occupies an important place in the food processing industries of India. The economic potential and marketing aspects of canning baby corn as a small scale food processing venture can be explored. Canning and pickling industries of baby corn offer huge export potential. Demand for baby corn as a health food is increasing in class hotels and middle clas~ consumers. After the harvest of babies, the economic potential is further enhanced since it supplies green, soft, succulent, nutritious, palatable fodder with higher digestibility.

Uses of Baby Corn

- Eaten afresh directly
- Used as a vegetable
- In the preparation of salads, soups, appetizers, chowders, stews and fried dishes
- Preparation of pickles - Tamarind baby corn pickle, baby corn masala pickle, baby corn sweet hot pickle and mixed vegetable pickle.
- Baby corn Manchurian and chilly baby corn preparations
- It is used in poriyal, kurma, kuzhambu and butter milk kuzhambu
- It is a part of delicacies such as milk payasam, alwa bajji, pakoda, biriyani and curd pachadi
- Its green nutritious, palatable fodder is fed directly to cattle or ensiled

Nutritive value of baby corn (on dry weight basis)

Protein	:	15-18%
Sugar	:	0.016 - 0.020 %
Phosphorus	:	0.6 - 0.9 %
Potassium	:	2-3 %
Fibre	:	3 -5 %
Calcium	:	0.3 - 0.5 %
Ascorbic acid	:	75 - 80 mg. $100g^{-1}$

In addition, it is a rich source of thiamine, riboflavin and folic acid and it is an attractive low calorie vegetable high in fibre without cholesterol.

Scope lor baby corn cultivation

- In traditional belt and malnad areas in place of upland rice where water is insufficient for paddy crop
- Irrigated areas
- In the traditional rainfed maize areas which suffers due to vagaries of monsoon baby corn is a best alternate dual purpose crop by virtue of short duration (65-75 days)
- In North-Eastern Indogangetic plains of Bihar, UP, Karnataka and Andra Pradesh
- In traditional sorghum areas in place of late sown jowar which is likely to be infested with shoot fly in the early stage and ear head midge at the later stages
- During *rabi* season in rice fallows with residual moisture
- In place of fodder maize for both baby corn and green fodder
- In a double cropping system as an early crop with protective irrigation followed by a regular crop
- Baby corn will be a solution to the vegetable needs of the increasing population and to the innovative thinking of enthusiastic faimer who want to have commercialized agricultural wealth scenario.

Quality of baby corn as measured at the international level standard

1. Ear length : 4-9 cm
2. Ear diameter : 1-1.5 cm
3. Ear Colour : Cream yellow
4. Ovule arrangement : Regular

Local food processors grade baby corn as follows

1. Supar small : 3 cm
2. Small : 3-6 cm
3. Medium : 6-9 cm
4. Large : 9-11 cm
5. Extra large : >11 cm

- While measuring diameter, basal, mid and tip are considered
- No. of rows and No. of columns in baby corn is also considered by food processors

- Rejection per cent must be less than 10 % in any hybrid
- Rejection includes long cobs, grain, filled cobs, different shapes of cobs
- Stage of harvest play an important role in reducing the rejection percent

Problems associated with the Baby corn production in India

- Lack of knowledge about this potential dual purpose crop
- In appropriate genotypes and
- Lack of improved agro techniques are the major problems facing this industry in India.

Cultivation of baby corn in India leads to

- Maize diversification
- Value addition as a health food and foreign exchange earner
- Growth of food processing small scale industries and
- Generate gainful employment to rural poor since, it is possible to raise 3 to 4 crops of baby corn in a year depending on the Agroclimatic conditions.

Climatic *Requirements*

Baby corn an offshoot of maize is suited to tropical and subtropical climate. In areas receiving seasonal rainfall of 400 mm or more well distributed for 2 ½ months, baby corn can be successfully raised. Growing season temperature of 21 to 32°C is most desirable. It can be cultivated in all the three seasons provided minimum temperature does not go below 15° C and irrigation facilities are available during summer.

Seasons

Although baby corn can be grown round the year, the optimum time of sowing is June-July in *Kharif,* September - October in rabi and January February during summer seasons.

Soil Requirement

Baby Corn is grown in all type of soils. The ideal soil type would be well drained sandy loam to silty loam soils. Water stagnation is harmful to the crop. Therefore, proper drainages is must for the success of the crop especially during Kharifseason. Baby corn will not thrive on heavy clays especially low lands. It can be grown successfully in soils with pH ranges from 5.5 to 7.5.

Land Preparation

Baby corn needs a friable, well aerated, moist and weed free seed bed, so that the seed placed at a depth should come in contact with soil particles to ensure sufficient movement of moisture to the seed. The first ploughing should be done with soil inverting plough so that at least 20-25 cm deep soil may become loose. followed by two to three harrowing or intercrossing ploughing with local plough. Planking should be done after harrowing. A properly levelled and uniformly graded field is a pre-requisite for good water management and drainage. Application of about 10 t of Farm Yard manure per ha before last ploughing is essential.

Planting Method

Baby corn is sown at a depth of 3-5 cm. The planting depth to a considerable extent will depend on the moisture status of the field and the type of soil. If the soil is dry and sandy, it would be advisable to plant deeper. Usually planting is done by one of the following methods.

(a) Planting on the side *of* the ridge: This method adopted in high rainfall situations and on land not uniform.

(b) Planting in narrow furrows: This method is adopted in low rainfall areas.

(c) Planting in a flat bed with no earthing up: in normal conditions

(d) Planting on flat bed and earthing up after 30 days *of* planting: In areas where there are heavy storms during rainy season.

(e) Row Direction: Planting in North-South Direction will have better light interception and enhanced growth and yield than planting in East-West direction.

Selection of *suitable variety*

Selection criteria for baby corn production differs from grain or sweet corn.

- Each plant bears multiple babies to realize higher yield
- Babies should emerge in sequence to facilitate multiple harvests
- Sturdy stalk resistant to breakage when multiple harvests are done
- Babies should be long and slender
- The wrapper husk should provide protection to the baby during handling and storage.

In India, development and release of baby corn variety or hybrid is of recent venture in the maize diversification process. At the Vivekananda Parvatiya Krishi Anusandha Sansthan, Almora seven yellow flint grain maize varieties were developed and released for commercial cultivation in the NorthWestern hills of India. Among these early duration double cross hybrid VL-42 produced the highest baby corn yield (1,428 kg ha-l) with an average of more than one baby per plant. It was earliest in maturity (45 days). The babies of this variety were cylindrical, longer, uniform and more attractive. Recently the Directorate of Maize Research, New Delhi identified VL-42 and MEH-44 for baby corn production at the national level. Composite VL-16 is another suitable variety for baby corn production with potential yield of 11 02 kg ha-l in 49 days (Table 17.1).

Table 17.1 Baby Corn of different maize varieties.

Variety	Yield (kg har^{-1})
VL-16	1102
VL-41	1031
VL-42	1428
VL-78	971
VL-88	1048
VL Amber Pop Corn	846
Dhari Local	819

Results of the studies conducted at Himachal Pradesh Krishi Vishvavidyalaya, Regional Research Station, Bajaure of All India Coordinated Maize Improvement programme, revealed the suitability of 4 cultivars viz., hybrids" VL-42, MEH-114, MEH-133" and a composite, 'Early composite' for baby corn production (Table 17.2).

The results of the study conducted by Sukanya *et ai.* (1998) indicated significantly higher baby corn yield of 37.85 q ha^{-1} with YBC-705 compared to 25.90 q ha^{-1} with C-6 and 21A8 q ha-l with ITC-ZENECA.

At the Department of Agronomy, University of Agricultural Sciences, GKVK, Bangalore a grain maize hybrid "Pro Agro 4642" ,composite "Shakthi" and three baby com hybrids "Golden baby, PAC-792 and PAC793" were evaluated for their performance of baby com production (Fig. 17.1). The

Table 17.2 : Mean yield and agronomic characteristics of maize cultivators for baby corn production

Cultivars	Yield (kg ha^{-1})		Green fodder yeild (t ha^{-1})	Size of young cob (cm)				Cobs plant^{-1}	Days to harvest	Period of harvest (Days)
				With husk		Without husk				
	With husk	Without husk		Length	Diameter	Length	Diameter			
VL-42	8091	1913	24.9	16.8	1.53	8.2	1.20	2.68	48	19
MEH-133	8797	1744	30.9	17.0	1.70	8.6	1.16	2.31	54	22
MEH-114	8292	1720	31.1	17.1	1.70	8.6	1.16	2.28	54	22
Early composite	7884	1512	39.8	18.8	1.74	9.3	1.18	1.86	58	21
CD. (p=0.05)	245	190	2.6	-	-	-	-	0.40	2.8	NS

Table 17.3 : Mean yield and agronomic characterstics of maize/baby corn cultivars for baby corn production

Cultivars	With husk	Without husk	Green fodder yeild (t ha^{-1})	Size of young cob (cm)				Babies plant^{-1}	Days to harvest	Period of harvest (Days)
				With husk		Without husk				
				Length	Diameter	Length	Diameter			
Golden baby	9423	1803	17.55	23.31	8.71	10.39	6.45	2.31	41	8
PAC-792	8862	2571	29.90	19.91	7.47	10.39	5.06	1.87	48	10
PAC-793	10458	2213	47.36	21.50	7.52	8.35	4.89	2.52	48	10
Pro-Agro 4642	9740	2195	34.50	21.05	7.85	10.00	5.57	2.67	50	10
Composite (Shakti)	10159	2559	27.26	21.25	7.86	10.13	5.33	3.75	50	10

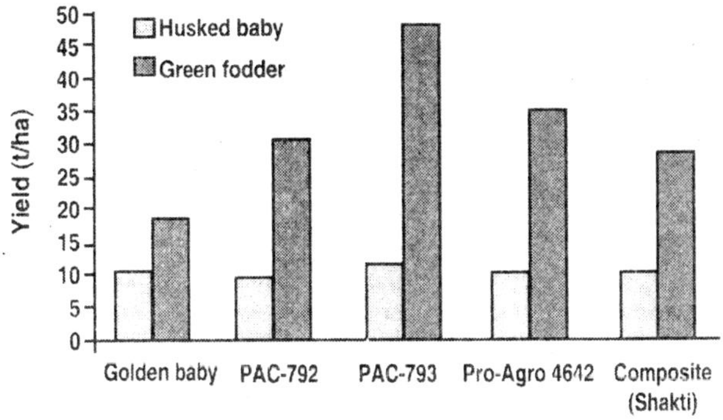

Fig. 17.1 Husked and fodder yield as influenced by the cultivars in the corn

Table 17.4 : Sensory parameters as influenced by varieties in baby corn (in 5 points scale)

Varieties	Appearance	Colour	Texture	Taste	Juiciness
Golden bay/ PAC 792	4.07	3.98	4.04	3.37	3.56
Hybrid maize	3.53	3.54	3.24	2.80	3.02
Composite	3.70	3.43	3.48	3.10	2.85

Agronomic characteristics of these cultivars in relation to baby com production are presented in Table 17.3.

The results indicated the superiority of P AC-792, P AC-793, composite and grain maize hybrid in terms of dehusked baby com and green fodder yield compared to golden baby. This may work well when the produce is bulked for marketing. But when grading and iabeling is done, the preference of the consumer is certainly for baby com hybrid.

Golden baby/ P AC-792 graded the best for characters like appearance, colour, texture, taste and juiciness followed by composite for appearance, texture and taste. Whereas maize hybrid ranked second with respect to colour and juiciness. Golden baby/ P AC-792 is the best choice of consumer with respect to quality (Table 17.4).

The results of the nutritional parameters indicated that both Hybrid maize and composite were found to contain higher percentage of sugar (0.025 and 0.022 per cent respectively) and potassium (3.05 and 2.93 per cent respectively) as compared to Golden baby/ PAC-792. While, Golden baby/ PAC-792 and Hybrid maize contained higher percentages of protein (14.67 and 15.28 respectively) and phosphorus (0.81 and 0.77 respectively) as compared to protein (13.33) and phosphorus (0.75) content of composite variety. In case of calcium and fibre content, composite (0.34 and 4.67 per cent respectively) and Golden baby/ P AC-792 (0.33 and 4.57 per cent respectively) were found to be superior as compared to Hybrid maize (Table 17.5).

Other Varieties

NAC 6002

HIM 129

Madhuri sweet com

Priya sweet com

Other Hybrids

Ganga - 9

Decan - 1

DHM 107

Hybrid Makka - 1

Hybrid Makka - 2 are also recommended for baby corn purpose with 7 to 7.5 t ha-l of husked baby com and 25 to 30 t ha^{-1} of green fodder.

Seed Rate

To maintain the desirable population of baby corn ten to twenty per cent more seeds are required to compensate for various field losses and reduced germination. Based on the seed weight and the required plant population per hectare the normal seed rate required is 35-40 kg per hectare for hybrids to maintain two plants per hill.

Optimum *Plant Population*

The yield of baby corn depends to a great extent on the number of plants per unit area. It is of great importance to establish the optimum plant population for the region concern, because unlike tillering plants such as rice or wheat, babycom can not compensate for lost space. The number of plants per unit area depends on the variety, its duration, productivity of soil and the water supply.

Earlier study by Sukanya *et al.* (1998) revealed the yield level of 29.62 qha^{-1} with 45 X 30 cm spacing which was 11.06 per cent higher compared to 45 X 15 cm spacing.

The results of the experiment have indicated that 60 X 20 cm, 45 X 20 cm and 45 X 30 cm spacing recorded higher husked babies (95.06, 91.65 and 87.02 q ha-l respectively) and dehusked babies (20.05, 19.39 and 18.41 q ha^{-1} respectively) and fodder yield (36.45,39.03 and 34.23 t ha^{-1} respectively) as compared to 60 X 30 cm spacing (84.36,17.85 q ha-l and 31.7 t ha-l offiusked, dehusked and fodder yield respectively) (Table 17.6).

Baby corn production requires detasseling and harvesting of babies. Detasseling has to be done as soon as the emergence of tassel and before it sheds pollens. This continues for about 5-6 days and harvesting of babies involves 8-10 pickings since all plants doesn't produce babies at a time and each plant produces on an average of 2-3 babies. It is economical to plant baby corn at 60 X 20 cm (83,333 hills ha-l) or 45 X 20 cm (1,11,111 hills ha-l) spacings.

Table 17.5 : Sugar, protein, phosphorus, potassium, calcium and fibre content as influenced by varieties.

Varieties	Sugar (%)	Protein (%)	Phosphorus (%)	Potassium (%)	Calcium (%)	Fibre (%)
Golden baby/ PAC-792	0.015	14.67	0.81	2.90	0.33	4.57
Pro-Agro 4642	0.025	15.28	0.77	3.05	0.30	4.47
Composite	0.022	13.33	0.75	2.93	0.34	4.67

Table 17.6 : Husked, dehusked and fodder yield of baby corn as influenced by spacing

Spacing (cm)	Plant Population	Husked yield (q ha^{-1})	Deusked yield (q ha^{-1})	Fodder yield (q ha^{-1})
45 X 20	1,11,111	91.65	19.39	39.03
45 X 30	74,074	87.02	18.41	34.23
60 X 20	83,333	95.06	20.05	36.45
60 X 30	55,555	84.36	17.85	31.70

Table 17.7: Sensory parameters as influenced by spacing in baby corn (in 5 points scale)

Spacing (cm)	Colour	Taste	Juiciness	Texture	Appearance
45 X 20	3.42	3.42	3.66	3.83	3.42
45 X 30	4.17	3.84	4.00	4.00	3.84
60 X 20	3.42	3.59	3.59	3.50	3.42
60 X 30	3.17	3.59	3.17	2.84	3.17

Table 17.8: Phosphorus, potassium, calcium, sugar, ascorbic acid, protein and fibre as influenced by spacing in baby corn

Spacing (cm)	Phosphorus (%)	Potassium (%)	Calcium (%)	Sugar (%)	Ascorbic acid (mg 100 g^{-1})	Protein (%)	Fibre (%)
45 X 20	1.35	3.77	0.34	0.013	75	17.87	5.80
45 X 30	1.21	3.70	0.39	0.012	94	15.60	6.00
60 X 20	1.17	3.96	0.37	0.013	94	16.48	5.90
60 X 30	1.18	3.76	0.46	0.014	94	17.57	5.93

The sensory evaluation indicated the superiority of the 45 X 30 cm spacing in terms of colour (4.17), taste (3.84), juiciness (4.00), texture (4.00) and appearance (3.84) compared to other spacings. However, optimum sensory parameters were observed with 45 X 20 or 60 X 20 cm spacings (Table 17.7).

The nutritional parameters indicated that wider spacing of 60 X 30 cm recorded higher values of calcium (0.46%), sugar (0.014%), ascorbic acid (94 mg 100g^{-1}), protein (17.57%) and fibre (5.93%) but the optimum quality babies can be realized with 45 X 20 cm or 60 X 20 cm spacing (Table 17.8).

Number of Plants per Hill

Baby corn is harvested at the emergence of silk. It can prove well with high plant population. But, increasing plant population by reducing spacing would be inconvenient for detasseling and harvesting. Hence increasing the

Table 17.9 : Husked, dehusked and fodder yield of baby corn as influenced by number of plants per hill in baby corn (mean data of 2001 and 2002)

Number of plants per hill	Husked yeild (q ha^{-1})	Dehusked yeild (q ha^{-1})	Fodder yeild (t ha^{-1})
One	84.27	17.82	30.05
Two	94.78	20.03	38.67

Table 17.10 : Sensory parameters as influenced by number of plants per hill in baby corn (in 5 points scale)

Number of plants per hill	Colour	Taste	Juiciness	Texture	Appearance
One	3.42	3.66	3.70	3.37	3.41
Two	3.67	3.54	3.50	3.70	3.50

number of plants per hill is a better option in realizing higher baby corn and fodder yield. In this regard the experiment conducted under ICAR ad-hoc project at Bangalore revealed that the maintenance of two plants per hill produced superior husked (94.78 q ha-l), dehusked (20.03 q ha-l) and fodder yield (38.67 t ha-l) as compared to single plants per hill (84.27,17.82 q ha-l and 32.05 t ha-l respectively) (Table 17.9). The percent increase was by 12.47,12.40 and 20.65 percent respectively over single plant per hill.

With respect to sensory parameters, two plants per hill graded the best for its characters like colour (3.67), texture (3.70) and appearance (3.50) as compared to single plant per hill (3.42, 3.37 and 3.41 respectively) while, single plant per hill was judged best in terms oftaste (3.66) and juiciness (3.70) (Table 17.10).

Table 17.11 : Phosphorus, potassium, calcium, sugar, ascorbic acid, protein and fibre as influenced by number of plants per hill in baby corn.

No. of plants per hill	Phosphorus (%)	Potassium (%)	Calcium (%)	Sugar (%)	Ascorbic acid (mg 100 g^{-1})	Protein (%)	Fibre (%)
One	1.24	3.83	0.39	0.013	87.5	16.00	5.93
Two	1.21	3.77	0.39	0.013	90.6	16.26	5.88

The results of the nutritional analysis revealed that single plant per hill recorded higher phosphorus (1.24 %), potassium (3.83 %) and fibre (5.93 %) content as compared to two plants per hill (1.21, 3.77 and 5.88 % respectively). Two plants per hill was found to be superior in terms of ascorbic acid (90.6 mg 100g^{-1}) and protein (16.26 %) as compared to single plant per hill (87.5 mg 100g^{-1} and 16.00 % respectively) (Table 17.11).

Fertilizer Management

Fertilizer management plays an important role in the baby corn cultivation. Hybrids and composite varieties exhibit their full yield potential only when supplied with adequate quantities of nutrients at proper time. The time of fertilizer application is as much important as the quantity applied. As far as nitrogen is concerned, major part of the nitrogen uptake by the crop is over by the tasseling stage. In general it would be better to apply the total quantity of P and K and half of N at planting and remaining half of N at knee high stage (above 30 days after planting). The extra quantity of the fertilizer that has to applied to the soil will depend not only on the plant requirement of individual nutrient but also on how much of them the soil can supply. In this regard the fmdings of the experiment conducted under ICAR ad-hoc project at Bangalore indicated the superiority of 200: 100:53 Kg NPK ha-l + lot FYM, 200: 100:53 kg NPK ha-l and 150:75:40 kg NPK ha-l + 10 t FYM in terms of husked yield (85.78, 85.17 and 82.40 q ha^{-1} respectively) and fodder yield

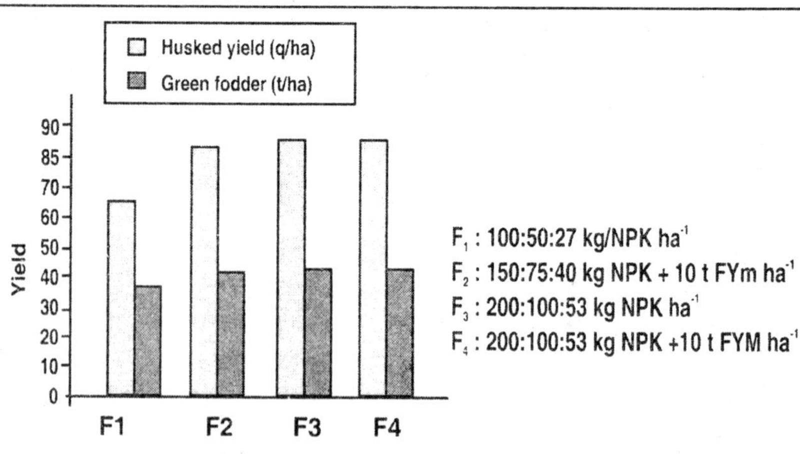

Fig. 17.2 : Husked and fodder yield as influenced by fertility levels in baby corn.

Table 17.12 : Yield and returns as influenced by fertility levels in baby corn.

Fertility level (kg NPK ha^{-1})	Husked yield (q ha^{-1})	No. of babies Plant	Fodder yield (t ha^{-1})	Cost of Cultivation (Rs ha^{-1})	Gross returns (Rs ha^{-1})	Net returns (Rs ha^{-1})	B : C ration
100:50:27	63.30	1.88	35.86	20928	68570	47642	1:2.27
150:75:40 + 10 t FYM	82.40	2.14	40.26	24944	86050	61106	1:2.45
200:100:53	85.17	2.22	42.37	23154	89321	66167	1:2.86
200:100:53 + 10 t FM	85.78	2.23	43.16	26054	90204	64150	1:2.46
CD at 5%	3.24	0.16	4.03				

Table 17.13 : Sensory parameters of baby corn as influenced by fertility levels (in 5 points scale)

Fertility levels (kg NPK ha^{-1})	Appearance	Colour	Texture	Taste	Juiciness
100:50:27	3.47	3.38	3.46	3.37	2.87
150:75:40 + 10 t FYM	3.92	3.72	3.92	4.18	3.65
200:100:53	3.60	3.38	3.92	3.96	3.62
200:100:53 + 10 t FYM	3.52	3.60	3.75	3.70	3.26

(43.16,42.37 and 40.26 t ha^{-1} respectively) as compared to 100:50:27 kg NPK ha-l (63.30 q ha-l and 35.85 t ha-l respectively) (Fig. 17.2). Yield of baby corn increased with increase in fertilizer upto 200: 100:50 kg NPK ha-l with Rs.66, 167 /- net returns and 1 :2.86 benefit cost ratio (Table 17.12).

The sensory parameters indicated the superiority of the 150:75:40 kg NPK ha^{-1} + 10t FYM fertility levels in terms of appearance (3.92), colour (3.72), texture (3.92), taste (4.18) and juiciness (3.65) followed by 200:100:53 kg NPKha^{-1} and 200:100:50kg NPKha^{-1} + 10 tFYM fertility levels Table 17.13).

The nutritional parameters revealed that fertility levels of 150:75:40 kg NPKha^{-1} + 10 tFYM was found to be optimum in terms of protein (19.94 %), phosphorus (0.84 %), potassium (2.78 %), calcium (0.58 %), sugars (0.015 %), ascorbic acid (0.75 mg $100g^{-1}$) and crude fibre (5.22 %) as compared to higher doses (Table 17.14).

IRRIGATION MANAGEMENT

Nature and importance of irrigation management

Water management of baby corn is an important aspect for higher production. Traditional crop of maize is greatly affected by vagaries of weather conditions. Rainfall is uncertain and may either cause prolonged drought or waterlogged conditions. It is therefore essential to consider both the aspects.

Water requirement to produce one kg of dry matter is the lowest in case of maize. Thus, a very high water use efficiency can be achieved as compared to other cereal crops. Although maize needs less water than soybean or pea but its water requirement for germination is 10 to 30 times more than that of wheat, berseem and mustard. It is therefore imperative

Table 17.14 : Nutritional parameters of baby corn as influenced by fertility levels

Fertility levels (kg NPK ha^{-1})	Protein	Phosphorus (%)	Potassium (%)	Calcium (%)	Sugar (%)	Ascorbic acid (mg $100g^{-1}$)	Crude fibre (%)
100:50:27	16.59	0.55	2.53	0.52	0.014	0.74	4.80
150:75:40 + 10 t FYM	19.94	0.84	2.78	0.58	0.015	0.75	5.22
200:100:53	19.86	0.84	2.88	0.55	0.015	0.76	5.27
200:100:53 + 10 t FYM	19.96	0.81	2.81	0.54	0.016	0.77	5.32

that at the time of germination available moisture in case of baby corn should be high so that each and every seed may germinate properly. Availability of moisture at later stage has direct bearing on the growth and yield of baby corn.

Methods of Irrigation

Various methods of irrigation to be adapted to baby corn depends on soil type, climate, source and head of available water resource etc. The objective of selecting a particular irrigation method is to use minimum water to get optimum yield.

(i) **Surface method**: In this surface system water flows by gravity either through furrows, basins on borders. In this type water loss by conveyance and deep percolation is heavy and the efficiency of irrigation is only 40-50 per cent at field level.

(ii) **Sprinkler method**: Water is applied in the form of rain. Water is conveyed through pipes and sprayed through sprinklers. This method is most suited for steep slopy and sandy soils

(iii) **Drip irrigation**: Drip irrigation is adopted in water scarce areas for conserving water. In this method water is applied in drops around the root zone through a network of mains, sub-mains and lateral on line drippers. Studies at UAS, Bangalore indicated irrigations at 0.8 E Pan daily produced higher yields of quality babies.

Scheduling of Irrigation

Irrigating crop with required amount of irrigation water at appropriate growth stages is of at most importance for increasing water use efficiency under irrigated conditions. Excess or deficit amount of irrigation water at sensitive crop growth stage will affect their productivity considerably. So irrigation can be scheduled based on

1. The soil moisture status
2. Meteorological approach
3. Phenological stage of crop plants and

Optimum depletion of soil moisture for scheduling irrigation is 50 per cent depletion of available soil moisture from the 90 cm surface soil on sandy loam to clay loam soils.

Irrigation scheduled at 0.8-1.0 IW/CPE could be followed for higher baby corn and fodder yields.

The results indicated the superiority of continuously non-stressed irrigations at IW/CPE ratio of 1.0 in terms of husked (66.02 q ha^{-1}) and fodder yield (43.38 t ha^{-1}) (Fig. 17.3). The next best treatments were IW/CPE ratio of 0.6 at 10-26 days and 1.0 IW/CPE in the rest of the crop stages which recorded husked (60.44 q ha^{-1}) and green fodder yield (38.67 t ha^{-1}) as compared to delayed irrigation at IW/CPE ratio of 0.6 throughout (38.19 q ha^{-1} and 24.08 t ha^{-1} respectively) (Table 17.15).

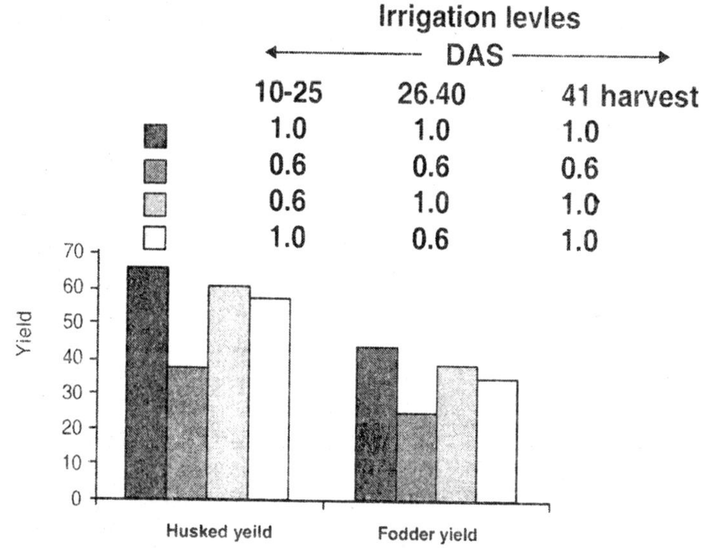

Fig. 17.3 Husked (q ha^{-1}) and green fodder ycild (t ha^{-1}) of baby corn as influenced by irrigation levels

Table 17.15 : Husked and green fodder yield of baby corn as influenced by irrigation level

Irrigation level (DAS) 10-25	26-40 IW/CPE	41-harvest	Husked yield (q ha^{-1})	Fodder yield (q ha^{-1})
1.0	1.0	1.0	66.02	43.38
0.6	0.6	0.6	38.19	24.08
0.6	1.0	1.0	60.44	38.67
1.0	0.6	1.0	57.42	35.81
	CD at 5%		4.85	3.50

The sensory parameters indicated that scheduling of irrigation at IW / CPE ratio of 1.0 throughout the crop growth recorded higher grade in terms of appearance (4.10), colour (4.00), texture (4.10), taste (3.50) and juiciness (3.60) followed by irrigation at IW/CPE ratio of 0.6 either at 10-26 DAS or at 26-40 DAS (3.90, 3.80, 4.00, 3.70 and 3.60 respectively). While, irrigation scheduled at 0.6 IW/CPE throughout graded higher with respect to taste (4.60) and juiciness (4.10) but remained low with other parameters like appearance (3.40), colour (3.20) and texture (3.80) (Table 24).

Table 17.16 : Sensory parameters of baby corn as influenced by irrigation levels (in 5 points scale)

Irrigation levels (DAS)			Appearance	Colour	Texture	Taste	Juiciness
10-25	26-40 IW/CPE	41-harvest					
1.0	1.0	1.0	4.10	4.00	4.10	3.50	3.60
0.6	0.6	0.6	3.40	3.20	3.80	4.60	4.10
0.6	1.0	1.0	3.90	3.80	4.00	3.70	3.60
1.0	0.6	1.0	3.90	3.70	3.90	3.90	3.70

The results ofthe nutritional parameter indicated that scheduling of irrigations at IW /CPE ratio of 1.0 throughout showed higher content of crude protein (18.90%), calcium (0.51 %), phosphorus (0.44%), potassium (2.74%) and crude fibre (5.41%) closely followed by delayed irrigations at IW/CPE ratio of 0.6 in the early stage. While continuous moisture stress at 0.6 registered higher sugars (0.025 %) and ascorbic acid (1.06 mg $100g^{-1}$) compared to other treatments but, remained lowest with respect to other parameters like crude protein (12.65%), calcium (0.41 %), phosphorus (0.28%), potassium (1.89%) and crude fibre (4.66%) (Table 17.17).

Water requirement

Water requirement is defined as the quantity of water regardless of its source required by a crop in a given period of time for its normal growth under field condition at a given place.

Baby corn is highly sensitive to water stress and water logging. Submergence of soil for 3-5 days during seedling to flowering stage reduces the yield considerably. Water requirement of the crop is 400-450 mm. Irrigation requirement varies with the type of soil and the season in which the crop is grown.

Table 17.17 : Reducing sugar, protein, calcium, phosphorus, potassium, crude fibre and ascorbic acid as influenced by irrigation levels in baby corn.

Irrigation levels (DAS)			Sugars	Crude	Calcium	Phosphorus	Potassium	Fibre	Ascorbic acid
10-25	26-40	41-harvest							
	IW/CPE		(%)	protein (%)	(%)	(%)	(%)	(%)	(mg 100 g^{-1})
1.0	1.0	1.0	0.013	18.90	0.51	0.44	2.74	5.41	0.17
0.6	0.6	0.6	0.025	12.65	0.41	0.28	1.89	4.66	1.06
0.6	1.0	1.0	0.014	18.30	0.50	0.40	2.63	5.35	0.74
1.0	0.6	1.0	0.016	17.47	0.50	0.38	2.51	5.17	0.79

Effect of water stress on growth, yield and quality of baby corn

Water deficit in plants at different stages of growth leads to increase in leaf water potential and reduction in relative water content causing increase in canopy temperature. Leaf expansion and height of plant get reduced resulting in reduction in size of babies, eventually reduction in production potentiality of baby com. Reduction of photosynthesis under water deficit is due to closer of stomata and this leads to reduced translocation of assimilates to different plant parts and ultimately to the sink. Stress at the later stage enhances reducing sugar in the baby com and ascorbic acid content. While, it brings down the protein and other mineral contents.

There was 42 per cent reduction in yield due to delayed irrigations at 0.6 IW /CPE ratio throughout the crop growth for baby corn . While, the reduction was 44 per cent for fodder and total yield. This was closely followed by delayed irrigation at 0.6 IW/CPE consecutively from 26 DAS to harvest with 37 per cent reduction in yield of baby com. The extent of reduction in yield was 25-30 per cent due to continuous stress from 10-40 DAS with irrigations at 0.6 IW/CPE ratio. Scheduling irrigations at 0.6 IW/CPE ratio from 41 DAS to harvest registered 19 per cent reduction in yield. Thus, it could be inferred that baby development (41 DAS-harvest) and baby initiation (26-41 DAS) stages are the most critical stages for irrigation in baby com. During these stages adequate moisture through frequent irrigations needs to be maintained to realize higher yield and quality babies.

***Water* use efficiency**

Efficient use of irrigation water has always been an important factor in irrigation system design and operation.

In irrigated conditions, efficient utilization of irrigation water and increasing productivity per unit of irrigation water depends on two factors. Firstly, being efficient conveyance of irrigation water to the plot head and second being soil and plant characteristics. Water use efficiency is 17-19 kg ha mm-l for baby com and 75-85 kg ha mm-l for green fodder. This could be further enhanced by adopting trickle irrigation with paired row planting.

Intercultivation

Intercultivation operations in baby corn crop are carried out for manipulating the soil after the seed is planted or young plant has emerged. The objective is to control weeds and to have dust mulch in the soil surface. Large area can be easily weeded with the use of intercultural implements. Loosening the surface soil due to intercultivation enable to maintain high

Table 17.18 : Stress day index as influenced irrigation schedules at different phenophases in baby corn

	Irrigation schedule CPE (mm)			Yield (t ha^{-1})			Crop susceptibility (t ha^{-1})				SDI		
	10-25	26-40	41-har	Baby corn	Fodder	Total	Baby corn	Fodder	Total	SD mm of CPE	Baby corn	Fodder	Total
I_1:	50	50	50	6.602	4.34	49.99	-	-	-	-	-	-	-
I_2:	83.33	83.33	83.33	3.82	2.40	27.90	0.42	0.445	0.44	83.33	34.99	37.08	36.66
I_3:	83.33	50	50	6.04	3.86	44.72	0.085	0.11	0.10	83.33	7.08	9.16	8.75
I_4:	50	83.33	50	5.74	3.58	41.56	0.13	0.17	0.16	83.33	10.83	14.58	13.74
I_5:	50	50	83.33	5.29	3.36	38.9	0.19	0.23	0.22	83.33	16.24	18.74	18.74
I_6:	83.33	83.33	50	4.94	2.97	34.69	0.25	0.31	0.30	83.33	24.83	25.83	25.41
I_7:	50	83.33	83.33	4.34	2.70	3140	0.345	0.37	0.37	83.33	28.75	31.24	30.83

porosity and provides aeration in the root zone. Two intercultivations with blade hoe at 15 and 30 days would be beneficial in maintaining good soil physical condition and control of weeds.

Earthing up

This operation is done to provide anchorage to the crop to facilitate safe disposal of excess water during the rainy season. The most beneficial effect of earthing up in baby corn is reduced lodging which is expected to be more due to high plant density in baby corn fields. A ridge is formed in the cropped rows. Ridge plough can also be used for this purpose. Earthing up operation is usually followed at the time of last intercultivation.

Weed management

The baby corn crop is found to be badly infested with numerous types of weeds in initial stages, which suppress the crop growth badly. Therefore weeding is done between the rows with bullock drawn implements. Whereas the weeding with in the rows is done by hand. Two to three hand weedings at 15 days interval is necessary to keep the weeds under check. Effective weed control can also be obtained by spraying simazine or atrazine (@ 1-1.25 kg ha 1 of 50 % WP) as pre-emergent application followed by hand weeding if required. Early control of weeds and maintaining weeds below the threshold level upto 30 days stage ensures higher yield of baby corn because the crop matures in 50-60 days.

Diseases and insect pests

Leaf blight caused by *Helmithosporium tuicicum* is the common prevalent disease. Selection oftolerant varieties would be the best option. In areas with high disease infestation spraYIng Dithane M - 45 @ 0.20 to 0.25 % as soon as the first symptom of disease appear is found to be effective in controlling the diseases. If need arise a second spray may be given after 15 days.

Among the insect pests shoot fly and stem borer are minor pests. However, they can be controlled by soil application of thimet @ 25 kg ha^{-1}.

Detasseling and stage of harvest

Detasseling is the process of removal of tassels in all the plants as and when they emerge, since the cobs have to be harvested for edible purpose before pollination. Tassel emergence in maize usually occurs between 45th - 55th day depending upon the variety. The tassel will emerge at least a minimum of 5 days earlier to silk emergence. All the tassels in the plant

Tassel emergence

Detasseling

rows must be removed before shedding of pollen. This operation is necessary for getting good quality babies. The tassels are removed by holding firmly with hand and giving an upward jerk. Though it is a labour consuming operation still essential to avoid pollination and to get quality babies acceptable in the international markets. Detasseling helps in harvesting faster and gives better baby development. It also helps to increase the number of ears, quality and prevent seed growth. The labour for detasseling is estimated to be around 8-10 man days per hectare.

Stage of harvest

In baby corn since cobs are harvested for vegetable purpose, right time of harvest of babies will help in optimizing the yield and realizing the quality

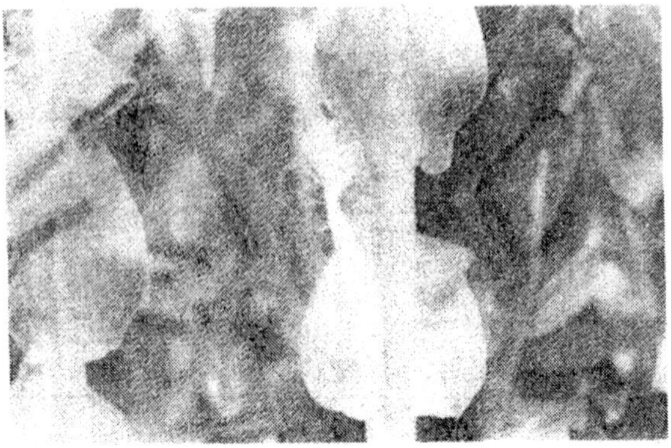

Silk emergence

babies. Harvesting of baby corn is done by hands before pollination so that the deterioration of quality doesn't occur as a consequence of fertilization. Care should be taken so that stem and leaves do not break to avoid damage to other emerging baby corn ears. Systematic work under ICAR ad-hoc project at Bangalore revealed that delay in harvesting of babies resulted in increased yield of husked and dehusked babies, but from quality point of view and also the preference of the consumer harvesting babies within three days after silk emergence would result in 97 to 102 q ha-l of husked baby yield and 25 to 29 t ha^{-1} green fodder yield (Table 19.19).

Sensory parameters showed highest score for appearance, colour, texture, taste and juiciness when harvested soon after cob emergence followed by after silk emergence. While, nutritional parameters viz. protein, phosphorus and calcium declined progressively with delay in harvest from soon after cob emergence to 5 day after silk emergence. On the contrary sugar and fibre progressively increased with delay in harvest. Hence it could be possible to strike a balance between optimum yield and quality babies by harvesting with in three *days* after *silk* emergence are more acceptable or palatable (Table 17.20).

Generally 2-3 pickings should be done at an interval of 2-3 days. Harvesting of baby com earlier than this stage may reduce the yield and the reduced ear size may pose problem in marketing. However, harvesting can also be followed every day which lasts for 8-10 harvests to avoid over maturity of baby com because the right stage for harvest is the critical criteria for better price in the market.

Table 17.19 : Husked, dehusked, fodder yeild and sensory parametes as influenced by stage of harvest in baby corn

Stage of harvest	Husked yeild ($q\ ha^{-1}$)	Dehusked yeild ($q\ ha^{-1}$)	Fodder yeild ($t\ ha^{-1}$)	Appearance	Colour	Texture	Taste	Juiciness
Soon after cob emergence	84.33	19.74	28.07	4.21	3.86	4.02	3.18	3.30
Soon after silk emergence	92.82	21.19	29.10	4.06	4.04	3.81	3.75	3.71
3 days after silk emergence	99.96	23.82	27.25	3.65	3.58	3.44	2.91	2.91
5 days after silk emergence	110.10	27.74	29.34	3.12	3.14	3.06	2.41	2.64

Processing and Marketing

The processed ear should be bright yellow and have a mild com taste, a crunchy texture and uniform length and shape. Crop, which is intended for retail fresh markets, need not have ears that are long and slender. Standards in Taiwan specify ears measuring 10 em long and 1-2 em in diameter. The optimum size requirements for the market / canning industry is 4.5 to 10 em long and 7 to 17 mm diameter of young dehusked baby com. Baby corn can be canned in a solution of3% salt, sugars (2%), acetic acid (1.4%) or vinegar and citric acid (0.3%).

Fresh baby com with the husk should be purchased from the market to maintain crispness and flavour. To retain sweetness, it should be refrigerated immediately. Husked baby com can be refrigerated for up to one week without loosing its quality. If kept at ambient temperature, the husked babies can stay for 2-3 days only. it should be kept in polyethylene bags with vents in a wellventilated place. Baby corn stays for months in freezers. Depending upon the size, one kilogram of baby com contains 20 to 30 cobs. The yield of dehusked cob varies from 400 to 450 gms per kilogram of husked baby com. A 200 gm pack of freshly harvested baby com is being sold for Rs. 40-50 in the vegetable stalls of Delhi posh colonies. In Bangalore husked baby com is being sold in HOPCOMS at Rs. 12-15 a kilogram and dehusked corn in attractive tin foil with 200 g is priced at Rs. 25-30. In Himachal Pradesh, the fruit processing unit of Himachal Pradesh fruit processing and marketing Corporation (HPMC) at Jarol near Sunder Nagar in Mandi District is packing 230 g baby corn ears in a tin having 425 g net weight and marketing the canned product in Mumbai market. In Bangalore sterling Agro of Banneraghatta Road, IQF Indiranagar and Namdhari seeds are the potential buyers of baby corn for processing and exporting. In addition there are many contract farms which works on buy back system.

Since 1987, Thailand produced approximately 77,750 tonnes of baby com annually of which almost 33% is canned, exported earning 18 million US $ annually. In India this industry is still in the developing stage.

Marketing of Baby Corn

Decision regarding the marketing is the prime consideration in the production of baby corn. When the crop is new to the farmer/ region, before planting baby com on a large scale, planting a small plot to familiarize with the operations like detasseling, harvesting, storage, and marketing techniques is essential. Detasseling stimulates fast baby corn development and improved weight. If the silks are pollinated, the quality of baby corn declines fetching

Table 17.20 : Sugar, protein, phosphorus, potassium, calcium and fibre content as influenced by stage of harvest in baby corn.

Stage in harvest	Sugar (%)	Protein (%)	Phosphorus (%)	Potassium (%)	Calcium (%)	Fibre (%)
Soon after cob emergence	0.0173	17.31	0.864	2.91	0.39	3.18
Soon after silk emergence	0.0182	14.97	0.854	3.05	0.30	4.32
3 days after silk emergence	0.0217	13.61	0.743	2.87	0.36	4.98
5 days after silk emergence	0.0259	11.78	0.651	3.02	0.24	5.79

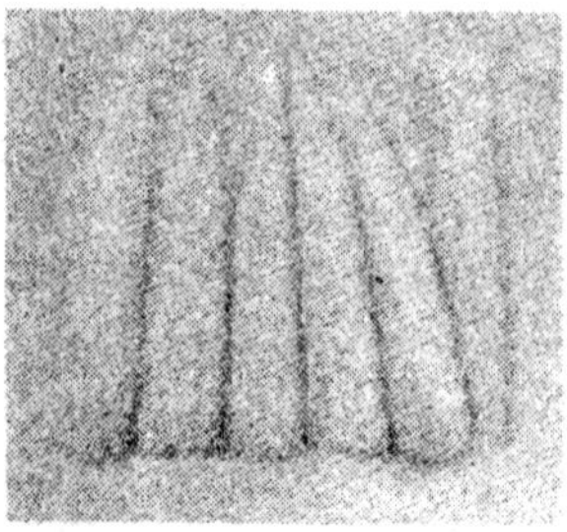

Dehusked baby corn

normally less price. Husked baby corn should be sold to maintain moisture and ear quality. If the husks are removed, that leads to damaged, discolored, and desiccated babies. Direct marketing to restaurants and at farmers market by the local growers have the advantage of providing a fresh, tasty product for consumers who have not had the pleasure of experiencing fresh baby corn.

Harvesting of baby corn at optimum maturity stage (soon after silk emergence) can ensure the quality criteria viz., uniform maturity, color, shape, size, and kernel coverage and be free from defects. Although, each plant can bear 2-3 babies, first formed baby is very good to good, while the second is good to fair and the third is poor to very poor in quality. Careful handling to prevent mechanical damage while harvesting and transportation, controlling temperature and moisture until the product reaches the market can extend the shelf life as high as 7-10 days. Inadequate or slow cooling, poor temperature maintenance or inappropriate packaging can rapidly lead to post harvest problems and quality loss in baby corn.

Harvesting should be carried out in the morning, when the cob moisture content is higher and ambient temperatures are lower. This also saves the energy costs and time needed for precooling. Harvesting should be conducted in every alternate days and normally lasts 8 to 14 days. Ears are harvested using a knife or secateurs and should not be snapped or broken to avoid mechanical damage. Harvested ears should be kept in shade and precooling must be carried at the earliest to avoid heating up. Cooling process can be started with the application of a constant flow of clean water. Water must be distributed evenly over the load of corn at a rate of 2 liters per kilogram of corn per hour. For every hour delay in cooling after harvest, baby corn loses shelflife by 10-12 hours.

Precooling

The best method of precooling baby corn is hydrocooling, where in baby corn (husked and dehusked) is drenched or immersed in near-freezing water for 20 to 30 minutes to remove field and respiratory heat and other heat emitted while transportation or storage can also be removed by top ice cooling. Here one kg ice is used for every 5 kg of baby corn. With these cooling methods, the baby corn is protected from water loss and in some cases may even absorb water. Crushed ice is normally used in small-volume operations. Several types of hydro cooling methods are suitable for baby corn, including the conveyorshower system, the batch-shower system, and the conveyor-immersion system.

In conveyor-shower hydrocooling process, baby corn is passed along a conveyor and under a shower of chilled water. The conveyor moves one foot per minute. Uniform stacking of the baby corn was necessary to prevent water channeling and nonuniform cooling.

In batch shower system, the product remaining stationary. Cold water is poured over the top of the pallet load, collected at the bottom, recooled, and recycled. Here care must be ensured to see the uniform water movement and cooling.

In conveyor-immersion system, hydrocoolers are normally large boxes of chilled moving water. Crates of corn are loaded onto the conveyor at its entrance, submerged, moved through the chilled water, and removed at the other end. This system is most efficient than others, because the cold water comes in contact with the entire product and ensures uniform cooling.

When hydro cooling operations are used, post harvest diseases may develop, particularly in products that have sustained mechanical damage. With recirculating systems, disease may spread to entire product. This can be reduced by using chlorine as a disinfectant in the water at the rate of 100 to 150 ppm in the form of sodium hypochlorite or dry as calcium hypochlorite.

Grading and Packaging

Baby corn is graded by size. The size requirements vary according to the market. Generally 6 to 8 cm, 8-10 cm and 10-12 cm long grades are used. In the outlets offood world, 200 g dehusked baby corn wrapped in polystyrene bags is being sold at Rs. 25/- while, 500 g fresh husked baby corn costs Rs. 12/-.

Packing is normally carried out after cooling. Dehusked baby corn is placed in perforated plastic clamshells or punnets for retail markets. Polystyrene or plastic trays wrapped with film can also be used.

Packaging for export consists of either one- or two-piece self-locking telescopic cartons with ventilation in all four side walls. Carton dimensions vary depending on net weight and market. The most common packs weigh 2 to 2.5 kilograms of 40 cm long by 30 cm wide and 9 cm height ISO pallets. Packages should bear all the labeling information required by the importing countries like country of origin, Product / variety, Net weight and Exporter name/ importer name.

Processed Baby corn often packed in metal cans and glass jars. Baby corn preserved in brine and packed in glass jars is more expensive than canned baby corn, and consequently has higher quality. Baby corn in glass jars is a speciality item found mostly in supermarkets. Restaurants and other food industries usually do not purchase baby corn in glass jars because it entails difficulty in storing, is prone to damage, and more costly than canned baby corn.

Packaging of baby corn

Storage

Baby corn should be stored at 5°C to 7°C, with a relative humidity of 90 per cent. The respiration rate increases 8 to 10 times at 28°C than 0°C. Low temperatures reduce the rate of the conversion of sugar to starch. As much as 80 per cent of the sugar lost within 24 hours of harvest in ears stored at 30°C.

Transportation

Because baby corn is highly perishable, exports are made by air. Packages shoul.d be transported from the packing facility to the airport in cool trucks, especially if the corn has been cooled. In all cases, trucks should be covered to prevent contact with wind, rain, and sun.

Air shipments are made in aircraft containers or pallets. Heat can build up in the containers, especially if they are left exposed to the sun while awaiting loading in the airport. This is obviously detrimental to the corn. Attempts should be made to ensure that the aircraft containers are held in shady or cool locations until loading.

Nutritive value of baby corn fodder

Baby corn is harvested at about 65-70 days depending on the variety and as a dual purpose crop also provides soft, succulent, green, palatable and nutritious fodder suited for direct feeding or could also be ensiled for off-season feeding. It consists of

Protein	:	9-10%
Neutral detergent fibre (NDF)	:	67.21%
Acid detergent fibre (ADF)	:	80.15%
Lignin	:	8.86%
Lignin/ADF	:	0.175%

On the contrary, the popularity grown exclusive fodder maize variety south African Tall has

Protein	:	10-11%
Neutral detergent fibre (NDF)	:	68.96%
Acid detergent fibre (ADF)	:	43.40%
Lignin	:	9.68%
Lignin/ADF	:	0.223

Table 17.21 : Quantity of ingredients used in the preparation of baby corn snacks and savouries

Products	Baby corn* (g)	Rice flour (g)	Coriander leaves (No.)	Onion (g)	Green chillies (No.)	Cooking oil (ml)	Turmeric	Bengalgram flour (g)	Chilli powder (tsp)	Wheat flour (g)	Water (ml)
Vada	100	60	10	10	5	250	A pinch	-	-	-	-
Kofta	100	-	10	30	1-2	250	A pinch	30	1/2	-	-
Finger frys	100	60	-	-	-	250	-	-	1	-	100
Roti	40	-	5	5	2	5	-	20	-	80	50
Raita	25	-	5	5	1-2	-	-	-	-	-	-

Salt to taste; tsp; tea spoons ; Add 225 ml curd to Raita ; Add 5 ginger to Vada ; Add ½ tsp omum to Finger frys ; * : Dehusked

Table 17.22 : Ingredients used in the preparation of baby corn sweet products

Products	Baby corn* (g)	Sugar (g)	Small wheat grits	Milk (g)	Cardamom (No.)	Food colour	Raisins (g)	Cashew nuts (g)	Ghee (g)	Water (ml)
Burfi	100	75	25	15	2	Orange red	-	-	10	15
Kheer	40	40	-	200	3	Yellow	5	5	-	100
Halva	100	60	-	50	1-2	Orange red	10	10	15	-
Khesari	100	75	25	150	2	Yellow	5	5	10	-

Table 17.23 : Ingredients used in the preparation of baby corn salt products

Products	Baby corn* (g)	Green chillies (No.)	Cooking oil (ml)	Red Chilli powder (tsp)	Cumin seed (mg)	Garlic pods (No.)	Tamarind (g)	Fenugreek powder (tsp)	Mustard powder (tsp)	Lemon juice (ml)
Chutney	100	12	10	-	3	2	5	-	-	-
Pickle	100		20	2	-	10	-	1/4	1/4	15

* Dehusked. These should be followed by seasoning in both the cases

Procedure for Preparation of differet baby corn products

Cut dehusked cobs, ginger, green chillies to small pieces
↓
Grind to coarse paste
↓
Add chopped onion, rice flour, coriander leaves, turmeric and salt
↓
Make small round balls
↓
Flatten on polythen sheet
↓
Deep fry till goden brown

Fig. 17.4 Flow chart for preparation of vad a (Anita and Rajyalakshimi, 2005)

Cut dehusked cobs, ginger, green chillies to small pieces
↓
Grind with chilli powder, coriander leaves, turmeric and salt to smooth paste
↓
Add Bengalgram flour
↓
Make medium size balls
↓
Deep fry till golden brown

Fig. 17.5 Flow chart for preparation of Kofta (Anita and Rajyalakshimi, 2005)

Cut dehusked cobs into thin pieces of 1 inch long and ¼ width

↓

Boil for 10-15 min

↓

Wipe off surface water with muslin cloth

↓

Shift rice flour into a bowl with chilli powder and salt

↓

Make thick batter with water

↓

Dip the boiled corn pieces in the batter

↓

Deep fry till golden brown

Fig. 17.6 Flow chart for preparation of ginger crisps (Anita and Rajyalakshimi, 2005)

Wheat flour and Bengalgram flour

↓

Add chopped onions, rice flour, coriander leaves, turmeric, salt and grated baby corn

↓

Make a well in the center and gradually stir in the water

↓

Work to a soft, supple dough

↓

Knead the dough again and divide into balls

↓

Press ball into thin round pan cake

↓

Pan fry with little oil both sides to light brown cake

Fig. 17.7 Flow chart for Preparation of roti (unleavened bread) (Anita and Rajyalakshimi, 2005)

Beat curd to a smooth consistency

↓

Cut baby corn to ¼ width

↓

Chop onions and green chilli

↓

Add all pieces into beaten curd and mix

↓

Garnish with chopped coriander leaves

Fig. 17.8 Flow chart for preaparation of Raita
(Anita and Rajyalakshimi, 2005)

Soak tamarind pods in ½ cup ht water for 10-15 min

↓

Shallow frybaby corn pieces and green chillies separately using a little oil

↓

Grind chilli, corn pieces, cumin seeds, garlic and soaked tamarind to smooth paste

↓

Add salt to taste and season the mix

↓

Fig. 17.9 Flow chart for preparation of chutney
(Anita and Rajyalakshimi, 2005)

Cut dehusked cobs into ½" pieces

↓

Shallow fry to 1-2 min (till they become golden brown)

↓

Mix a little juice and keep aside

↓

Prepare a spice mixture with chilli powder, salt, mustard powder, fenugreek powder, garlik pods, cloves

↓

Add the spice mixture to cut pieces

↓

Finally add sesame/groundnut oil

↓

Store in air tight glass bottles

Fig. 17.10 Flow chart for preparation of pickle (Anita and Rajyalakshimi, 2005)

Grate dehusked cobs

↓

Melt ghee in vessel

↓

Fry grated corn adn rava separately for 2-3 min to golden brown colour

↓

Prepare sugar syrup

↓

Stir and cook continuously until the mixture leaves sides of the pan

↓

Remove from fire, add ground cardamom

↓

Pour mixture into greased plate and flatten surface

Fig. 17.11 Flow chart for preparation of burfi (Anita and Rajyalakshimi, 2005)

Cut dehusked cobs into small pieces and grind to a smooth paste (keep aside)

↓

shallow fry ground paste and rava separately with a little ghee to a golden brown colour

↓

Take half quantity of milk and sugar in vessel

↓

Heat till sugar dissolves

↓

Add fried corn pieces and rava to sugar solution

↓

Cook for 5 min stirring continuously

↓

Add remaining milk, colour and ghee

↓

Cook till mixture starts leaving sides

↓

Spread on a greased and garnish with raisins, cashew nut

Fig. 17.12 Flow chart for preparation of Kesari (Anita and Rajyalakshimi, 2005)

Grate dehusked cobs

↓

Add milk to grated corn and cook

↓

Cook to thick consistency

↓

Add ghee, sugar and raisins and continue cooking for 15-20 min

↓

Stir and cook the mixture till it starts leaving sides of pan

↓

Garnish with fried cashew nut / almond

Fig. 17.13 Flow chart for preparation of hulwa (Anita and Rajyalakshimi, 2005)

Cut dehusked cobs into small pieces and ground to a smooth paste

↓

Take half quantity of milk and sugar into a cooking pan

↓

Boil milk at simmering temperature for 10-15 min
(till it reduced to half the quanity)

↓

Add the remaining milk, raisins and colour

↓

Garnish with fried cashew nut

Fig. 17.14 Flow chart for preparation of kheer
(Anita and Rajyalakshimi, 2005)

Baby corn products

In animal nutrition, digestibility of fodder is an important parameter apart from absolute nutrient content in the fodder. Lignin/ ADF ratio is an index of digestibility is lower in 'baby corn compared to South African Tall indicating higher digestibility of baby corn fodder. Thus, in places where exclusive fodder maize is grown, baby corn can be a profitable substitute with 35-40 t ha^{-1} of green fodder.

Product development using baby corn

Baby corn apart from its wide uti l ity for the preparation of Manchurian salads, and vegetable is also used for the preparation of various baby corn snacks and sweet products such as vada, kofta, finger frys, roti, raita,burfi,kheer,halva,kesari, chutney and pickles. The various ingredients used and procedure followed for the preparation of these products as developed by Anita and Rajyalakshimi (2005).

Problems and Research needs

- Lack of awareness about the crop, use, taste, nutritive value of quality baby corn as a vegetable free from pesticides among the common men is a major limitation for its cultivation as a dual purpose commercial crop. There is a need for popularizing this crop and increasing area under its cultivation in view of its demand in the international market as a potential foreign exchange earner in the changing scenario of agriculture after WTO.

- To explore the possibility of transplanting baby corn crop to suit the stagger planting to minimize the seeding cost.

- Detasseling is an essential but labour intensive operation in baby corn. Development of male sterile baby corn varieties/ hybrids would reduce the cost of baby corn production and makes it further more remunerative.

- Small scale processing industries should be encouraged in rural areas for easy accessibility and to reduce the transportation cost apart from increasing the employment potential for the rural poor.

- Prolific hybrids with multiple ears emerging in sequence are the need of the hour. It is a challenge for the breeders to develop baby corn hybrids or varieties with multiple ears to maximize the productivity and profitability.

- Mechanization of baby corn dehusking would economize and improve the efficiency

- At present it is contract farming with buy back system and any venture by the farmer should be after ensuring the market and staggered planting at 15-20 days interval in small areas needs to be done to ensure

Table 17.24 : Cost of baby corn production and economic returns

Sl. No.	Particulars of operation	Item/quantity	Rate (Rs)	Total amount (Rs.)
1.	Pre-ploughing irrigation	Daily wage labours (6)	45 /day	270.00
2.	Land preparation (2 ploughing +passing cultivator and leveling)	Bullock pair (5) Men labours (8)	200 /day 45 / day	1000.00 360.00
3.	Seed	40 kg	125 / kg	5000.00
4.	Sowing	Bullock pair (3) Women labour (10)	200 / day 42 / day	600.00 420.00
5	Manures and fertilizers	FYM 10 tons Urea 326 kg SSP 469 kg MOP 67 kg Men labour (6)	200 / ton 5.00 /kg 3.20 / kg 4.60 / kg 45 / day	2000.00 1630.00 1501.00 308.00 270.00
6.	Irrigation	Men labour (12)	45 / day	54.00
7.	Weeding (twice)	Women labour (20)	42 / day	840.00
8.	Hoeing (twice)	Bullock pairs (2)	200 / day	400.00
9.	Detasseling	Women labour (20)	42 / day	840.00
10.	Harvesting (8-10 picking)	Women labour (100)	42 / day	4200.00
10. 11.	Harvesting of green fodder	Men labour (15)	45 /day	675.00
		Total		**20854.00**

Out put and returns

	Husked baby yield (q ha^{-1})	Green fodder yeild (t ha^{-1})	Gross returns (Rs.)	Net returns (Rs)
Golden baby	94.23	17.55	84159	63305
PAC -792	88.62	29.90	85846	64992
PAC-793	104.58	47.36	107344	86490

@ baby corn Rs. 8 kg^{-1} and fodder Rs. 500 t^{-1}

availability of labour for picking and continuity with respect to flow of income.

Cost of baby corn production and returns

Baby corn hybrids on an average can yield 85-105 q ha-l of husked baby and 15 to 45 t ha-l of green fodder. Despite high cost on seeds, detasseling and picking the average cost of cultivation is Rs.20,000 to 2 i ,000 ha-l and the net returns could be Rs. 60,000 to 85,000ha-l from a single crop of baby corn and on an average. 3 to 4 crops can be raised in a year depending upon the climatic conditions and availability of irrigation water.

Tips for baby corn production

- PAC- 792, PAC- 793, Golden baby are the suitable varieties for quality baby corn production
- Baby corn can be sown throughout the year (May-July, Sept-Oct, Jan-Feb)
- 45 cm X 20-30 cm / 60 cm X 20 cm spacing are the appropriate planting geometry
- Maintenance of two plants per hill is superior in achieving higher yield and returns than one plant per hill
- 35-40 kg ha-l baby corn seeds required to maintain two plants per hill
- Application of 150: 75: 40 kg NPK + 10 t FYM ha^{-1} is the optimum fertilizer dose for quality baby corn production
- Application of 50 % Rec. N with 100% P and K as basal and remaining 50% N at 30 DAS was the appropriate fertilizer schedule
- Baby corn initiation (26-40 days) and baby development (41 harvest) are the critical stages for irrigation
- Baby corn needs 400-425 mm of water for successful completion of its growth
- Irrigation once in 8 days (7-8 irrigations) is essential for baby corn production during summer
- Two hand weedings at 20 and 35 DAS or one hand weeding with a pre-emergent application of Atrazine or Simazine @ 1-1.25 kg a.i. ha^{-1} can substantially reduce the weed menace in baby corn
- One earthing up at knee-high stage provides anchorage to the crop and avoids lodging

- Detasseling, an important operation in baby corn production should be carried out soon after tassel emergence to avoid pollination and fertilization
- Harvesting baby corn soon after silk emergence (2-3 cm of silk length) is essential to maintain the quality of babies
- Baby corn hybrids on an average can yield 85-105 q of husked babies and 15-45 t green fodder per hectare
- Baby corn fodder is superior than South African Tall due to higher digestibility
- Net returns of Rs. 60,000 - 85,000 per hectare can be realized from a single crop of baby corn and on an average 3 to 4 crops can be raised in a year depending on availability of irrigation water.

18

Extruded Snacks

Consumers today are demanding an ever-broadening selection of snack foods. Extrusion has provided a means of manufacturing new and novel products and has revolutionized many conventional snack manufacturing processes. Extrusion equipment offers many basic design advantages that result in minimizing time, energy, and cost while at the same time introducing a degree of versatility and flexibility that was not previously available.

Many common snack foods such as fried or baked collettes (corn curls) are corn based and produced on rather simple single-screw highpressure extrusion cookers. Other snack products (for example, half-products or third-generation products) may require more sophisticated twin-screw extrusion equipment.

Snack producers today are faced with an increasing number of extrusion equipment styles and suppliers. In one respect this will, complicate the snack producers' choice of equipment but on the other hand will lead to a wider use of extrusion and increased availability in terms of lower cost.

The influx of the so-called "new technology" twin-screw extruder in recent years will require the snack food manufacturer to acquire a better understanding of the mechanism of single- and twin-screw extruders. This will increase one's ability to apply and use each of the processes for the applications in which they perform most efficiently. No individual extruder type, whether single- or twin-screw, will be compatible with all specific processes and/or raw materials.

TERMINOLOGY

Food or snack extruders are- generally divided into two major categories: (1) single-screw and (2) twin-screw. Single-screw extruders may be divided into four subcategories: low-shear forming; low-shear cooking; medium-shear cooking; and high-shear cooking. Twin-screw extruders may be divided into several subcategories: corotating intermeshing; corotating nonintermeshing; counterrotating intermeshing; counterrotating nonintermeshing; and conical intermeshing. In the past, the most popular and successful extruders in the snack food production plant have been the single-screw extruders; and there are many applications today where these extruders are ideal from an economic point of view. However, in recent years the twin-screw extruder has begun to challenge the dominance of the single-screw extruder for snack food production.

The food extruder must exercise a number of functions in a short time under controlled, continuous or steady-state operating conditions. These functions may include heating, cooling, conveying, feeding, compressing, reacting, mixing, melting, cooking, texturing, and shaping.

Energy sources to provide heat for cooking, texturing, or melting may include:

- *Conversion:* Mechanical energy is dissipated into the extruder in the form of heat caused by shearing or friction generated by pumping or conveying inefficiencies. For high-shear extruders it is possible that / 100% of the heat may be generated through shear. This type is referred to as an adiabatic extruder.
- *Conduction:* Heat is transferred through the barrel of the extruder from a thermal fluid or other external source.
- *Convection:* Heat is transferred to the extrudate by direct contact such as steam injection.

Each energy source has its advantages and disadvantages. In most cases, a combination of the three will be most practical.

There are several basic components having specific functions common to all extrusion systems (Fig. 18.1):

1. A holding bin for mixed raw material capable of discharging raw premixed dry ingredients continuously and uniformly
2. A variable speed metering/feeding device to feed the raw dry mixed ingredients uniformly and in an uninterrupted manner at the desired flow rate

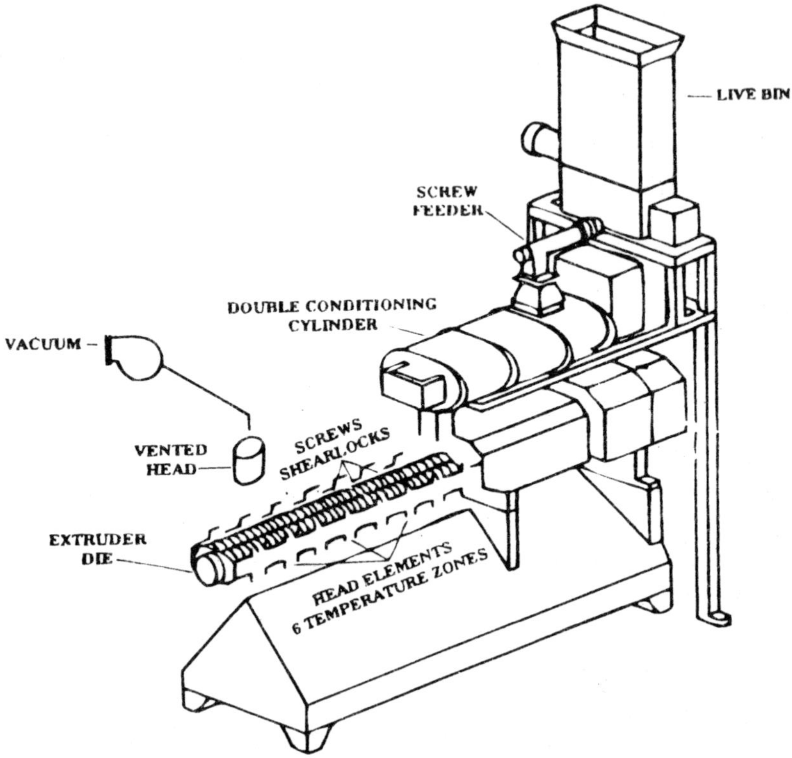

Figure 18.1 Cutaway view of twin-screw extruder.

3. A preconditioner in which liquids and/or steam, and/or other vapors may be uniformly combined with the premetered dry (or pretempered) ingredient mix
4. An extruder assembly whose configuration of barrel segments, screws, and shearlocks has been preselected to properly feed, knead and cook the dry or premoistened process material
5. A final die to restrict the extruder discharge and to shape the final product
6. A cutting device to cut the extruded profile to the desired length

EXTRUSION PROCESS

The most important criterion for extruding a wide range of raw materials to produce a wide range of finished products is the selection of a proper extruder configuration. The term extruder configuration is subdivided into three distinct categories: (1) the feeding and preconditioning configuration; (2) the screw and barrel profile of the extruder; and (3) the die configuration.

Preconditioning Configuration

Preconditioning may be defined as a prerequisite processing step of putting a substance into the proper or desired condition. Preconditioning is a very important part of the extrusion process. Mixing, hydration, cooking, pH modifications, and addition of vapors, flavors, lipids, colors, etc., may all take place in a properly designed preconditioning process. The single most important aspect of the preconditioning system is the added mixing and retention time, which is imperative for all reactions, chemical or physical.

There are basically two types of continuous preconditioners available:

- Pressurized preconditioners
- Atmospheric preconditioners

Pressurized conditioning chambers normally provide approximately 1-3 minutes residence time at temperatures up to 240°F (115°C). Research indicates that pressurized preconditioners have a negative effect on the nutritional quality of food and feed products. Their design and operation are more complex than those of atmospheric preconditioners.

Atmospheric conditioning chambers provide from 20 to 240 seconds retention during which time a product formulation is preheated and the moisture is allowed to penetrate the individual particles. Preconditioning is known to enhance flavor development and to aid in the final product texture. This has been most evident in the production of cereal and snack products, especially corn- and oat-based products. Oats, for example, have a bitter aftertaste that may be removed by preconditioning.

In addition to flavor development, preconditioning reduces extruder component wear, refines cell structure and permits increased throughput of the extruder.

The method of water addition is an important part of preconditioning a product formulation. The residence time of the raw material in the' conditioning cylinder after water injection along with steam injection permits the moisture to penetrate the grain particles equally throughout each particle. This equilibration of moisture assures a more uniformly cooked and textured final product.

The conditioning cylinders typically used in the extrusion cooking processes may be equipped with either a single agitator, dual agitators, or

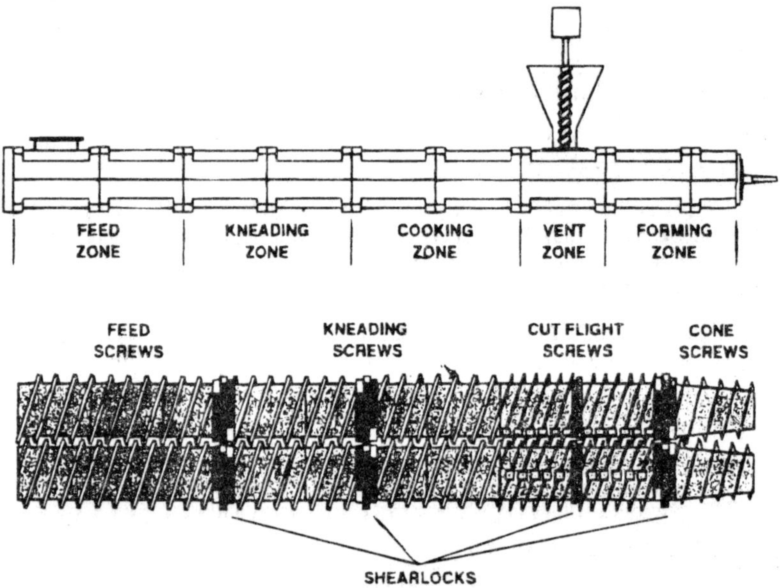

Figure 18.2 Extruder components.

dual agitators with differential speed. Single-agitator mixing cylinders are used in extrusion applications of low to moderate capacity where steam and water are mixed and continuously blended with the dry raw material substrate.

Dual agitator/differential speed preconditioners provide the longest controlled residence time and therefore the best and most thorough blending of moisture into dry raw materials. This preconditioning usually pays for itself quickly through improved flavor, increased production capacity of the final product and reduced extruder component wear.

Before purchasing an extrusion system, careful consideration should be given to the effect preconditioning will have on the final product and how these changes or improvements will influence the product sales potential.

Extruder Configuration

The barrel of the extruder is made up of screws, heads, and flow restrictors or shearlocks (Fig. 18.2). Typically a number of different segmented screw designs and configurations may be placed on an extruder shaft. Each screw is designed to perform a specific function. Some screws must convey raw material and/or preconditioned material into the extruder barrel while other ,

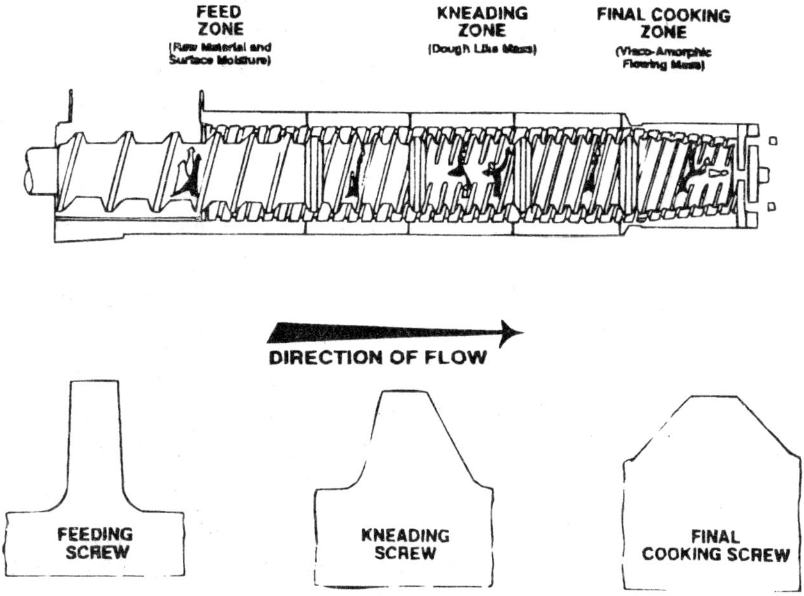

Figure 18.3 Extruder configuration design.

screw elements must compress and degas the extrudate. Other screw elements must create backflow and shear or perform other tasks. Where kneading is required, kneading screws may have one or multiple flights. Some kneading screws may be cut-flighted or have interrupted flighting in order to add turbulence, increase backflow, or increase mechanical energy dissipation into the extrudate. The cut-flighted screw elements reduce conveying efficiently and thus' add residence time to the product being conveyed through the barrel of the extruder. The screws may also have various pitches to control (usually to increase) residence time within the extruder processing chamber without changing the free volume of the screw. The final cooking screws may be conical. These conical final screw elements cause a rapid pressure increase, a uniform pressure distribution around the screw periphery, and dampening of any pulsations that may be present in the final section of the extruder.

Screws are not the only component that affect shear energy input or mechanical energy dissipation within the barrel of the extruder. Heads or the barrel segments that surround the screws have a profound effect as well.

The barrel segments may be ribbed to increase the function of each specific extruder segment. For example, the ribbing may be used to increase the volume in the inlet of the extruder barrel for achieving higher throughputs.

Special attention should be given to the use of conical sections at the discharge of an extruder barrel. In a twin-screw extruder, conical end sections separate the product flow channel into two isolated flow channels. This concept contributes to unique product textures and increased flexibility, and also minimizes screw and barrel wear, which is problematic and costly in most twin-screw systems. Wear is minimized because the two isolated conical flow channels distribute the product uniformly around the periphery of each extruder shaft. This uniform product distribution centers each shaft or screw within its respective flow channel. much like the function of an internal bearing.

Both single-screw and corotating twin-screw extruders may be subdivided into processing zones: the feeding zone, the kneading zone, and the final cooking zone (Fig. 18.3).

The feeding zone of the extruder is that area where the low-density discrete particles of raw materials are introduced into the extruder barrel inlet. This low-density, often preconditioned, material is then transported into the interior of the extrusion processing chamber. The flow channel of the screw is typically filled with low-density material in this zone. The density is low because of the air entrapped in the incoming material and because of the granular nature of the material. The incoming material is 1 compressed slightly in this zone, with the air being expelled. Water is typically injected into the extruder barrel to facilitate textural development and viscosity development, and to enhance conductive heat transfer.

The kneading zone of the cooking extruder continues the compression started in the feeding zone, and the flow channels of the extruder achieve a higher degree of fill as a result of the extrudate being compressed. Within this zone of the extruder barrel the extrudate begins to lose some of its granular definition, extrudate density begins to increase, and pressure begins to develop in the extruder barrel. The mechanism of shear begins to play a dominant role in the kneading zone because of the barrel fill condition that exists here.

Within the kneading zone of the extruder barrel the discrete particles of material begin to agglomerate because of the increasing temperature resulting from conduction, direct steam injection, and viscous energy dissipation. The extrudate begins to form a more integral flowing doughlike mass and as it moves through the kneading zone will typically reach its maximum compaction.

The final cooking zone of the extruder barrel is that area where homogeneity is achieved and texturizing occurs. Temperature and pressure typically increase rapidly. In this region shear rates are highest because of the extruder screw configuration and maximum compression of the extrudate. The pressure, temperature, and resulting fluid viscosity are such that the extrudate will be expelled from the extruder die to yield the desired final product texture, density, color, and functional properties.

The single-screw extruder has some definite process limitations in the food processing industry. The most obvious limitation centers around the inability of the single-screw extruder to transport sticky and/or gummy raw materials. From a process application and quality control point of view, the single-screw extruder may sometimes be limited in its . ability to maintain process stability. Process instability on the singlescrew extruder generally manifests itself in product inconsistency, i.e., nonsteady-state flow at the extruder die.

In special cases, venting and forming zones may be added downstream of the cooking zone (Fig. 18.2). These zones are normally used for moisture removal applications or forming of high-bulk-density products.

Die Configuration

Die design and its effect on functional properties and quality of a final product is frequently overlooked. Die shear rates may be altered dramatically by changing from a single-die with one opening to a triple or quadruple die with multiple openings and flow channels (Fig. 18.4). When changing from a single-die configuration to a multiple die configuration, the degree of barrel fill is also increased. In general, dies. with high shear rates cause starch-bearing products to have increased stickiness, increased water absorption characteristics, and increased solubility.

EXPANDED SNACKS

The majority of extruded snacks on the market fall into this category, which may also be classified as second-generation snacks. Expanded snacks may take on various marketing styles including: high-fiber, lowcalorie, high-protein, nutritional, etc. They are usually "light," having low bulk density, and are seasoned with an array of flavors, oils, and salt (Fig. 18.5).

Fried Collettes

One of the most familiar expanded snacks is the so-called "fried collettes" produced from com meal or grits and normally coated with cheese powders and flavors.

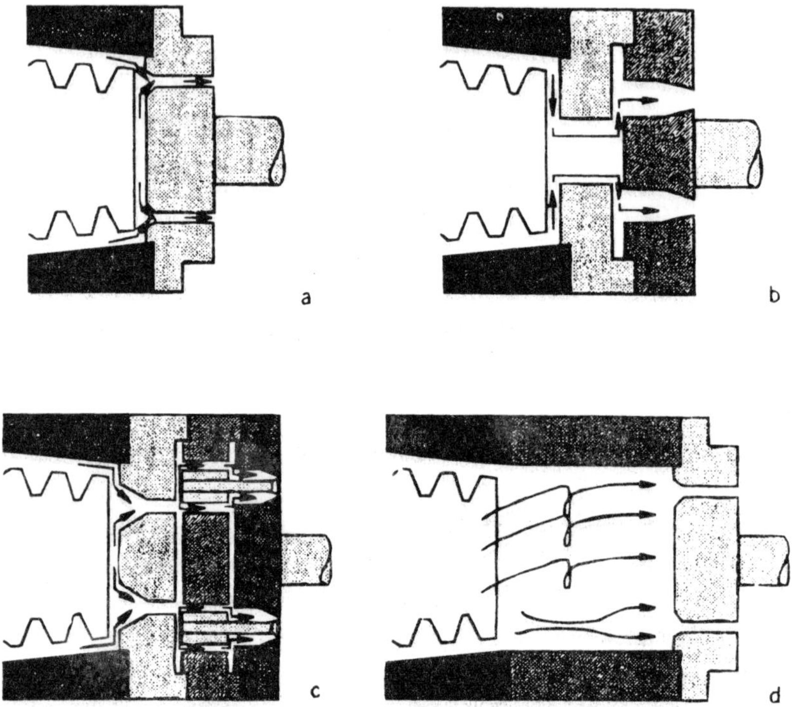

Figure 18.4 Die types : (a) single die; (b) double die; (c) triple die; (d) single die with spacer

Product Description Corn meal with a properly quantified and equilibrated rated moisture content is fed into an extruder. The pressure and heat generated inside the extruder vaporizes the moisture in the corn meal. As this heated mixture is forced between two brass rotating heads, the pressure of the steam vapor is released very rapidly causing a "popping" or "puffing" of the com meal. This leaves a rough, cylinder-shaped product known as a *collette*. The extruded collettes are then sifted, fried in vegetable oil, and coated with a mixture of vegetable oil, cheese, and salt.

Process Description A variety of equipment is used in the manufacture of fried cheese puffs. A brief description of the major pieces follows:

1. The blender moisturizes com meal through use of a vertical auger moving the meal from bottom to top of the mixing tank with water being added in measured amounts.

2. Bucket elevators are used to transfer moisturized corn meal from the blender to the extruder holding hopper.
3. The extruder consists primarily of a screw and a set of heads called rotors and stators through which the corn meal is forced. As the corn meal passes through the extruder, it is compressed. The work performed on the corn meal during the extrusion is transformed into heat. This pressure and heat causes the corn meal to become a very viscous and substantially homogeneous mass. As this material passes through the heads, the superheated moisture instantaneously vaporizes, causing the "popping" or "puffing" of the com meal.
4. A perforated tumbler that is designed to remove most small pieces and unpopped meal from the good collettes before frying.
5. The fryer is designed to remove moisture and introduce oil into the collettes; both direct-fired and heat-exchanger type fryers work well. Because of the short residence time of the product in the fryer, proper sizing is critical to achieve correct oil turnover rates.
6. The coating tumbler is designed for a uniform and positive flow of product down the length of the unit. Longitudinal flights turn the' bed of collettes over while liquid cheese slurry is dispensed inside the tumbler at the infeed end.
7. The cheese mix system consists of constant-temperature, hot-water jacketed kettles equipped with mixers and recirculating pumps where cheese, oil, and salt are homogeneously mixed together. The temperature of the cheese-oil mix is held to 120-130°F (49-55°C) and must never exceed 145°F (63°C).

Formulation Corn meal is the primary ingredient for this type of product. Typical Corn meal specifications used are shown in Table 18.1.

Final Product Specifications

Bulk density (before frying)	4.0-6.5 lb/ft^3 (80-104 g/litre)
Moisture (finished product)	1.0-2.0%
Salt	1.8-2.8%
Oil (finished product)	32-38%
Cheese	5.0-6.5%

Baked Collettes or Shapes

Product Description The other most popular example of expanded,

TABLE 18-1. TYPICAL CORN MEAL SPECIFICATIONS FOR FRIED COLLETTES

Granulation (mesh)	Percent retained on screen
16	0
20	0-2
25	0-10
30	25-50
40	45-65
50	0-8
60	0-2
Moisture	11-12
Fat	<1

extruded snacks is the baked collette (corn curl). There are spin-offs of the expanded snack concept utilizing other cereal grain flours, tuber flours, fibers, and proteins. Potato is commonly added to com or rice to make potato-flavored snacks. Snacks containing high levels of potato flour or granules (greater than 65%) are better suited for the twin-screw extruder because of the sensitivity of potatoes to heat. The bland flavor of rice makes it desirable for preservin~ more expensive flavour attributes.

Fiber, cellulose, bran, and fruit-derived pectins may be blended with cereal grain or protein blends to make healthy nutritional snacks. Fiber and proteins may each be added at 20% levels to expanded snack formulation with little effect on flavor and expansion. Higher levels may be added when more soluble fibers and proteins are utilized. Low levels of low-molecular-weight starches will also counter the effects of fiber and protein additions. Extrusion-reacted fiber or bran yield softer-textured snacks when high levels of fiber are desired.

Process Description Properly selected ingredients are fed into an extruder at a constant rate. The ingredients are exposed to moisture, heat, and pressure as they are transported through the extruder into the extruder die. *As* the material exits the extruder die it expands owing to pressure release and is sized to the proper length with a rotating knife to produce a collette, ball shape, or multiple shapes depending on the shape of the extruder die. These collettes or shapes are then dried or baked and coated with oils, flavors, and/or seasoning.

There are many extruders on the market today that are capable of making good-quality expanded snacks. Single-screw extruders can do an excellent job and have been well proven in this market. The twin-screw extruders, however, offer some advantages in flexibility of raw ingredients and process control, but their basic functions are the same.

The extruder includes a feeder for providing a means of getting a uniform flow of material into the extrusion process. Any instability or nonuniformity in the feed flow will affect the rest of the process. For a raw ingredient such as corn meal, small vibratory feeding systems are the most commonly used.

Extruders for second generation snack products are normally short in length (less than 10: 1 length: diameter *(L/D)* ratio). Typical processing conditions are:

Extruder	300-400 rpm
Extruder barrel temperature	250-320°F (120-160°C)
Extruder barrel pressure	70-150 atm
Dry ingredient feed rte	205 lb/hr (450 kg/hr)
Moisture added into the extruder	5.9 lb/hr (13 kg/hr)
Moisture of extruded product	8-10 MCWB
Bulk density of extruder product	3.0-4.0 lb/hr^3 (48-64 g/litre)

It is important that the proper extruder configuration, consisting of screws, steamlocks, and barrel segments be selected to properly feed, knead, and cook the process material as it passes through the extruder.

The die configuration used to produce corn snack products is a critical part of the extrusion process. Single, double and even triple die plates may be used to alter or change the final product texture and mouthfeel. The speed of the rotating knife assembly regulates the length of the final product.

Moisture of the extruded product is normally between 8 and 10% moisture content on a wet basis and it requires additional drying to produce the desired product crispness. Temperatures of 300°F (150°C) and retention times of 4-6 minutes are used to lower the moisture of these products to 1-2% moisture.

Before coating the extruded products with flavors, the fines that have been produced during the conveying and drying must be separated. The fines tend to absorb the flavor and oil coatings, causing agglomerations of fines and flavors into forms that are undesirable.

The most popular flavoring for extruded corn-based snack products is cheddar cheese. Two methods of application are most common. When using the dry flavor application method, the extruded product is first sprayed with vegetable oil and then dusted with a variety of dry flavors and/or seasonings. Alternatively, the oils, flavors, and spices may be mixed together in a tank and applied to the extruded product as it is tumbled in a flavor-application reel.

Formulations

Some typical formulations are listed in Table 18.2.

The particle size of corn meal or the cereal grains used may actually influence the texture and mouthfeel of the final snack product. Degermed corn meal most commonly used in extrusion systems today would have particle size analysis and specifications as listed in Table 18.3.

Many other grades or granulations of degermed corn meal are available. If a finer texture or cell structure, or softer bite for a snack are desired, a snack producer may wish to use raw materials having particle size as listed in Table 18.4.

On the other hand, some consumers prefer extruded snacks that exhibit a more crunchy texture with a slightly larger cell structure. For this type of texture, a coarser granulation of degermed corn grits is desired.

Premoistening of coarse granulation ingredients may be required to eliminate grittiness in the final product.

TABLE 18-2. TYPICAL SECOND-GENERATION SNACK FORMULAS

	Percent
High protein snack	
Rice flour	35
Wheat flour	35
Soy concentrate	20
Sugar	6
Cornstarch	2
Vegetable oil	2
Potato Stick snack	
Potato granules	64
Degermed corn meal	35
Vegetable oil	1
Corn curls	
Degermed corn meal or grits	100

TABLE 18.3. SPECIFICATIONS FOR MOST CQMMONLY USED DEGERMED YELLOW CORN MEAL

Analysis performed	Typical analysis e%)	Analysis range (%) Minimum	Maximum
Moisture	12.0	11.0	13.0
Protein	7.0	6.0	8.0
Oil	0.7	0.5	1.0
Fiber	0.5	0.4	0.6
Ash	0.4	0.3	0.5
Nitrogen free extract (%)	79.4		
Bulk density, loose (lb/ft^3)	39.0		
Percentage granulation U.S. sieve			
On 16	0	0	0.1
On 20	0.3	0	2
On 25	8.7	4	18
On 30	43	30	50
On 40	45	35	55
On 50	2	0	8
Thru 50	1	0	2

TABLE 18.4. SPECIFICATION FOR SOFTER TEXTURE DEGERMED YELLOW CORN MEAL

Analysis performed	Typical analysis (%)	Analysis range (%) Minimum	Maximum
Moisture	11.0	10.0	12.0
Protein	8.0	7.5	9.0
Oil	0.6	0.3	0.9
Fiber	0.4	0.3	0.5
Ash	0.3	0.1	0.5
Percent nitrogen free extract	79.7		
Bulk density, loose (lb/ft^3)	44		
Percent granulation US sieve			
On 30	0.1	0	0.5
On 40	0.4	0	1
On 60	80	70	90
On 80	15	10	20
Thru 80	4.5	1	7

TABLE 18.5. SPECIFICATIONS FOR CRUNCHY TEXTURE DEGERMED YELLOW CORN GRITS

Analysis performed	Typical analysis (%)	Analysis range (%) Minimum	Maximum
Moisture	11.5	11.0	12.0
Protein	7.5	6.5	8.5
Oil	0.7	0.4	1.0
Fiber	0.5	0.3	0.6
Ash	0.4	0.3	0.6
Bulk density, loose (lb/ft^3)	42		
Percentage granulation U.S. sieve			
On 10	0	0	0.1
On 14	2.5	0	5
On 20	65	60	75
On 30	31	25	40
On 40	1	0	2
Thru 40	0.5	0	2

A large amount of flour or fines in coarse .meals is undesirable for extrusion, especially when using a single-screw extruder. Flour tends to segregate in the feeding system and in the inlet portion of the extruder barrel. When water is added in the extruder barrel, the flour will absorb the water quickly leaving less moisture available for the coarser particles.

This circumstance may disrupt the product and cause fluctuations in the final product quality.

Listed in Table 18.6 are some typical cheese-oil coating formulations.

Quality Control Considerations

Always consider the functionality, organoleptic characteristics, product image, and nutritional value of your product. Quality control considerations include:

1. Determination of moisture, oil, and salt in the final product
2. Determination of cheese coating on final product
3. Oil absorption characteristics

TABLE 18.6. TYPICAL CHEESE COATING FORMULATION

Ingredient	Fonnula A (%)	Fonnula B (%)
Extruded corn product	57.8	66.0
Coconut oil	28.0	24.0
Cheddar cheese powder	7.0	9.3
Acid whey powder	3.5	-
Cheese flavor	3.5	0.7
Salt	0.2	-
Total	100.0	100.0

4. Final product color
5. Final product bulk density

THIRD GENERATION SNACKS

Product Description

Third-generation snack products or pellets are sometimes referred to as semi or half-products. Following extrusion cooking and forming, they are dried. Once they reach their final texture, they are ready to be consumed after frying in hot oil, puffing with hot air, or by secondary expansion extrusion by the snack processor or by packers prior to packaging. They can also be sold as a consumer item to be fried in the home, in restaurants, etc., for immediate consumption. After the final puffing step, the products can be salted or flavored externally. Some products have flavoring within the pellet itself. The stability during storage and the high bulk density of the packaged, nonexpanded thirdgeneration snack adds an interesting dimension to its marketing potential. New variants of the original third-generation snacks can now be expanded or puffed by infrared or microwave heating.

Process Description

A typical flow diagram for the production of third-generation snacks.

After the dry ingredients have been uniformly blended, the liquid ingredients such as shortenings, flavors, or water are applied as a spray in the batch mixer or injected into the preconditioning cylinder of the cooking extrusion system. In the extrusion cooking step, the raw materials must be completely cooked unless the formulation contains pregelled starches. Cook is defined as the combination of temperature, residence time, and moisture content during extrusion to fully gelatinize the starchy components in the formulation. The temperature profile in the extruder must be above the

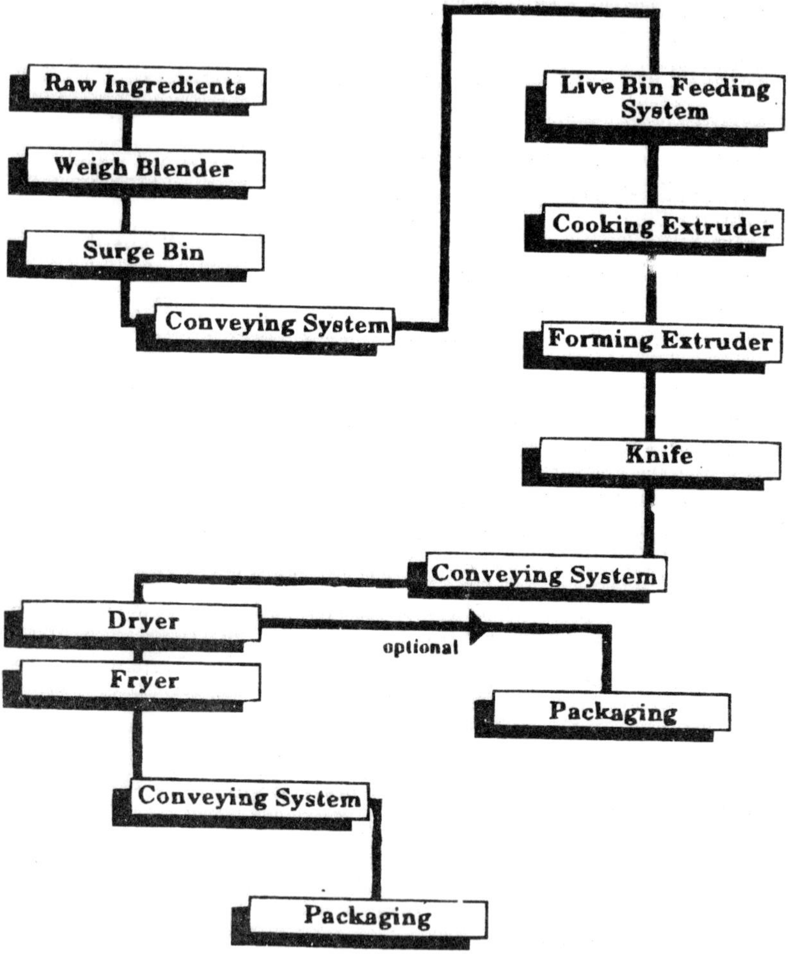

Figure 18.6 Typical flow for extrusion cooking of third generation snacks

gelatinization temperature of the starches found in the formulation unless they have been precooked.

Typical extrusion cooking processing conditions include:

Extruder rpm	180-250 rpm
Barrel temperatures	212-300°F (100-150°C)
Moisture content (extruder)	25-35%

Residence times

Cooking zone	15-20 seconds
Forming zone	30-45 seconds

The specific mechanical energy input is usually quite low as the main proportion of energy required for the gelatinization of the starch is supplied from conductive or convection energy sources.

Conductive and convection energy sources include steam, hot water, or other thermal fluids circulated through the jacketed barrel to provide external heat and/or steam and hot water injected directly into the product in the mixing cylinder or extruder barrel. Various heads, screws, and steamlock designs can be incorporated into the configuration to. produce the desired cooking conditions. The most common configurations provide a moderate- to low-shear input in the cooking zone of the extruder.

Forming, which includes cooling and densifying, may be accomplished in the secondary zone of the cooking extruder or a separate extruder. The forming zone is configured to contain a minimum of restrictions except' for the final die. Positive forward transport configurations complement maximum cooling to reduce product temperatures to 195-230°F (90-110°C). The cooled, visco-elastic mass is shaped by the final forming die, which contains sufficient open area to preven. expansion of the cooked dough. Varlous shapes of third-generation snacks before and after 'frying may be produced (Fig. 18.7).

Drying is very critical in the production of good -quality third-generation snacks. Proper drying will reduce the moisture content of the pellet to approximately 12%. Temperatures of 167-208°F (70-95°C) and retention times of 1-3 hours are required.

Some moisture in the extruded pellet is distributed close to its periphery but most is located in the center.

Properly dried third-generation snack pellets fry or expand better following a minimum -1-day period during which the moisture migrates eventually to reach an equilibrium.

Prior to consumption, third-generation snacks are usually expanded in hot oil or air. Frying involves complete immersion of the pellets in oil at 300-350°F'(150-175°C) for.30-40 seconds. The expansion of pellets in hot air is relatively new and *has* gained popularity owing to the low caloric content in the final product.

It must not be forgotten that these half-products may also, after moistening, be used-'as a feedstock in the most simple form of expansion

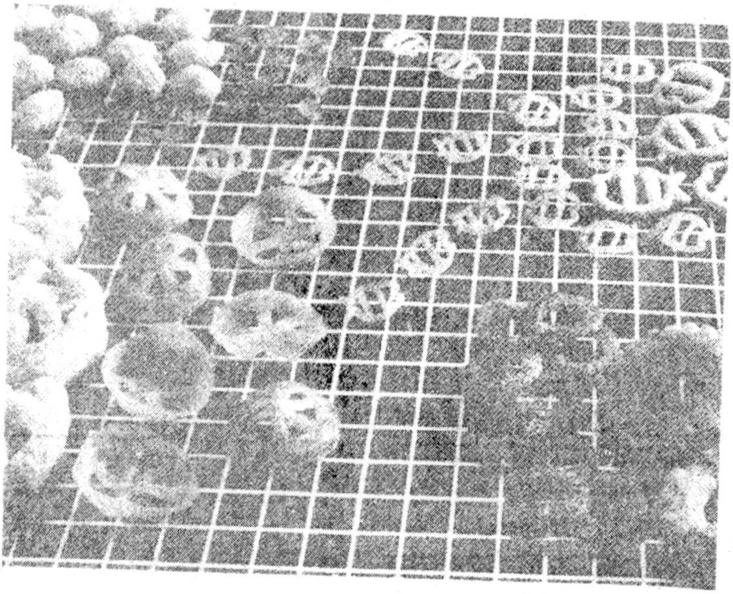

Figure 18.7 Some third generation snacks before and after frying.

extruder to produce a variety of shapes and sizes and flavors of final product for local consumption. For geographic situations where transport of delicate, fragile, and bulky product with a short shelf-life makes it impossible (technically and economically) to import it and where volume of production does not warrant a complete manufacturjng facility, this alternative to frying or hot air expansion of half-products to give a more locally "tailored" product has proved very helpful and has proved popular in North Africa and the Middle East.

Formulations

A wide range of raw ingredients may be selected suitable for thirdgeneration snack formulations. Combined ingredients must contain high levels of starch to maximize the expansion of the final product during exposure to hot oil or air. Levels of 60% or less of total starch in the formulation will give only slight expansion in the final processing step and will yield a final product with a crunchy, hard texture. Examples of this type of product would be those containing mainly whole ground corn, such as the traditional corn chip snack.

As the total starch level is increased above 60%, the final product will expand more, resulting in a light, frothy texture.

Shortening or vegetable oils (1-3%) and emulsifiers (0.5-1.0%) are usually included in the formulation as processing aids, to reduce stickiness and to impart a more uniform cellular structure in the final product.

Table 18.7 contains generic formulations representing two different textures.

Hard, crunchy texture	Soft, frothy texture
94.5% Ground corn	55.2% Cornstarch
5.0% Cornstarch	27.5% Wheat starch
0.5 % Monoglyceride	14.0% Tapioca starch
	2.5% Liquid shortening
	0.8% Monoglyceride

Examples of a suitable monoglyceride or emulsifier are Eastman Chemical's Myvaplex 600 or Grinstead's Dimodan P.V.

Extrusion systems for the production of third-generation snacks are efficient, economical to run, and produce a product with built-in marketing flexibility, owing to long shelf-life and high bulk density prior to frying, hot air" expansion, or secondary expansion extrusion.

19

Corn Flakes

Introdution

Corn flakes being one of most nutritious foods and is consumed as breakfast food not only in India but - elsewhere in the world.

Basically, it is prepared from maize, this is the main raw material. Flavours, like sugar or salt, are also added.

Maize, the main raw material, is itself a corn grain. India a predominantly an agricultural country. Due to the progressive increase in farm produce a need has been felt to develop more agrobased food processing industries to make gainful utilisation of the raw material resources and to provide remunerative prices to the growers. Maize is one of the important commercial food-grains food abundantly in our country. The maize is processed for the manufacture of oil, flour, starch, liquid glucose etc. Besides popcorn, another snack foods made from maize, maize is also used for the manufacture of corn flakes. Roasted corn flakes are generally used as breakfast food with milk. Raw corn flakes are used by the liquor manufacturing units for manufacturing of beer. Fried corn flakes are also served as snack foods.

Maize provides invaluable substances, which act as nutrients and these substances are very necessary of balance of human diet. The various substances are proteins, carbohydrates, starch, fat and water, proteins, carbohydrates and starch are main nutrients of maize.

Plant Economics of Corn Flakes

Rated Plant Capacity = 1.00 Ton/Day

LAND & BUILDING

(Land Area 2000 Sq.mts.) =	Rs.	73,00,000.00

PLANT & MACHINERY

1. Silo for storing corn grain constructed by brick of R.C.C.
2. Air Classifiers with all accessories
3. Separator
4. Storage bin
5. Weight balance
6. Rotary steam cooker
7. Agitator or lump breaker
8. Pan cooler or steamer
9. Germ Separator
10. Heavy flaking machine
11. Rotary oven
12. Conveyor
13. Inspection conveyor
14. Packing Machine
15. Mixer for flavouring syrup
16. Boiler (Mini)
18. Sifter

FIXED CAPITAL

1.	Land and Building	Rs.	73,00,000.00
2.	Plant and Machinery	Rs.	13,30,000.00
3.	Other Fixed Assets	Rs.	5,29,000.00
	TOTAL	Rs.	91,59,500.00

RAW MATERIALS

1. Corn Grain
2. Sugar
3. Salt
4. Polythene bags of different sizes

TOTAL WORKING CAPITAL/MONTH

1.	Raw Material	Rs.	6,27,000.00
2.	Salary and Wages	Rs.	2,49,109.00
3.	Utilities and Overheads	Rs.	68,350.00
	TOTAL	Rs.	9,44,459.00

TOTAL CAPITAL INVESTMENT

Total Fixed Capital	Rs.	91,59,500.00
Total Working Capital for 2 Months	Rs.	18,88,915.00
TOTAL	Rs.	1,10,48,418.00

TURN OVER/ANNUM

By sales of 300 tonne of Corn Flakes

TOTAL	Rs.	1,80,00,000.00

PROFIT SALES RATIO = Profit / Sales x 100 = 24.35%
RATE OF RETURN = Operating profit / T.C.I x 100 = 39.67%
BREAK EVEN POINT (B.E.P) = 46.48%

20

Liquid Glucose

Starches

Starch is a group of polysacchrides, composed of glucopyranose units joined together by glucosidric linkages. It conforms to the molecular formula $(C_6H_{10}O_5)u$, where n varies from a few hundred to over one million. Starch is found as the reserve carbohydrate in various parts of plants and is enzymaticallybroken down to glucose to other carbohydrates according to the metabollic needs of the plants.

Industrially, starch is broadly divided into two types, viz, natural and modifed. Natural starches, also designated as unmodified starches or simply starches, are obtained from grains such as the shorghum from roots like potato, tapioca and arrow root, and from the pith of the stems of certain palms such a sago. They are further classified into cereal starches and root starches. The characteristics of the natural starches are changed by chemical or enzymatic action and the products of these reactions are termed modified starches, oxidized starches, starch esters, starch ethers, dialddehyde, and catoionic starches.

Plant Economics of Liquid Glucose

Rated Plant Capacity = 1667.00 Kgs./Day

LAND & BUILDING

(Land Area 1500 Sq.mts.) = Rs. 36,40,000.00

PLANT & MACHINERY

1. Washing tank with paddles
2. Wet Milling machine
3. Centrifugal Separator.
4. Slurry tank complete with agitator and motor
5. Converter (Autoclave) made of manganese Bronze vessel, pressure
6. Filter Press
7. Refining with complete accessories
8. Neutralisation tank with agitator
9. Vacuum pan evaporator with vacuum pump
10. Boiler
11. Weighing machine, pumps, tanks etc.
12. Miscellaneous

FIXED CAPITAL

1.	Land and Building	Rs.	36,40,000.00
2.	Plant and Machinery	Rs.	17,25,000.00
3.	Other Fixed Assets	Rs.	3,30,000.00
	TOTAL	Rs.	56,95,000.00

RAW MATERIALS

1. Maize
2. Activated Carbon
3. Soda Ash & Hydrochloric Acid and Chemicals
4. Packing Materials

TOTAL WORKING CAPITAL/MONTH

1.	Raw Material	Rs.	2,79,000.00
2.	Salary and Wages	Rs.	1,71,250.00
3.	Utilities and Overheads	Rs.	1,87,000.00
	TOTAL	Rs.	6,67,750.00

TOTAL CAPITAL INVESTMENT

Total Fixed Capital	Rs.	56,95,000.00
Total Working Capital for 3 Month	Rs.	19,13,250.00
TOTAL	Rs.	76,08,250.00

TURN OVER/ANNUM

By sales of 500 tonne of Liquid Glucose Rs. 1,25,00,000.00

PROFIT SALES RATIO = Profit / Sales x 100 = 25.10%
RATE OF RETURN = Operating profit / T.C.I x 100 = 41.24%
BREAK EVEN POINT (B.E.P) = 52.22%

21

Maize / Corn Oil

Maize oil is produced as the big product of the maize product industries. In wet milling industries starch and its product, corn syrup, dextrose dextrin etc are the principal products, gluten feeds and corn oil are the main by-products. Corn products which mainly consists the endosper without separation of starch from gluten such a cornmeal, homing. In its pearl meal etc. are made by drymilling. In the Dry milling, corn oil maynot be produced as by product depending upon the size of the plant.

In any case the quality of the oil produced in wet milling process some distillers of alcohol used maize as raw material and some dry milling processor to determinate the corn before fermentation and recover the oil.

Plant Economics of Maize/Corn Oil

Rated Plant Capacity = 5.00 M.T./Day

LAND & BUILDING

(Land Area 1500 Sq.mts.) = Rs. 35,13,500.00

FIXED CAPITAL

1.	Land and Building	Rs.	35,13,500.00
2.	Plant and Machinery	Rs.	27,00,000.00
3.	Other Fixed Assets	Rs.	2,00.000.00
	TOTAL	Rs.	64,13,500.00

RAW MATERIALS

1. Germ
2. Petroleum either
3. Gunny Bags
4. Tin containers
5. Other chemicals for testing

TOTAL WORKING CAPITAL/MONTH

1.	Raw Material	Rs.	27,27,100.00
2.	Salary and Wages	Rs.	1,94,500.00
3.	Utilities and Overheads	Rs.	1,35,100.00
	TOTAL	Rs.	25,56,700.00

TOTAL CAPITAL INVESTMENT

Total Fixed Capital	Rs.	64,13,500.00
Total Working Capital for 3 Months	Rs.	51,13,400.00
TOTAL	Rs.	1,15,26,900.00

TURN OVER/ANNUM

By sales of 1500 M.T. of Maize /Corn Oil	Rs.	3,75,00,000.00

PROFIT SALES RATIO = Profit / Sales x 100 = 12.05%

RATE OF RETURN = Operating profit / T.C.I x 100 = 39.19%

BREAK EVEN POINT (B.E.P) = 46.23%

22

Malto Dextrin from Maize

INTRODUCTION

Maltodextrins are products with a low Dextrose Equivalent (DE) from 3 to 20, obtained by enzyme conversion (usually Alphamylase). They are usually spray dried powders (less than 5 per cent moisture) as the corresponding liquids have extremely high viscosities and tend to become cloudy on storage. Among Maltodextrins, the very low DE product is preapred from waxy corn starch, a natural starch that is almost entirely the amylopectin polymer.

Maltodextrin is a purified concentrated aqueous solution of nutritive saccharides obtained from edible starch, or the dried product derived from said solution and having a dextrose equivalent (DE) less than20:

Plant Economics of Malto Dextrin from Maize

Rated Plant Capacity = 5.00 M.T./Day

LAND & BUILDING

(Land Area 2500 Sq.mts.) = Rs. 59,00,000.00

PLANT AND MACHINERY

1. Washing tank with paddles
2. Wet milling Machine
3. Centrifugal Separator
4. Slurry tank complete with agitator and motor

5. Converter (Autoclave) made of manganese Bronze vessel, pressure
6. Refining press/Centrifuge
7. Refining tank with complete accessories
8. Neutralisation tank with agitator
9. Vacuum pan evaporator with vacuum pump
10. Heat Exchanger
11. Packing Machine
12. Spray Drier
13. Boiler
14. Weighing machine, pumps, tanks etc.
15. Miscellaneous viz. pipe fittings.

FIXED CAPITAL

1.	Land and Building	Rs.	59,00,000.00
2.	Plant and Machinery	Rs.	80,50,000.00
3.	Other Fixed Assets	Rs.	8,00,000.00
	TOTAL	Rs.	1,47,50,000.00

RAW MATERIALS

1. Maize
2. Activated Carbon
3. Soda Ash &Hydrochloric Acid and Chemicals
4. Packing Materials

TOTAL WORKING CAPITAL/MONTH

1.	Raw Material	Rs.	13,54,500.00
2.	Salary and Wages	Rs.	1,38,750.00
3.	Utilities and Overheads	Rs.	1,45,000.00
	TOTAL	Rs.	16,38,250.00

TOTAL CAPITAL INVESTMENT

Total Fixed Capital	Rs.	1,47,50,000.00
Total Working Capital for 3 Months	Rs.	49,17,750.00
TOTAL	Rs.	1,19,64,750.00

TURN OVER/ANNUM

By sales of 1500 Tons	Rs. 2,85,00,000.00

PROFIT SALES RATIO = Profit / Sales x 100 = 14.43%
RATE OF RETURN = Operating profit / T.C.I x 100 = 20.92%
BREAK EVEN POINT (B.E.P) = 59.68%

23

Plant Economics of Non Roasted Corn Flakes (POHA)

Plant Economics of Non Roasted Corn Flakes (POHA)

Rated Plant Capacity = 1.00 M.T./Day

LAND & BUILDING

(Land Area 1000 Sq.mts.) = Rs. 27,75,000.00

PLANT AND MACHINERY

1. Silo for storing corn grain constructed by brick & R.C.C.
2. Air classifiers with all accessories
3. Separators
4. Storage bin
5. Weighing Balance
6. Steam Cooker
7. Agitator or lump breaker
8. Pan Cooler or steamer
9. Germ Separator
10. Heavy flaking machine
11. Misc. Equipments.
12. Conveyor
13. Inspection Conveyor
14. Packing Machine
15. Screening and cooling Equipment
16. Mixer for flavouring syrup
17. Boiler (MINI)
18. Sifter

FIXED CAPITAL

1.	Land and Building	Rs.	27,75,000.00
2.	Plant and Machinery	Rs.	8,75,000.00
3.	Other Fixed Assets	Rs.	3,72,000.00
	TOTAL	Rs.	40,22,000.00

RAW MATERIALS

1. Corn Grain
2. Sugar
3. Salt
4. Polythene bags for different sizes

TOTAL WORKING CAPITAL/MONTH

1.	Raw Material	Rs.	2,02,250.00
2.	Salary and Wages	Rs.	1,02,258.00
3.	Utilities and Overheads	Rs.	68,350.00
	TOTAL	Rs.	3,72,858.00

TOTAL CAPITAL INVESTMENT

Total Fixed Capital	Rs.	40,22,000.00
Total Working Capital for 3 Months	Rs.	3,72,585.00
TOTAL	Rs.	43,94,858.00

TURN OVER/ANNUM

By sales of 300 MT. of Non Roasted corn Flakes	Rs.	90,00,000.00

PROFIT SALES RATIO = Profit / Sales x 100 = 39.39%

RATE OF RETURN = Operating profit / T.C.I x 100 = 80.67%

BREAK EVEN POINT (B.E.P) = 33.67%

24

Starch from Maize

Starches

Starch is a group of polysacchrides, composed of glucopyranose, units joined together by-glucosidric linkages. It conforms to the molecular formula, $(C_6H_{10}O_5)u$, where n varies from a few hundred to over one million. Starch is found as the reserve carbohydrate in various parts of plants and is enzymatically broken down to glucose to other carbohydrates according to the metabolic needs of the plants.

Natural Starches

Starch occurs naturally in the plants and its percentage varies with the plant and also in different parts of the same plant. Corn (maize) sorghum grain wheat, rice, potato, topioca, arrow root and sago are among the important sources of natural starches. The grains of barley, rye, oat, and the millets are also employed in the production of starches.

Plant Economics of Starch from Maize

Rated Plant Capacity = 200.00 M.T./Day

LAND & BUILDING

(Land Area 2.5 Acres=2617.5 sq.mtr.) = Rs. 1,27,55,000.00

PLANT AND MACHINERY

1. Weighing machine
2. Silos

3. Screening machine
4. Rotary burner
5. Steep tanks
6. Recirculating pumps
7. Acid tank storage
8. Evaporator
9. Condensor
10. Attrition mills
11. Hydroclones Cyclones
12. Fine Mill (pulveriser)
13. Centrifuge
14. Storage Tanks
15. Elevator
16. Tray dryer
17. Flash Dryer
18. Miscellaneous

FIXED CAPITAL

1.	Land and Building	Rs.	1,27,55,000.00
2.	Plant and Machinery	Rs.	45,90,000.00
3.	Other Fixed Assets	Rs.	17,10,000.00
	TOTAL	Rs.	1,90,55,000.00

RAW MATERIALS

1. Maize
2. Sulphur
3. Fuel Oil
4. Lubricating oil

TOTAL WORKING CAPITAL/MONTH

1.	Raw Material	Rs.	1,06,58,750.00
2.	Salary and Wages	Rs.	1,58,129.00
3.	Utilities and Overheads	Rs.	6,27,800.00
	TOTAL	Rs.	1,14,44,679.00

TOTAL CAPITAL INVESTMENT

Total Fixed Capital	Rs.	1,90,55,000.00
Total Working Capital for 3 Months	Rs.	3,43,34,038.00
TOTAL	Rs.	5,33,89,038.00

TURN OVER/ANNUM

By sales of 6000 M.T. of Starch	Rs.	16,50,00,000.00

PROFIT SALES RATIO = Profit / Sales x 100 = 11.66%

RATE OF RETURN = Operating profit / T.C.I x 100 = 36.03%

BREAK EVEN POINT (B.E.P) = 38.81%

25

Snack Food

Today a whole new generation of food products floods the market, catering a entirely new breed of consumers. Rapid industrialization and rising standards of living have not only pushed the boundings of the market but have also brought about general changes in the profile of Indian consumers.

Every year around Rs. 60,689 crores worth of agro-food material are converted into processed foods by the different food industries. The Indian government has recently acknowledged the importance of this sector. A separate ministry was set up for the food processing industries, the first of its kind in developing countries, in July1988. The major objectives of the ministry have been identified as providing a dynamic and synchronized mesh between the former and the industry in order to facilitate better utilization of agricultural products, greater addition of value of rural products, generation of employment in rural areas, enhancement of the net level of rural incomes and induction of modern technology in food processing.

Plant Economics of Snack Food (Crax Size), (Roll & Ball Type)

Rated Plant Capacity = 2400.00 Nos./Day

LAND & BUILDING

(Land Area 800 Sq.mts.) = Rs. 18,32,500.00

PLANT AND MACHINERY

1. Grinding Machine
2. Dough making machine
3. Humidiffer

4. Grain Puff Machine (extruder)
5. Cutting Machine
6. Rotary Oven
7. Rotary Seasoning Machine
8. Seasoning Spray System
9. Automatic Weighing Machine
10. Automatic Packing Machine
11. Conveyor
12. Genset
13. Lab testing equipment, Pumps, Compressors, Valves etc.

FIXED CAPITAL

1.	Land and Building	Rs.	18,32,500.00
2.	Plant and Machinery	Rs.	14,65,000.00
3.	Other Fixed Assets	Rs.	5,70,000.00
	TOTAL	Rs.	38,67,500.00

RAW MATERIALS

1. Rice
2. Edible oil
3. Salt, Spices, Masala & Other Flavours
4. Packing Materials

TOTAL WORKING CAPITAL/MONTH

1.	Raw Material	Rs.	4,01,800.00
2.	Salary and Wages	Rs.	81,875.00
3.	Utilities and Overheads	Rs.	1,17,900.00
	TOTAL	Rs.	8,98,575.00

TOTAL CAPITAL INVESTMENT

Total Fixed Capital	Rs.	38,67,500.00
Total Working Capital for 2 Months	Rs.	11,95,150.00
TOTAL	Rs.	50,62,650.00

TURN OVER/ANNUM

By sales of 7,20,000 Nos. of Pouches of Snacks	Rs. 1,44,00,000.00

PROFIT SALES RATIO = Profit / Sales x 100 = 42.73%

RATE OF RETURN = Operating profit / T.C.I x 100 = 121.55%

BREAK EVEN POINT (B.E.P) = 24.67%

26

Yeast Dry Powder from Maize

There are two types of yeast as compressed yeast. It is convenient to use dry yeast powder for bakeries because its handling is simple and its preservation easy. Dry yeast which can be contained in the form of pillets of flakes in packets or tins. Can be kept for some time in cool, dry conditions.

It is important to remember that :

a. Approximately half as much dried yeast as fresh is required in any recipe.

b. Reconstitution is necessary before using dried yeast.

This is done by soaking the yeast is luke warm water at 85°F containing 2 oz, sugar to 2 pint water, the water and sugar used for reconstitution should be substracted from the quantities given in the recipe. Sugar can be omitted, but the proving is necessary very fresh yeast.

Yeast is a living organism which requires warmth (80-85°F) food and liquid so that it can live and reproduce. The ingredient and utensils used in bread making and the atmosphere in which the bread is proved must, therefore, be lukewarm; suden cooling hindes growth and anything hot will yeast before it has hand time to multiply.

Yeast powder is very important ingredient in bread making and if it is not added, the bakery breads will be produced like homely breads.

Plant Economics of Yeast Dry Powder From Maize

Rated Plant Capacity = 1.00 Ton /day

LAND & BUILDING

(Land Area 2000 Sq.mts.) = Rs. 58,00,000.00

PLANT AND MACHINERY

1. Washer with accessories
2. Steeping Tank (M.S.)
3. Germ Removal mill
4. Grinding mill (Attrition Mill)
5. Cyclone
6. Washing Tank (M.S.)
7. Centrifuge
8. Cyclone Washer
9. Fermenter (MS)
10. Plate & Frame Filter Press
11. Mixer (MS) fitted with agitator
12. Tray Drier
13. Packing M/c. (Semi-Automatic)
14. Lab Tray Equipment
15. Miscellaneous viz Pipe Fitting, Valves, Motor etc.

FIXED CAPITAL

1.	Land and Building	Rs.	58,00,000.00
2.	Plant and Machinery	Rs.	22,20,000.00
3.	Other Fixed Assets	Rs.	3,10,000.00
	TOTAL	Rs.	83,30,000.00

RAW MATERIALS

1. Maize
2. Sodium Phosphates, Magnesium Sulphate & Other additives & Fermentator Chemicals
3. Packing material

TOTAL WORKING CAPITAL/MONTH

1.	Raw Material	Rs.	3,01,250.00
2.	Salary and Wages	Rs.	1,74,895.00
3.	Utilities and Overheads	Rs.	45,000.00
	TOTAL	Rs.	5,21,145.00

TOTAL CAPITAL INVESTMENT

Total Fixed Capital	Rs.	83,30,000.00
Total Working Capital for 2 Months	Rs.	5,21,145.00
TOTAL	Rs.	88,51,145.00

TURN OVER/ANNUM

By sales of 300 M.T. of Dried Yeast Powder from Maize	Rs.	1,20,00,000.00

PROFIT SALES RATIO = Profit / Sales x 100 = 42.73%

RATE OF RETURN = Operating profit / T.C.I x 100 = 121.55%

BREAK EVEN POINT (B.E.P) = 24.67%

27

Suppliers of Maize/Corn Processing Machineries

FIT WELL ENGINEERING COMPANY

Manufacturer and exporters of maize processing plants, vegetable tanin powder, medicinal herbal and oil extraction plant, lemon powder plant.

Address: 2nd Pokhran Road, Thane-400 601 India
Phone: +91-022-25346436/25346121
Fax: +91-022-25333632/25333634

MAVERIK INCORPORATION

Exporters of vegetable, fruit, pulse processing & packaging plants, prawn crackers, chicken crackers, noodle, paste making plant, cold storgae, IQF, BQF, cold chain management, snack food & extruder snack food plants & machineries.

Address: 2, Giribaug, Behind Center Point,
Alkapuri, Baroda-390 005 India
Phone: +91-265-2343010
Fax: +91-265-2343010

MUKUL BROTHERS ENGINEERING WORKS LIMITED

Manufacturer and exporter of food processing plants and machinery, roller flour mills plant, chakki plants, besan plant, rice mills plants, grinding plants, seed cleaning plants, maize milling plants, etc.

Address: Near Jain Temple, Kunda,
Delhi Road, Partapur, Meerut-250 103 India
Phone: +91-121-2440731
Fax: +91-121-2440729

HUANG GROUP MACHNERY CO., LTD.

Our company's corn flour processing machine can grind corn into powder, and other production. The capacity from 10T-500T per day.

Ms. Wang Shuo
SHIDAI GARDEN, GUOTAI STREET,
SHIJIAZHUANG - 050081, HEBEI, CHINA
Phone Number 86-311-87260955
Fax 86-311-83618179

JINAN SAIBAINUO TECHNOLOGY DEVELOPMENT COMPANY

Cathy
No 18, Central street, tianqiao industry park, Jinan, Shandong, China
Phone: 86-531-85762891
Fax: 86-531-85762891

Corn Flakes Machinery, Corn Flakes Processing Line is a continuous and economical process with an easily controlled production cycle, Corn Snacks Machinery, Snack can be directly extruded from the extruder. Besides the dryer and seasonal, it does not need other equipment

SIFTER INTERNATIONAL

83, Sector-6, Faridabad - 06 (Hr.)
90-129-2240150/5060039
(Corn Flakes Machinery Supplier)

VIJSON ENGINEERS PVT. LTD.,

370/2C, Ahmednagar - Manmad State Highway,
Tal : Kopargoan - 423 601.
Dist : Ahmednagar. (M. S. India).
Tel. No. : +91 - 2423 - 221987, 221988.
Telefax : +91 - 2423 - 221987.
PUNE OFFICE :
203, legacy Apartments, Above Lifeline Hospital,
D. P. Road, Aundh, Pune - 411 007.
Telefax :+91 -20 -25881678, 25899006.
Mobile : +91 - 98220 15413.
Machineries for Starch Glucose, Dextrose, Monohydraulic

MUKUL BROTHERS ENGINEERING WORKS LTD

Mr Tushar Jain
Ph: +91-0121-2440731, 9837235657, +91-0121- 2440729

Addreass: Near Jain Temple, Kunda Road,
Partapur, Delhi Highway, MEERUT - 250103
(Uttar Pradesh) India
Maize mill Machinery Supplier

MICMAC SOAP MACHINERY & SOAP PLANT
Mr. SARJU KALARIA
Ph: +91 281 2368564, +91 98242 17600, +91 281 2366010
Add: PLOT NO. 2, DHARMAJIVAN INDUSTRIAL ESTATE,
GOKULDHAM MAIN ROAD END,
RAJKOT - 360 004
(Gujarat) India
Pulverizer Maize mill

BASANT INDUSTRIES
We are Manufacturers and Exporters of Diesel Engines, Diesel Generators, Centrifugal pumps, Corn mills and spare parts
Mr. Puneet Mittal
Ph: +91-562-3103649 / 2280779 / 2280774, +91-562-2280778
Add: I. E., Nunhai, AGRA - 282006
(Uttar Pradesh) India

TINYTECH PLANTS
Manufacturer, Supplier and Exporter of -
Cooking oil machinery, sugar machinery, oil expellers, edible oil refinery.
Cooking Oil Machinery, Sugar Machinery, Oil Mill Machinery, Maize Mills
Wind Mills, Jaggery Making Plant
Mr. Gopal Desai
Ph: +91-281-2480166, +91-9227606264, +91-281-2467552
Tagore Road, RAJKOT - 360002
(Gujarat) India

VIJSON ENGINEERS PVT. LTD.,
MR.SUNIL CHAVAN - DIR.
Address: 203, Legacy Apts.,
Above Lifeline Hospital,
D.P.Rd., Aundh, Pune - 411007
Tel.No: (020) 25881678 / 25890006
Fax No : (020) 25881678 / 25890006
Machineries for Maize to Starch Plant & Machineries

HEBEI HUANGPAI MACHINE CO., LTD
Contact Person: Mr. Hussin Ali
#302 Xinhua Rd, Shijiazhuang, P.R.China, shijiazhuang, CHINA
Phone: 0086-311-87038225
Fax: 0086 311 87037468
Contact: Yang Poping Headship: Chief Director
Tel: 0086-372-5153917 Mobile:0086-136-83726800
E-mail: afpmcc@yahoo.cn,afpmcc@yahoo.com.cn Website: http://www.afpm.cn
Agriculture & Food Processing Machinery Consultative Center
Address: NO.6 Beichang Street, Anyang, Henan, China Postcode:455000

COSMOS INTERNATIONAL
Food and Agro Products, Rice, Wheat, Tea, Edible Oil, Soya Meal &Sunflower Meal, Other Flour, Pulses, Indian Spices, Agriculture Equipment &Machinery, Agriculture Equipment, Agriculture Implements, Centrifugal Pump Sets, Agricultural Trailers, Hand Pumps, Agriculture Tractors, Food Processing Plants, Maize Processing Plant, Cassava Processing Plant, Honey Processing Plant, Multi Purpose Fruit/V... More.
Aradhana Colony, Sector-13,
R.K. Puram, New Delhi-110066, India

UNIVERSAL PROCESS ENGINEERS
Manufacturers & Exporters of Starch Glucose Plant and Machinery, Derivates of Starch, Dextrin, Dextrose, Sorbitol, Modified Starches. Grinding mills, Consultancy & Turnkey Assignments for the Complete Plant.
Plot No. A28/1/10,IDA, Nacharma
New Delhi 500076
Phone: 91-40 -271 72573
Fax: 91-40 -271 79701

M.SON INDUSTRIES
D-33, Sector-2,
NOIDA-201301 (U.P)
Tele Fax: 95120-2552177,2538397
Tel:(R):95120-2536955,2543119
Website:www.food-machines.com
*Email:msons2002@yahoo.com
CORN FLAKES MACHINE

28

Present Manufacturers/Exporters/Suppliers of Maize and Maize Products

RAJKUMAR AGRO ENGINEERS PVT. LTD.
Profile : Manufacturers & exporters of mini oil mill machinaries, pulverisers, paddy [rice] threashers decorticators, maize threashers.
Address : Ghat Road, Nagpur 440 018, India
Telephone : +(91)-(712)-725171 Fax : +(91)-(712)-725271
Contact : Mr. Naresh Gambhir

MALLOYS INDIA
Profile : Manufacturer & Exporter of Agriculture Implements like multicrop thrasher for wheat, soyabean, gram, mustard, maize sheller for maize etc.
Address : 12, Old Vijay Nagar, Agra 282 004, India
Telephone : +(91)-(562)-352219-352447-357852
Fax : +(91)-(562)-520014
Contact : Mr. Gupta

P.GURUSAMY & SONS
Profile : Manufacturer of Sulphuric Acid, Hydrochloric acid, Activated Carbon Powder, Maize Starch, Liquid Glucose, Tapiaco Starch, Aluminium Sulphate, Magnesium Sulphate, Ferrous Sulphate etc
Address : 631 Sivakamipuram Street, Rajapalayam 626 117, India
Telephone : +(91)-(4563)-22697-21471
Contact : Mr. S.M.Murali

WELCHEM CHEMICALS
Profile : Distributors of Wipro Ltd for glycerine, stearic acid, maize starch, liquid paraffin, pvc stabilizers etc.
Address : 137, Raheja Arcade, Koramangala, Bangalore 560 095, India

Telephone : +(91)-(80)-5536417-5520553
Contact : Mr. Mukesh Khanna

B.M. SAVLA & CO.
Profile : distibutors of magnesium carbonate, calcium carbonate, all types of gum, maize starch, acid slurry, starch powder, chemicals(for detergent industries)precipitate silica, soda ash,caustic soda,tri sodium phosphate,sodium sulphide, sodium bi sulphide,etc.
Address : 26-55 Birhana Road, Kanpur 208 001, India
Telephone : +(91)-(512)-312348
Fax : +(91)-(512)-312410
Contact : Mr. Ashok Savla

MANIKSEM ENTERPRISES
Profile : Exporters & Suppliers for Rice,maize, Ground Nut Seeds(HPS)
Address : #G-1, Soundarya Apartments,
Punnamathota, Vijaywada 520 010, India
Telephone : +(91)-(866)-481652-481653-430015
Fax : +(91)-(866)-471780
Contact : Mr. Manubhai M. Sthankiya

A. MANGALARAJ
Profile : Exporter & Importer of Agro & Agro Based Products like Mustard Seeds, Groundnuts, turmeric, dry red chilly, coriander, black pepper, cumin, mustard, anise, big onion, sesame seedsdry ginger, rice, maize, potato
Address : 114-South Raja Street,
Tuticorin 628 001, India
Telephone : +(91)-(461)-321758-320388
Fax : +(91)-(461)-322988
Contact : Mr. A. Mangalaraj

RAMA ASSOCIATES LTD.
Profile : Exporters of Rice, Wheat, Maize, Jowar, Pulses, Sugar
Address : B-10, Lawrence Road, New Delhi 110 035, India
Telephone : +(91)-(11)-7186557 Fax : +(91)-(11)-7184709
Contact : Mr.Anil Gupta

PREMJI GHELLABHAI & CO.
Profile : Exporters of Food Grains like rice, wheat, bajra, jowar, maize.
Address : 3 Keshavji Nayak Road, Mumbai 400 009, India
Telephone : +(91)-(22)-3776856-3743945 Fax : +(91)-(22)-3738394
Contact : Mr. Anand Kothari

PKS LIMITED
Profile : Deals in rice, maize, soyabean, etc.
Address : 7.Camac Street, 4th Floor, Kolkata 700 017, India
Telephone : +(91)-(33)-2425061-2425605-2425909
Fax : +(91)-(33)-2429577
Contact : Mr. Ajay Bhalotia

MAGANUR DISTRIBUTORS
Profile : Exporters & suppliers of Indian rice, maize etc.
Address : Chowkipet,, Davangere , India
Telephone : +(91)-(8192)-60467-60812 Fax : +(91)-(8192)-60986
Contact : Mr. Aman Jain

M.S. EXPORTS
Profile : Exporters of rice, pulses, flours of wheat, maize, rice, corn, etc.
Address : 5, Wadi Plot, Porbandar 360 575, India
Telephone : +(91)-(286)-243377
Fax : +(91)-(286)-246147
Contact : Mr. Soni Agarwal

KENWIN TRADING (AGRI BULK)
Profile : suppliers-exporters of wheat, corn, sorghum, maize, etc. from India, Brazil, Argentina, Unites States of America
Address : 3974 Roshan Ara Road,
New Delhi 110 007, India
Telephone : +(91)-(11)-2516374-3985410
Fax : +(91)-(11)-3985410
Contact : Mr. Ajay Khandelwal

G & A EXPORTS
Profile : Deals in Non-Basmati Rice, Yellow Maize, etc
Address : 261, 6th Street, Gandhipuram, Coimbatore 641 012, India
Telephone : +(91)-(422)-495251 Fax : +(91)-(422)-495251
Contact : Mr. Suresh Kumar

HARI AND CO. EXPORT HOUSE
Profile : Exporter Of Onion, Rice, Maize and other Food Products
Address : 133, Great Cotton Road,
Tuticorin 628 001, India
Telephone : +(91)-(461)-323276, 325276, 321605
Fax : +(91)-(461)-323684,
Contact : Mr. Annamali Swamy

UNIVERSAL ENTERPRISES

Profile : Merchant exporters- dealing in non-basmati rice, wheat, maize, soya d-oiled cake (poultry feed), cotton yarn, etc.
Address : 7, Rabindra Sarani,1st Floor,
Kolkata 700 001, India
Telephone : +(91)-(33)-2253425-2253006-2254052
Fax : +(91)-(33)-2153113
Contact : Mr. Dipak Goenka

ASHWIN VANASPATI INDUSTRIES LIMITED

Profile : Vanaspati, Maize-Corn, Coconut, Sunflower oil and all types of Edible Oils
Address : Premier Chambers, 3rd floor, R. C. Dutt Road,
Alkapuri, Baroda 390 007, India
Telephone : +(91)-(265)-342101-342104-342105
Fax : +(91)-(265)-341726
Contact : Mr. Manohar G. Chawla

ROSHAN OVERSEAS

Profile : Exporters of edible oils, sugar, soyabean meals, maize, wheat etc.
Address : F-29 , Rajouri Garden,
New Delhi 110 027, India
Telephone : +(91)-(11)-5450745-5465149-5121136
Fax : +(91)-(11)-5121136
Contact : Mr. Sanjeev Kapoor

S.PRASAD BROTHERS

Profile : Exporters of spices & produces like arecanuts, black pepper, cloves, coconut (fresh), cardamom, cinnamon, garcinia cambogia fruits (goraka), maize, nutmeg, mace, tamarind, tea (all grades of branded and bulk) etc
Address : No-11-1-11, Sea Street, Colombo 11, Sri Lanka
Telephone : +(0094)-(1)-380722-380721
Fax : +(0094)-(1)-710638
Contact : Mr. S.Gagendra Prasad

SERVICES INTERNATIONAL PTE. LTD.

Profile : Exporters of beans, maize, legumes, pulses, rice
Address : 10 Melrose Court #04-08 Lorong Limau,
Whampoa District 328754, Singapore
Telephone : +(65)-(254)-5817
Fax : +(951)-253225
Contact : Dr. Mya Thidar

BHUIYAN GROUP

Profile : Exporters of grains like wheat, maize
Address : 39, Agrabad C-A,
Chittagong 40000, Bangladesh
Telephone : +(880)-(31)-720671-615408
Fax : +(880)-(31)-611692-716338
Contact : Mr. Md. Irshad Ali Bhuiyan

GLOBAL IMEX

Profile : Exporters of Fishmeal, Maize, Green Beans, White corn, Sharkfinns, Mangoes.
Address : 12 Wickens Cres, Ajax L1T 3M7, Canada
Telephone : +(1)-(905)-6264561 Fax : +(1)-(905)-4282502
Contact : Mr. Paul Ponce De Leon

HASAN SEKER LTD CO.

Profile : Processors of lentils, chick peas, beans, cumin seeds, peas in Turkey and Canada. International traders of Wheat, Barley, and Maize.
Address : Uray Cad, 5207 Sk., No.2-1, Mersin 33060, Turkey
Telephone : +(90)-(324)-2381010
Fax : +(90)-(324)-2373214
Contact : Mr. Irfan Burian

AFG WAREHOUSE

Profile : Exporters of rice, corn, maize meal, sugar, sunflower oil and wheat.
Address : Stella Street 61A, Vryburg 8600, South Africa
Telephone : +(27)-(53)9270779
Fax : +(27)-(53)9270410
Contact : Mr. Arthur Maddocks

KUWAIT FLOUR MILLS & BAKERIES CO.

Profile : Importers of Raw & Packaging Materials for Mill Plant (Wheat Barley Maize), Biscuit Plant Macaroni Plant, Oil & Ghee Plant, Bakery Plant, Feed Mill
Address : Jamal Abdul Naser Street,
next to Shuwaikh Port, Kuwait 13007, Kuwait
Telephone : +(965)-4841866
Fax : +(965)-4841590
Contact : Mr. Abdullah Al Wahaibi

SANHO VIETNAM CO. LTD.
Profile : Importers of maize wheat bran pellet pollard, maize, wheat gluten, pure lactose & lysine, methionine & threonine etc.
Address : 617-60 Nguyen Kiem St,
Phunhuan Dist, HoChiMinh City 848, Vietnam
Telephone : +(84)-(8)-8957380 Fax : +(84)-(8)-8957380
Contact : Mr. Nguyen Tuan

MJENGO LIMITED
Profile : Importers of Rice,Maize Flour,Wheat Flour etc.
Address : P.O.Box 1536, Thika , Kenya
Telephone : +(254)-(151)30180-30085
Fax : +(254)-(151)31733
Contact : Mr. Kaushik Purohit

K.S.TRADING ASSOCIATES
Profile : Importers of wheat, maize, corn , pulse & rice
Address : 261, Khatungonj, Chittagong 4000, Bangladesh
Telephone : +(880)-(31)-623117-671351-610482
Fax : +(880)-(31)-610482
Contact : Mr. M.K.Saifullah

ASIAN MERCANTILE COMPANY
Profile : Importers of Wheat,Maize, Soyabean Meal, Rice, etc.
Address : 9-G, Motijheel C-A, 2nd Floor, Dhaka 1000, Bangladesh
Telephone : +(880)-(2)9562377
Fax : +(880)-(2)9564729
Contact : Mr. Tanjir D Shagar

ALI STORES
Profile : Importers of rice, wheat, pulses, chickpeas, dunpeas, whitepeas, maize, soya meal
Address : 319-D.T.Road, P.O. Pahartali,
Chittagong 4202, Bangladesh
Telephone : +(00880)-(31)-751053 Fax : +(00880)-(31)-751763
Contact : Mr. Mohammed Ali Khan

THE ANIL STARCH PRODUCTS LTD.
Profile : Importers of maize
Address : Anil Road, Post Box No 10009, Ahmedabad 380 025, India
Telephone : +(91)-(79)-2123222 Fax : +(91)-(79)-2110731
Contact : Mr. Pravine Chester

SHREE NILKANTH STARCH & ALLIED PRODUCT
Profile : Importers of maize germs 600 MT
per month and peagion peas 200 MT per month.
Address : Khatraj Chokdi (Khatraj),
Ahmedabad 380 001, India
Telephone : +(91)-(79)-44847
Fax : +(91)-(79)-44848
Contact : Mr. Pragnesh Patel

RITURAJ IMPEX
Profile : Importers of wheat & yellow maize
Address : 3C, 3rd Floor, 3 Royd lane,
Park street, Calcutta 700 016, India
Telephone : +(91)-(33)-2260886 Fax : +(91)-(33)-2260888
Contact : Mr. Sajjan Kumar Agarwal

MIMA FLOUR MILLS PVT.LTD
Profile : Importers of red & white wheat,
gram , maize & bread making machine
Address : 88, Burtolla Street,
Calcutta 700 007, India
Telephone : +(91)-(33)-2191288/2192455
Fax : +(91)-(33)-2410264
Contact : Mr. Rajesh Mimani

AMRIT FEEDS LTD.
Profile : Importers of maize.
Address : M-28, Old DLF Colony,
Sector-14,, Gurgoan 122 001, India
Telephone : +(91)-(124)-6300326/6300327
Fax : +(91)-(124)-6334297
Contact : Mr. Rajesh Bagla

359. DI ETHYL OXALATE
360. DI METHYL ORTHOPHTHALATE
361. DI-METHYL PHTHALATE
362. DICLOFENAC GEL
363. DIOCTYL PHTHALATE (DOP)
364. DI PHENYL GLYCERINE
365. DI PHENYL OXIDE
366. DINITRO-CHLORO BENZENE
367. DISTILLED WATER
368. DODECYL BENZENE SULPHONATE
369. DUSTLESS CHALK
370. EDTA & ITS SALTS
371. ELECTROLESS NICKEL PLATING ON PLASTICS
372. ENDOSULFAN
373. EPOXY RESIN BASED COMPOUND
374. ETHYL ACETATE
375. EHTYL ETHER
376. ETHYL ALCOHOL (POTABLE LIQUOR)
377. ETHYL HEXANOL
378. EXTRACTION OF ESSENTIAL OILS BY SUGAR CRITICAL FLUID (CARBON DIOXIDE) METHOD FROM FLOWERS, HERBAL & SPICES
379. FERRIC ALUM
380. FERRO CHROME LIGNO SULPHONATE
381. FERRO MANGANESE
382. FERRO SILICONE
383. FERRO VANADIUM FROM VANADIUM SLUDGE
384. FERROUS SILICATE
385. FERROUS SULPHATE
386. FERTILIZER FROM ANIMAL BLOOD & LEATHER WASTE
387. FLUORESCENT TUBE LIGHT POWDER
388. FOAMED PVC COMPOUNDING & ITS PRODUCTS
389. FORMALDEHYDE
390. FRACTIONAL DISTILLATION OF D.M.O (DEMENTHOLIZED OIL)
391. FRACTIONAL DISTILLATION OF ESSENTIAL OIL & MEDICINAL PLANT EXTRACT
392. FRICTION DUST (LIQUID & POWDER) FROM CNSL
393. FRUIT FLAVOURS
394. FURFURAL FROM RICE HUSK
395. GARLIC ACID
396. GASKET SHELLAC COMPOUND
397. GEAR OIL
398. GIBBERELLIC ACID
399. GLASS PUTTY
400. GLYCERINE
401. GOSSYPOL (POLY PHENOL) FROM COTTON SEED OIL
402. GUAR GUM POWDER
403. HAIR FIXER (HAIR GEL TYPE)
404. H - ACID
405. HENNA PASTE MAKING
406. HEPTAL DEHYDE
407. HIGH CARBON FERRO CHROME
408. HYDRATED CALCIUM SILICATE BRICK
409. HYDRATED LIME FROM SEA SHELL
410. HYDROCHLORIC ACID
411. HYDRO FLUORIC ACID
412. HYDROGEN PEROXIDE (BY AUTO-OXIDATION PROCESS)
413. ICE PACKS (SOLUTIONS TYPE, WHITE GEL TYPE, VIOLET SEMI SOLID POLYMER TYPE)
414. IMPROVING DROP POINT PARAFFIN WAX FROM 45-50ºC TO 75-80ºC
415. INDUSTRIAL ALCOHOL
416. INTEGERATED COMPLEX OF EASTER & ALLIED PRODUCTS (D.O.P, D.B.P, ETHYL ACETATE WIRE ENAMEL & CABLE JELLY)
417. IMFL (WHISKY) & COUNTRY LIQUOR
418. IRON OXIDE FOR MAKING FERITTE
419. IRON SULPHIDE
420. JUTE BATCHING OIL
421. KESH KALA TEL (HAIR DYE LOTION) (VASMOL 33, BLACK NITE TYPE)
422. L-LYSINE MONOHYDROCHLORIDE
423. LACTIC ACID FROM WHITE SUGAR BY FERMENTATION PROCESS
424. LDPE GRANULES FROM VIRGIN (LDPE RESIN)
425. LEAD EXTRACTION FROM BATTERY SCRAP
426. LEAD OXIDE (A) LEAD MONOXIDE
(B) LEAD TETRA OXIDE
(C) GREYLEAD OXIDE
427. LIQUID GLUCOSE & ITS BY PRODUCTS
428. LIQUID OXYGEN BOTTLING PLANT
429. LIQUID SHOE POLISH
430. LIQUID FLOOR POLISH
431. LUBE OIL VISCOSITY IMPROVED FOR P.P.G/P.E.G
432. LUBRICANTS ASHLESS 100% COMBUSTION
433. MAGNESIUM CARBONATE AND MAGNESIUM BICARMONATE
434. MAGNESIUM HYDROXIDE POWDER
435. MAGNESIUM SILICATE
436. MAGNESIUM SULPHATE
437. MALACHITE GREEN
438. MALEIC ANHYDRIDE
439. MANGANESE SULPHATE
440. MANUFACTURING OF CARBON MONO-OXIDE WATER GAS
441. MENTHOL BOLD CRYSTALS FROM FLAKES
442. MENTHOL CRYSTAL & MENTHA OIL
443. MERCURIC OXIDE
444. METAL PRE-TREATMENT CHEMICALS
445. METHANE GAS BY SODIUM ACETATE & SODA LIME
446. METHYL ACETYL RICINOLATE
447. METOL
448. METOL FROM HYDROQUINONE & METHYLAMINE
449. MICANITE
450. MICRO NUTRIENT MIXTURE
451. MINERAL WATER
452. MINERAL WATER AND PET BOTTILNG PLANT
453. MINERAL WATER IN BOTTLES, GLASS AND POUCHES
454. MINI CEMENT PLANT (BY ROTARY KILN PROCESS)
455. MIXED FERTILIZER
456. MOSQUITO & FLIES REPELLENT AGARBATTI (INCENSE STICKS)
457. MONO CHLORO ACETIC ACID
458. MONOCROTOPHOS (TECHNICAL)
459. MOSQUITO COIL
460. MOSQUITO COIL & MAT
461. MOSQUITO MAT
462. MOTHER TINCTURE & BIO CHEMIC MEDICINES
463. NAPHTHALENE & PHENYL (INTEGRATED UNIT)
464. NATURAL MINERAL WATER BY REVERSE OSMOSIS PROCESS
465. NICKEL PLATING BRIGHTNER (PRIMARY OR CARRIER BRIGHTNER & SECONDARY BRIGHTNER)
466. NICKEL SULPHATE
467. NICOTINE FROM TOBACCO WASTE
468. NICOTINE SULPHATE FROM TOBACCO WASTE
469. NITRO BENZENE
470. NITRO CELLULOSE SANDING SEALER/LACQUER
471. NITRO MUSK
472. NITROGEN & OXYGEN GAS PLANT
473. NON-IONIC SURFACTANT (WETTING AGENT)
474. NO-CARB PASTE
475. OCTANOL
476. ORTHO NITRO PHENOL
477. OXALIC ACID FROM MOLASSES
478. OXALIC ACID FROMRICE HUSK
479. OXALIC ACID FROM TREE BARK
470. OXALIC ACID FROM WASTE VEGETABLES
471. OXYGEN GAS PLANT
472. OXYGEN GAS PLANT (AIR SEPERATION METHOD)
473. PARA-AMINO BENZOIC ACID
474. PARA-AMINO PHENOL
475. PARA TOLUENE SULPHONIC ACID
476. PECTIN FROM RAW PAPAYA
477. PERFUME (LEMON & OTHERS)

CRUDE NAPHTHA
570. TRIMETHYL AMMONIUM CHLORIDE
571. TRIPHENYL PHOSPHITE (T.P.P)
572. ULTRAMARINE BLUE (LIQUID)
573. UREA FORMALDEHYDE & MELAMINE FORMALDEHYDE POWDER
574. UNDECYLINIC ACID
575. VINYL ACETATE MONOMER
576. VITAMIN C
577. VITAMIN E
578. WASTE WATER TREATMENT PLANT FOR INDUSTRIAL SECTOR IN INDIA (ONLY MARKER SURVEY)
579. WIRE DRAWING LUBRICANT
580. WIRE ENAMEL
581. XANTHATES
582. YELLOW DEXTRIN
583. ZINC CHLORIDE
584. ZINC OXIDE
585. ZINC PHOSPHATING BY COLD PROCESS
586. ZINC SILICATE
587. ZINC STEARATE
588. ZINC SULPHATE
589. ZINC SULPHATE MONOHYDRATE
590. ACID BLACK
591. AURAMINE 'O'
592. AZO DYES STUFF
593. DYE & DYE INTERMEDIATE
594. DYE INTERMEDIATES
595. MALACHITE GREEN
596. METHYLENE BLUE
597. PHTHALOCYANINE BLUE
598. PHTHALOCYANINE BLUE & GREEN
599. REACTIVE DYES
600. SULPHUR BLACK DYE
601. VAT DYES
602. WATER CHILLING PLANT
603. WADDING OIL (100%) FOR WADDING OF COTTON HOSIERY CLOTH IN THE DYEING PROCESS
604. WHITE OIL
605. WAX FLOOR POLISH

ELECTRICAL, ELECTONICS, COMPUTERS AND INFOTECH/IT PROJECTS

606. AIR CONDITIONING
607. ALUMINIUM ALLOY CONDUCTOR
608. ALUMINIUM CABLE
609. ALUMINIUM ELECTROYTIC CAPACITORS
610. AUDIO CASSETTE ASSEMBLING & RECORDING
611. AUDIO CASSETTES DUPLICATING RECORDING
612. AUDIO CASSETTES & AUDIO STUDIO
613. AUDIO CASSETTES PLANE & RECORDED
614. AUDIO MAGNETIC HEADS
615. AUDIO MAGNETIC TAPE
616. AUDIO/VIDEO CASSETTES
617. AUTO BULB/LAMPS
618. AUTOMATIC VOLTAGE STABILIZER
619. BATTERY PLATES
620. BACK OFFICE (Rs. 5000/-)
621. B/W TV & COMPUTER MONITOR PICTURE TUBE
622. BREAD BOARDS
623. CALL CENTRE
624. CAMERA (35 MM)
625. CAPACITORS
626. CARBON ELECTRODE USED FOR BATTERY CELL
627. CARBON POTETIOMETERS
628. CEILING FAN
629. CERAMIC INSULATOR
630. CHILDREN INFOTECH TRAINING INSTITUTE (Rs. 5000/-)
631. CHOKE AND PATTI
632. CHOKE AND STARTER
633. CHOKE USED FOR FLUORESCENT LAMPS
634. COLOUR TELEVISION
635. COLOUR AND BLACK & WHITE TELEVISION
636. COMPACT DISC
637. COMPACT DISC PLAYER (AUDIO/VIDEO)
638. COMPUTER EDUCATION INSTITUTE
639. COMPUTER ASSEMBLY
640. COMPUTER HARDWARE
641. COMPUTER KEYBOARD
642. COMPUTER PERIPHERALS
643. COMPUTER PRINTERS
644. COMPUTER RIBBON
645. COMPUTER RIBBON REINKING OR REFILLING
646. COMPUTER STATIONERY
647. COMPUTER STATIONERY &

IMPORTED HARDWARE PARTS
648. COMPUTER TERMINALS
649. COMPUTERISED WASHING MACHINE (AUTOMATIC)
650. COMPUTER SOFTWARE
651. CONDENSER FOR MOTOR USING MPP FILM
652. CONTENT DEVELOPMENT CENTRE (EOU) (Rs. 5000/-)
653. CONTROL PANEL BOARD
654. COOLING COIL FOR AIR CONDITIONERS
655. COPPER STRIP COIL FROM SCRAP
656. CORDLESS TELEPHONES
657. CYBER CAFE
658. CYBERKIOSK (Rs. 5000/-)
659. DATA PROCESSING CENTRE (Rs. 5000/-)
660. D.C. MICRO MOTORS
661. D.G.SETS
662. DISH ANTENNA AND CABLE T.V. NETWORK EQUIPMENT
663. DISTRIBUTION TRANSFORMERS & REPAIRS
664. DOMESTIC ELECTRICAL APPLIANCES- ROOM COOLER, WASHING MACHINE, WATER HEATER, ELECTRIC ROOM HEATER
665. E-SCHOOL
666. E-COMMERCE/BUSINESS
667. ELECTRIC ENERGY METER
668. ELECTRIC FANS
669. ELECTRIC HORN FOR AUTOMOBILE
670. ELECTRIC LAMP/GLS (INCANDESCENT LAMP)
671. ELECTRIC MIXER
672. ELECTRIC MOTORS UP TO 10 HP. REWINDING OF ALL TYPES OF MOTORS WATER PUMPS
673. ELECTRIC MOTOR WINDING (FOR FAN, MIXIES, ETC.)
674. ELECTRIC STEAM IRON
675. ELECTRICAL APPLIANCES
676. ELECTRICAL FIXTURES
677. ELECTRICAL STAMPING
678. ELECTROLYTIC CAPACITORS
679. ELECTROMAGNETIC RELAY
680. ELECTRONIC BALAST/CHOK
681. ELECTRICAL CHOKE
682. ELECTRONIC DIGITAL WATCHES
683. ELECTRONIC DIGITAL WEIGHING MACHINE
684. ELECTRONIC FIRE ALARM
685. ELECTRONIC GAS STOVE LIGHTERS
686. ELECTRONIC PRESSURE INDICATORS, ELECTRICALS, ELECTRONIC LIQUID LEVEL INDICATORS, ELECTRONIC TEMPERATURE INDICATOR, DIGITAL TACHOMETER
687. ELECTRONIC TELEPHONE INSTRUMENTS
688. ELECTRONIC TOYS
689. ELECTRONIC WATCHES & CLOCKS
690. FAX MACHINES
691. F.H.P MOTORS
692. FLOPPY DISKETTES
693. FLUORESCENT LAMP STARTER
694. FLUORESCENT TUBULAR

LAMPS WITH INTRODUCTION TO MERCURY VAPOUR LAMP
695. FRANCHISEE COMPUTER EDUCATION CENTRE (Rs. 5000)
696. GAS DETECTOR (L.P.G)
697. GENERATOR SET & PUMP SETS
698. GENERATOR (BATTERY OPERATED)
699. GIS SERVICE CENTRE (GEOGRAPHICAL INFORMATION SYSTEMS)
700. HARDWARE FITTING FOR TRANSMISSION LINE OVERHEAD LINE MATERIAL
701. HEADERS FOR TRANSISTOR ICS SEMI CONDUCTOR
702. H.T & L.T INSULATORS
703. H.T & M.V INDUSTRIAL CUBICAL SWITCH BOARD
704. INFORMATION MOVING DISPLAY (L.E.D TYPE)
705. INSURANCE CLAIM PROCESSING CENTRE (EOU) (Rs. 5000/-)
706. INTEGRATED CIRCUITS
707. INTERNET BASED STOCK TRADING (Rs. 5000/-)
708. INTERNET SERVICE PROVIDER (I.S.P.)
709. JELLY FILLED TELEPHONE CABLES
710. LAP TOP COMPUTERS
711. LEAD ACID BATTERIES
712. LEAD ACID BATTERY PLATES AND ASSEMBLING OF BATTERY
713. LEGAL TRANSCRIPTION & SECRETARIAL SERVICES CENTER (EOU)(Rs. 5000/-)
714. LIGHT EMITTING DIODES (L.E.D)
715. LINEAR ICS TRAINER KIT
716. LOUD SPEAKER
717. L.T TRANSFORMER REPAIRING
718. MEDICAL TRANSCRIPTION CENTRE
719. METAL FILM RESISTORS
720. METALLISED POLYPROPYLENE, POLYESTER FILM CAPACITOR
721. MICA BASE ELECTRONIC COMPONENTS
722. MICA PAPER WASTE PAPER FROM MICA WASTE
723. MICRO PROCESSORS TRAINER KITS BASED ON MICRO PROCESSORS
724. MINI COMPUTER (PERSONAL COMPUTER)
725. MINIATURE CIRCUIT BREAKER (M.C.B)
726. MINIATURE WATCH BATTERIES (BUTTON CELL)
727. MIXER/GRINDER (MIXI)
728. MONO CHROME COMPUTER MONITOR
729. MOTOR START ELECTROLYTIC CAPACITOR
730. MULTI LAYER P.C.B
731. MULTIPLE RELAY FOR LOW VOLTAGE
732. NEON INDICATOR
733. NEON SIGN MANUFACTURE
734. OPTICAL FIBRE CABLES
735. ON LINE SHOPPING MALL (Rs. 5000/-)
736. OPTO MECHANICAL & ELECTRICAL EQUIPMENTS
737. PHOTO COLOUR LAB
738. PICTURE TUBE (B/W)
739. PLAIN PAPER COPIER
740. PLASTIC FILM CAPACITORS
741. POLYESTER CAPACITORS
742. PORTABLE GENERATOR SET
743. PORTAL
744. PORTABLE TELEVISION(TV)
745. POWER CAPACITORS
746. POWER INVERTERS
747. POWER PLANT
748. POWER TRANSFORMERS UP TO 600 KVA
749. PRINTED CIRCUIT BOARD
750. PVC WIRES & CABLES
751. RE-CONDITIONING OF PICTURE TUBE
752. RESIN CAST CT & PT (1 KV)
753. SEMI CONDUCTOR DEVICE
754. SEMI CONDUCTORS FOR TRANSISTORS & DIODES
755. SETTING UP OF A VIDEO STUDIO
756. SMOKE DETECTORS
757. SOLAR CELLS
758. SOLAR MODULES
759. SOLAR PHOTO VOLTAIC SYSTEM
760. SOLDER FLUXES
761. SOLAR WATER HEATING PANELS
762. STEEL FURNITURE & ELECTRICAL APPLIANCES
763. STEREO AMPLIFIERS
764. STEREO CASSETTE RECORDERS/PLAYERS
765. STREET LIGHT FITTINGS SURGE SUPPRESSOR
766. TANTALUM CAPACITORS
767. TEFLON COATED ELECTRIC CABLE
768. TELEMEDICINE (DISTANCE HEALTH CARE) (Rs. 5000/-)
769. TELEPHONE CORD/CABLE
770. TELEPHONE (PUSH BUTTON TYPE)
771. TELEPHONE (PUSH BUTTON & CORDLESS)
772. TELEVISION (CTV & B/W)
773. TELEVISION (3-D)
774. TELEVISION DEFLECTION COMPONENTS
775. TELEVISION SIGNAL BOOSTERS
776. TELEVISION TUNERS
777. TRACTION BATTERIES
778. TRAINING INSTITUTE OF MEDICAL TRANSCRIPTION
779. TRANSFORMER FOR B/W TV
780. TRANSFORMER FOR VOLTAGE STABILIZER & E.H.T
781. TRANSMISSION POWER LINE FITTING
782. TRANSMISSION TOWER FITTING
783. TV AUDIO EQUIPMENT CABINETS & THEIR ASSEMBLING UNIT
784. UN-INTERRUPTED POWER SUPPLY (U.P.S)
785. VARIABLE FREQUENCY
786. VARIABLE VOLTAGE A.C. DRIVE
787. VIDEO CASSETTES (COMPLETE MANUFACTURING & ASSEMBLING)
788. VIDEO CASSETTES RECORDER (V.C.R)
789. VIDEO FILM STUDIO
790. VOLTAGE REGULATOR FOR AUTOMOBILES
791. VOLTAGE STABILIZERS
792. VOLTAGE STABLIZER & T.V. GAIN BOOSTER
793. WAX AND CHEMICAL COATED, BRAIDED TINSEL WIRE
794. WEBSITE DESIGN & E-MAIL REGISTERING
795. WELDING ELECTRODES
796. WIND ENERGY POWER PROJECT (10 MW) WIRE WOUND POTENTIOMETERS

FOOD, AGRO FOOD, PROCESSED FOOD, AGRO PLANTATION, CULTIVATION, FARMING, DAIRY/MILK, TOBACCO/PAN MASALA, BREWERY & DISTILLERY, EDIBLE OILS, EOU FOOD PRODUCTS AND ALLIED PRODUCTS

797. ALCOHOLIC BEVERAGES & VENEGAR FROM COCONUT WATER
798. ALCOHOL DRINKS FROM ETHYL ALCOHOL BY MIXING OF VARIOUS FLAVOURS
799. ANTI SCALE COMPOUND FOR ADDING INTO SUGAR JUICE BOILING
800. APPLE JUICE CONCENTRATED & DEHYDRATED FRUIT & VEGETABLES
801. ARTIFICIAL FISH MEAL FOR POULTRY FEED
802. AUTOMATIC BISCUIT PLANT
803. BABY CEREAL FOOD AND MILK POWDER
804. BACTERIA FOR CANE JUICE
805. BAKER'S YEAST
806. BAKERY INDUSTRY
807. BANANA PUREE
808. BEER & WINE
809. BEER PLANT (BREWERY)
810. BIDI
811. BIDI & CIGARETTE
812. BISCUIT PLANT

1193. CANDLES (SEMI-AUTOMATIC)
1194. CORN OIL (MAIZE OIL)
1195. DEHYDRATED CASTOR OIL
1196. EUGENOL FROM CINNAMON LEAF OIL
1197. EXTRACTION OF ESSENTIAL OIL (CARDAMON, JEERA, AJOWAN, GINGER OILS ETC. & PACKAGING OF GROUND SPICES)
1198. EXTRACTION OF JASMINE ESSENCE
1199. EXTRACTION OF ESSENTIAL OILS BY SUPER CRITICAL FLUID METHOD FROM FLOWERS, HERBS & SPICES
1200. EUCALYPTUS OIL
1201. EXTRACTION OF OIL FROM OIL SEED EXPANDEREXTRUSION TECHNOLOGY)
1202. FAT LIQUOR SULPHATED OIL
1203. FLAVOURS FOR FOOD
1204. GARLIC OIL & POWDER
1205. GINGER OIL, SANDALWOOD OIL AND NAGARMOTHA OIL
1206. GINGER OIL
1207. GINGER OIL & GINGER DUST
1208. INTEGERATED WAX COMPLEX
1209. IONONE FROM LEMON GRASS OIL
1210. JASMINE & LILLY FLOWER OIL
1211. LEMON GRASS OIL
1212. LIQUID PARAFFIN
1213. LUBE OIL & GREASE
1214. LUBRICATING OIL
1215. MENTHOL CRYSTALS
1216. MENTHOL OIL & CRYSTAL
1217. MICRO CRYSTALLINE WAX
1218. MUSTARD OIL (EDIBLE OIL)
1219. OIL FROM ARTEMISIA HERBS
1220. PALM OIL CRUSHING UNIT
1221. PAN MASALA
1222. PARAFFIN WAX
1223. PARAFFIN WAX FROM SLACK WAX
1224. REFINED OIL-SUN FLOWER OIL, GROUNDNUT OIL, STAFF FLOWER OIL & COTTON SEED OIL
1225. REFINED VEGETABLE OIL
1226. RECLAMATION OF USED ENGINE OIL
1227. RICE BRAN OIL (R.B.O)
1228. ROSE OIL EXTRACTION
1229. SMOKE LESS CANDLE
1230. SPICE OIL & OLEORESINS
1231. SOLVENT EXTRACTION PLANT (OIL CAKE BASED)
1232. SYNTHETIC ALMOND OIL
1233. SYNTHETIC TALLOW
1234. SYNTHETIC GHEE
1235. VEGETABLE OIL EXTRACTION & REFINING
1236. WADDING OIL (100%) FOR WADDING OF COTTON HOSIERY CLOTH IN DYEING PROCESS
1237. WAX EMULSION FOR TEXTILE
1238. WAX FLOOR POLISH

PAINT, ENAMEL, SOLVENTS, THINNERS, INKS & VARNISH

1239. ACRYLIC EMULSION PAINTS
1240. ALUMINIUM PAINT
1241. AUTOMOBILE PAINTS
1242. BALL POINT PEN REFILL INK
1243. BITUMINIOUS ROAD EMULSION
1244. BITUMEN
1245. BITUMINIOUS FELTS FOR WATER & DAMP PROOFING
1246. BITUMINIOUS ROAD EMULSION RAPID MEDIUM & SLOW SETTING
1247. BUFFING & POLISHING
1248. CEMENT PAINT FOR WHITE & GREY CEMENT

1249. DISPERSANT
1250. DRY DISTEMPER
1251. DRY DISTEMPER & CEMENT PAINT
1252. DUPLICATING INK BLACK FOR GESTNER DUPLICATOR
1255. EMULSION PAINTS (WATER BASED)
1256. HAMMERTONE PAINT
1257. INSULATING VARNISH & WIRE ENAMEL
1258. IRON OXIDE PIGMENTS
1259. INSULATING VARNISH (POLY VINYL BUTYRAL BASED, FFC GRADE)
1260. LIME COLOUR (CEMENT COLOUR)
1261. SYNTHETIC RED OXIDE FOR FLOORINGS
1262. SOLVENT & THINNERS
1263. MARKING INKS (WATER PROOF)
1264. METAL NAPHTHANATE (AS DRIER FOR PAINTS)
1265. N.C.PUTTY
1266. OFFSET PRINTING INK
1267. OIL BOUND DISTEMPER PAINT
1268. PAINT BRUSHES
1269. PAINT REMOVERS
1270. PAINT INDUSTRY
1271. PAINT & VARNISH
1272. PICTURE VARNISH
1273. POWDER COATING PAINT
1274. PRINTING INKS (OFFSET, FLEXO & ROTO GRAVURE)
1275. PRIMER PAINT & ENAMEL PAINT
1276. PUTTY & WATER PROOFING PAINT
1277. PRINTING INKS (FLEXO-GRAPHIC INK)
1278. PUTTY (METAL CASEMENT)
1279. RED OXIDE PRIMER (ANTI CORROSIVE)
1280. REFRECTORY PAINT (GRAPHITE BASED)
1281. SCREEN PRINTING INKS
1282. SILK SCREEN PRINTING INK FORMULATION FOR PLASTIC, PAPER, CLOTH
1283. STAMP & PAD INK
1284. STOVING PAINT
1285. SPIRIT SOLUBLE MALEIC RESIN
1286. TEXTURE PAINT
1287. THINNERS AND ITS ALLIED PRODUCTS
1288. TONER INK
1289. VARNISH THINNER (SOLVENT)
1290. VACUUM METALLIZING LACQUERS
1291. WOOD PRIMER

PHARMACEUTICAL, DRUGS, AYURVEDIC/HERBAL COSMETICS & MEDICINES, HOMOEOPATHIC MEDICINES, DISPOSABLE SYRINGE, DENTAL COLLEGE & FINE CHEMICALS ETC.

1292. AROMATIC PILLS
1293. ASPIRIN
1294. AYURVEDIC PAIN BALM OINTMENTS
1295. AYURVEDIC CHURAN AND TABLETS
1296. AYURVEDIC TABLETS (HAJMOLA TYPE)
1297. AYURVEDIC/HERBAL PHARMACY
1298. AYURVEDIC SHERBATS
1299. AYURVEDIC PRODUCTS
1300. BULK DRUGS (E.O.U)
1301. BLOOD BAGS
1302. CALCIUM GLUCONATE
1303. CAPSULE, TABLET & INJECTION WITH MODERN INSTRUMENTS
1304. CASHEW FENI
1305. CHLOROQUINONE PHOSPHATE (BULK DRUGS)
1306. CLINICAL THERMOMETER
1307. DENTAL CLINIC

1308. DENTAL COLLEGE
1309. DENTAL GRADE EUGENOL
1310. DEXTROSE MONOHYDRATE, LIQUID GLUCOSE
1311. DEHYDRATED ONION & ONION POWDER
1312. DEXTROSE POWDER (ANHYDROUS FROM STARCH)
1314. DEXTROSE SALINE SOLUTION
1315. DISTILLERY (I.M.F.L)
1316. DISPOSABLE NEEDLES FOR SYRINGES
1317. DISPRIN
1318. DISTILLED WATER
1319. EMPTY HARD GELATINE CAPSULES
1320. FILLING & PACKING OF CAPSULES
1321. GLUCOSE - D - POWDER
1322. GLYCERINE
1323. HERBAL COSMETICS
1324. HERBAL SHAMPOO
1325. HERBAL HAIR OILS (AYURVEDIC)
1326. HOMOE & BIO-MEDICINES WITH MOTHER TINCTURE
1327. HOMOEPATHIC MEDICINES
1328. HYPODERMIC NEEDLES
1329. I.V. FLUIDS
1330. IBUPROFEN
1331. INFUSION & TRANSFUSION SETS (I.V. SET)
1332. INJECTABLE FOR PHARMACEUTICALS
1333. INJECTION AMPOULES PACKAGING BOX
1334. INTEGERATED SURGICAL COTTON
1335. ICE MAKING PLANT
1336. ICE & COLD STORAGE
1337. LACTOSE & BY PRODUCTS PROCESSING FROM MILK
1338. LICHEN (JATAMANSI CHARILA)
1339. LIQUID GLUCOSE AND ITS BY-PRODUCTS
1340. L-LYSINE MONOHYDRO CHLORIDE
1341. LIQUID GLUCOSE FROM POTATOES
1342. MEDICAL COLLEGE
1343. NICOTINE FROM TOBACCO WASTE
1344. OINTMENT-AYURVEDIC (YELLOW & WHITE)
1345. PHARMACEUTICAL AND FOOD GRADE GELATINE
1346. PHARMACEUTICAL INDUSTRY (TABLETS, CAPSULES, LIQUID, GEL, OINTMENT POWDER INJECTABLE)
1347. PHARMACEUTICAL UNIT (EOU) WITH FORMULA TIONS, INJECTABLES, ETC. PYRIDINE & DERIVATIVES
1348. SALT (IODIZED SALT)
1349. SALINE & INJECTION WATER
1350. SALINE WATER & DEXTROSE SOLUTION (I.V.FLUID IN PLASTIC BOTTLES)
1351. SORBITOL
1352. STARCH (MAIZE)
1353. SURGICAL ADHESIVE PLASTER
1354. SURGICAL BANDAGES
1355. SURGICAL GLOVES
1357. SURGICAL COTTON
1358. SURGICAL COTTON AND BANDAGE
1359. SYNTHETIC CAMPHOR POWDER
1360. TABLETS & CAPSULES
1361. TISSUE CULTURE
1362. TINCTURE FROM RECTIFIED SPIRIT
1363. TRIMETHOPIME
1364. VETERENARY MEDICINES (ONLY FORMULATIONS)
1365. VITAMIN 'C', SORBITOL' ANHYDROUS DEXTROSE, STARCH

PULP, PAPER, STRAW/GREY BOARD, KRAFT PAPER, PACKAGING, PAPER CARRY BAGE, PAPER FROM AGRO WASTE & STATIONERY ETC.

1366. AMMONIA PAPER
1367. AUTOMATIC BOOK BINDING
1368. ADHESIVE (FEVICOL TYPE)
1369. ALL PIN & GEM CLIPS
1370. CARBON PAPER
1371. CARD BOARD
1372. CARBON LESS PAPER
1373. CELLPHANE PAPER
1374. COMPUTER FORMS & SECURITY PRINTING PRESS
1375. CORRUGATED BOARD & BOX (PRINTED & LAMINATED)
1376. CORRUGATED BOARD AND BOXES FROM FROM CARD BOARDS
1377. CORRUGATED CARTONS FROM PLAIN PAPERS
1378. CORRUGATRED PACKING & MATERIAL (BULB & TUBES PACKING)
1379. DESK TOP PUBLISHING
1380. DEFOAMING AGENT FOR PAPER PLANT
1381. DRINKING STRAW PAPER
1382. D.T.P CUM OFFSET PRESS
1383. EGG TRAYS
1384. EXERCISE NOTE BOOK, REGISTER AND PAD
1385. FLEXOGRAPHIC INK
1386. GREETING CARD BY OFFSET PRESS
1387. HAND MADE PAPER FILTER PAPER
1388. HARD BOARD
1389. INJECTION AMPOULES PACKAGING BOXES
1390. INSULATIING PAPER
1391. KRAFT PAPER
1392. KRAFT PAPER FROM BAGASSE
1393. LAMINATED PACKAGING PAPER WITH PRINTING
1394. LAMINATION & COATING ON PAPER
1395. M.G. PAPER FROM WASTE PAPER
1396. MILL PAPER FROM WASTE PAPER
1397. MILL BOARD FROM RICE & WHEAT STRAWS
1398. MILL BOARD FROM WASTE PAPER
1399. MINI PAPER PLANT FROM SISAL
1400. MINI PAPER PLANT
1401. MULTI WALL PAPER SACKS
1402. NEWS PAPER FOR CHILDREN
1403. NEWS PRINT PAPER FROM RICE STRAW BAGASSE
1404. NEWS PAPER CHILDRENS
1405. NEWS PRINT PAPER
1406. OFFSET AND TREADLE TYPE PRINTING PRESS
1407. MILL BOARD BASED ON RICE STRAW
1408. PAPER AND BOARD FROM STRAW
1409. PAPER & PAPER PRODUCTS
1410. PAPER ENVELOPES
1411. PAPER CARRY BAGS
1412. PAPER BOARD CARTON
1413. PAPER CONES FOR LOUD SPEAKERS
1414. PAPER FROM AKRA
1415. PAPER FROM BAGASSE WITH CORRUGATED BOARD & BOXES
1416. PAPER FROM BAMBOO
1417. PAPER GLASSES FOR BEVERAGES
1418. PAPER FROM RICE HUSK & WHEAT HUSK
1419. PAPER FROM TREE BARK, EUCALYPRUS WOOD
1420. PAPER PRODUCTS
1421. PAPER PLANT (WHITE WRITING & NEWS PAPER FOR PULP & WASTE PAPER)
1422. PAPER PLATES, PAPER GLASS
1423. PAPER CONES & TUBES
1425. PAPER PLANT WITH DTP & PRINTING & PUBLISHING UNIT
1426. PAPER BASED PHENOLIC SHEET
1427. PAPER CUP FOR ICE CREAM
1428. PAPER TUBES SPIRAL WINDING COMPOSIT CONTAINER
1429. PAPER LABLE FOR BEER BOTTLES
1430. PARTICLE BOARD & BLACK BOARD WITH SANDING & LAMINATION OF PARTICLE BOARD
1431. PARTICLE BOARD FROM RICE HUSK
1432. POUCH FILLING & MAKING FOR TOMATO SAUCE
1433. POUCH MAKING &

GRAVURE PRINTING
1434. PROCESSING OF PAPER FOR FEEDING IN COMPUTER
1435. PULP FROM BAMBOO & WOOD
1436. PAPER FILES
1437. PLAYING CARDS
1438. ROSIN SIZING AGENT (FOR PAPER PLANT)
1439. SAND PAPER
1440. SANITRY NAPKINS
1441. SILICON COATED PAPER
1442. STENCIL PAPER
1443. STRAW BOARD AND GREY BOARD
1444. STRAW BOARD & MILL BOARD
1445. STRAW BOARD AND PAPER BOARD
1446. TISSUE PAPER FACIAL
1447. TISSUE MOIST TOILETERY CLEANSING TISSUE AND RELATED PRODUCTS
1448. TISSUE PAPER ROLLS
1449. TETRA PACK FOR MILK PACKAGING, GHEE & OTHER LIQUIDS
1450. TOILET PAPER ROLLS
1451. TOILET PAPER & NAPKINS
1452. WAX COATED PRINTED PAPER
1453. WET FACE FRESHNER TISSUE
1454 WHITE WRITING & PRINTING PAPER
1455. WRITING & PRINTING PAPER (PAPER MILLS)

PLASTIC, B.O.P.P, ACRYLIC, DISPOSABLE PLASTIC PRODUCTS, PET PRODUCTS, P.V.C, H.D.P.E, P.P, L.D.P.E., P.U, A.B.S, THERMOFOARMING, MASTER BATCHES, & POLYMER AND RUBBER PRODUCTS, TYRE, TUBE, ADHESIVE, SHEET, COIR & MANY OTHERS

1456. ABS GRANULES FROM ABS SCRAPS FROM OLD T.V. CABINETS, WHITE GOODS ETC.
1457. ACRYLIC BEADS
1458. ACRYLIC COPOLYMER EMULSION
1459. ACRYLIC LATEX
1460. ACRYLIC SHEET
1461. ACRYLIC SHEET & MOULDED PRODUCTS
1462. ACRYLIC TEETH
1463. AUTO TUBES
1464. AUTO FLAPS FOR TRUCKS & BUSES
1465. AUTO TYRES & TUBES
1466. BABY BOTTLES (PLASTIC) WITH WHITESILICON RUBBER NIPPLES
1467. B.O.P.P. FILM
1468. B.O.P.P. PRESSURE SENSITIVE SELF ADHESIVE TAPE
1469. BABY NIPPLE (SILICON)
1470. BABY NIPPLE (BIG SIZE)
1471. BALLOON PLASTIC ADVERTISING
1472 BLISTER FILM PVC
1473. BLISTER PACKAGING & POUCH PAKAGING
1474. BLOW MOULDING PLASTIC CONTAINER
1475. COATING ON METALIZED POLYESTER FILM/METALISED PAPER/ ALIMINIUM FOIL
1476. COATING ON PLASTIC (ELECTROLYSIS) & GLASS
1477. COIR FOAM (RUBBERISED)
1478. COLOUR COATING ON PLASTICS
1479. COLOUR MASTER BATCHES FOR VARIOUS PLASTICS
1480. CYCLE TYRES AND TUBES
1481. DISPOSABLE PLASTIC CUPS GLASSES, ETC.
1482. DISPOSABLE PLASTIC SYRINGES & NEEDLES
1483. DISPOSABLE PLASTIC SYRINGES
1484. DOUGH MOULDING COMPOUND (D.M.C)
1485. EPOXY RESIN
1486. EXPANDED POLYESTRENE MOULDING (THERMOCOLE)
1487. F.R.P AUTO, SCOOTER ROOFS & CEILINGS
1488. F.R.P PRODUCTS (HELMET, WASHBASIN SHEETS, ROOFING SHEETS)
1489. FIBRE REINFORCED PLASTIC (HIGH PRESSURE MOULDING WITH SMC BMC AND DMC)
1490. FIELD RUBBER CONVERTED TO THE 60% LATEX RUBBER
1491. FLEXIBLE P.U. FOAM
1492. FORMALDEHYDE CROCKERY & OTHER ITEMS
1493. FORMALDEHYDE RESIN (UREA, PHENOL, MELEMINE)
1494. GASKET SHEET
1495. GUM BOTTLE (PVC)
1496. GLASS BEADS
1497. HDPE COATED PAPER SACK
1498. H.D.P.E. BAGS
1499. H.D.P.E. CONTAINERS (BLOW MOULDING)
1500. H.D.P.E. CONTAINER, POLY JARS BY INJECTION MOULDING (FOOD GRADE)
1501. H.D.P.E. JERRY CANS
1502. HDPE MANUFACTURING FROM ETHYLALCOHOL
1503. H.D.P.E PIPE AND FITTINGS
1504. H.D.P.E. PIPES
1505. H.D.P.E PRINTED BAGS
1506. H.D.P.E TWINES AND ROPES
1507. H.D.P.E. & L.D.P.E PIPES AND FITTINGS
1508. H.D.P.E/PP BOX STRAPPING
1509. H.D.P.E/PP WOVEN SACKS USING PLAIN LOOMS
1510. HOLOGRAM STICKERS-3D
1511. H.M BAG PLANT WITH PRINTING UNIT
1512. HAWAI CHAPPALS (RUBBER)
1513. I.V PLASTIC BOTTLE
1514. ICE CREAM CUP (PLASTIC)
1515. INJECTION MOULDED AUTO COMPONENTS
1516. INJECTION & BLOW MOULDED PLASTIC PRODUCTS
1517. INJECTION MOULDED PLASTIC PRODUCTS
1518. INTEGERATED COMPLEX ESTER'S & ALLIED PRODUCTS (D.O.P.D.B.P. & ETHYL ACETATE, BUYTL ACETATE, WIRE ENAMELS, JELLY CABLE COMPOUND)
1519. L.D.P.E. (LOW DENSITY POLY ETHYLENE) GRANULES FROM VIRGIN (L.D.P.E. RESIN)
1520. INTEGERATED SURGICAL RUBBER GOODS INDUSTRY
1521. INJECTION MOULDED PLASTIC BALLS
1522. L.D.P.E FROM ETHYL ALCOHOL
1523. LDPE MOULDED PRODUCTS
1524. LAMINATION OF COEXTRUSION MULTILAYER FILM IN ROLL FORM
1525. LATEX RUBBER
1526. LATEX RUBBER CONDOM
1527. MASTER BATCHES (COLOURED, P.V.C, L.D.P.E, H.D.P.E, ETC.)
1528. MELAMINE FORMALHYDE RESIN
1529. MOULDED LUGGAGE
1530. MULTI-LAYER (3 LAYER BAGS)
1531. MULTI-LAYER (3 LAYER) FILM WITH LAMINATION & PRINTING
1532. OIL SEAL
1533. PET BOTTLE/CONTAINERS
1534. PET BOTTLES FROM PRE FORM
1535. PET BOTTLE & MINERAL WATER
1536. PET PRE-FORM FROM PET RESIN
1537. PET PRE-FORM CUM PET BOTTLES
1538. PET PRE-FORM PET BOTTLES CUM MINERAL WATERS
1539. POLY CARBONATE RESIN
1540. PTFE COMPONENTS
1541. PU/PVC SOLE FOR SPORT SHOE BY IMPORTED M/C.
1542. PVC BATTERY SEPARATOR
1543. P.V.C COMPOUNDS (FRESH)
1544. P.V.C COMPOUNDS (SCRAP)
1545. P.V.C ELECTRICAL INSULATING TAPE
1546. P.V.C. EXTRUSION PROFILES
1547. P.V.C FITTINGS
1548. P.V.C FLEXIBLE FUSIBLE POWDER HEAT FUSIBLE POWDER
1549. P.V.C GRANULES (FOR

INSULATION & SHEETS GRADES)
1550. P.V.C GRANULES FROM PVC SCRAPS (WITH POLLUTION CONTROL)
1551. P.V.C HOSES
1552. P.V.C LEATHER CLOTH
1553. P.V.C FLEXIBLE PIPES
1554. P.V.C PIPES AND FITTINGS
1555. POLYTHENE BAGS (PRINTED)
1556. PVC PLASTICS FILM SHEET SOFT/RIGID
1557. PVC RESIN AND COMPOUND
1558. PVC RULAR
1559. PVC STABLIZERS (SINGLE PACK SYSTEM)
1560. PVC WIRE AND CABLES
1561. PAPER BASED PHENOLIC SHEET FOR ELECTRICAL
1562. PHENOL FORMALDEHYDE RESIN
1563. PHENOLIC RESIN
1564. PLASTIC BEADS FROM PLASTIC SCRAPS
1565. PLASTIC BUTTONS
1566. PLASTIC CANS
1567. PLASTIC COLLAPSIBLE TUBE
1568. PLASTIC CORRUGATED SHEET & BOXES
1569. PLASTIC FILM AND SHEETS WITH PRINTING FLEXO & ROTO/LDPE/HDPE/PP/HM/PVC
1570. PLASTIC FILTER MASTER BATCH & OTHER MASTER BATCHES FOR VARIOUS PLASTICS
1571. PLASTIC JERRY CANS
1572. PLASTIC GRANULES OR POWDER FROM PLASTIC SCRAP
1573. PLASTIC INJECTION MOULDED T.V. CABINETS
1574. PLASTIC ITEMS MANUFAC TURE FROM POWDER MELAMINE
1575. PLASTIC GOODS
1576. PLASTIC PIPES & TARPAULINES
1577. PLASTIC SHEET FROM SCRAP
1578. PLASTIC PLANT (BLOW MOULDING & INJECTION MOULDING)
1579. PLASTIC PRODUCTS (GOLD, SILVER, NICKEL)
1580. PLASTIC TOYS
1581. POLYESTER BEADING
1582. POLYESTER FILM
1583. POLYTHENE BAGS & AUTOMATIC PRINTING
1584. POLYTHENE PRINTED BAGS
1585. POLYURETHANE FOAM AND ITS PRODUCTS
1586. PROPYLENE FILM (PRINTED) & BAG MANUFACTURING
1587. PLASTIC MATS
1588. RAINBOW COLOUR ON PVC FILM & SHEET
1589. RED MUD PVC PIPES AND FITTINGS
1590. RE-RUBBERISED OF SOLID TYPE
1591. RESIN COATED SAND REXINE
1592. REXINE CLOTH & ALLIED PRODUCTS
1593. RUBBER ADHESIVE
1594. RUBBER AUTO PARTS
1595. RUBBER BELTING
1596. RUBBER MOULDING UNIT INCLUDING LINING RUBBER SHEETING
1597. RUBBER RECLAIMING
1598. RUBBER ROLLERS FOR TEXTILE MILLS & PAPER INDUSTRIES
1599. RUBBER & PLASTIC SHEETS, MATS & FLAPS
1600. RUBBER SHEET AND ALLIED HOSPITAL RUBBER GOODS
1601. RUBBERIZED PVC GASKET
1602. RUBBERISED COIR
1603. RUBBER COMPOUND FOR AUTOMOBILES
1604. SAFETY BELTS
1605. SILVER AND GOLD PLATING ON PVC AND NYLON-6
1606. SILICONE RUBBER NIPPLES/ TEATS
1607. SPECTACLE FRAMES (PLASTIC)
1608. SPUNGE RUBBER
1609. SURGICAL EXAMINATION GLOVES
1610. SYNTHETIC PEARL COATING ON POLYSTYRENE BEADS
1611. SYNTHETIC RUBBER ADHESIVE
1612. TEFLON MANUFACTURING
1613. TEFLON TAPE
1614. TEFLON TAPES & CABLES
1615. THERMOCOLE SHEET AND MOULDED PRODUCTS EXPANDED POLYESTERENE EXTRUSION PROFILES
1616. THERMOFORMED PACKAGING (BLISTER PACKAGING & POUCH PACKAGING)
1617. THERMOPLASTIC POLYURETHANE
1618. THERMOFORMED CUPS, PLATES & GLASS WITH HIPS SHEET
1619. THERMOCOLE
1620. THERMOCOLE BASED DISPOSABLE GLASS, CUPS & PLATES
1621. TOOTH BRUSHES
1622. TOY BALLOON, DECORA TIVE & INDUSTRIAL BALLOONS
1623. TREAD RUBBER
1624. TYRE RETREADING (HOT)
1625. TYRE RETREADING BY COLD PROCESS
1626. TYRE TUBES & FLAPS
1627. TYRE & TUBES
1628. UNSATURATED POLYESTER FOR REXINE
1629. V-BELT AND FAN BELT
1630. VINYL ASBESTOS AND PVC WALL PAPER
1631. VITON (FLUORO ELASTOMER)

SOAP, COSMETICS & PERFUMES

1632. ACID SLURRY, SYNTHETIC DETERGENT POWDER
1632. ACID SLURRY
1633. AGARBATTI SYNTHETIC, PERFUMERY COMPOUND
1634. AFTER SHAVE LOTION
1635. ANTISEPTIC CREAM
1636. BETA IONONE
1637. BLEACHING POWDER
1638. BLUE DETERGENT POWDER
1639. CLEANING POWDER (VIMTYPE)
1640. COLD CREAM
1641. COLOURED FLAME & PERFUMED CANDLES (RED, BLUE, GREEN FLAME)
1642. COSMETIC INDUSTRY (MODERN)
1643. COSMETIC INDUSTRY (SHAMPOO, SPRAY PERFUME, TALCUM POWDER
1644. DETERGENT POWDER (ARIEL TYPE)
1645. DETERGENT POWDER (NIRMA TYPE) FULLY AUTOMATIC PLANT
1646. DETERGENT WASHING POWDER
1647. FISH OIL SOAP
1648. GLYCERINE TRANSPARENT SOAP
1649. HAIR REMOVING CREAM
1650. HERBAL COSMETICS
1651. HERBAL SHAMPO & CREAM
1652. HERBAL/AYURVEDIC COSMETICS
1653. INCENSE POWDER, INCENSE STICKS & INCENSE CAKE
1654. OPTICAL WHITENERS
1655. ROSE OIL EXTRACTION
1656. SHAMPOOS (COCONUT OIL BASED COLD PROCESS)
1657. SHAVING CREAM
1658. SINDUR (KUMKUM)
1659. SOAP COATED PAPER
1660. SPRAY DRIED DETERGENT POWDER
1661. STAIN REMOVER
1662. TALCUM POWDER (FACE & TOILET POWDER)
1663. TOILET AND HERBAL SOAP
1664. TOOTH PASTE & POWDER
1665. WASHING DETERGENT POWDER AND WASHING SOAP
1666. WASHING POWDER LIQUID DETERGENTS, LOTION & SHAMPOO

TEXTILE INDUSTRIES, READYMADE GARMENTS, COTTON, DYEING, BLEACHING, CLOTH, HOSIERY, POWER LOOM, HAND LOOM, WOOLLEN, SILK, SOCKS, SURGICAL COTTON & MANY OTHERS

1667. ANGORA RABBIT WOOL
1668. BUCKRAM
1669. CANVAS SHOES, JUNGLE BOOT, BOOT RUBBER KNEES & BOOT COMBAT
1670. CARPET FROM COTTON WASTE
1671. CERAMIC THREAD GUIDE
1672. COTTON BUDS/SWABS
1673. COTTON FROM WASTE YARN
1674. COTTON ROLLS
1675. COTTON SPIDERS FOR LOUD SPEAKERS
1676. DENIM CLOTH
1677. DENIM CLOTH (INTEGERATED UNIT WITH BLEACHING, DYEING AND PRINTING)
1678. DISPERSENT FOR TEXTILE
1679. DYEING & BLEACHING
1680. DYEING OF HANK YARN
1681. EMULSIFIER FOR WOOL BATCHING OIL
1682. EMBROIDERY ON FABRICS
1683. GARMENT DYEING, WASHING & STITCHING (JEANS, JACKETS, SKIRTS & SHIRTS)
1684. GOVES KNITTING
1685. GUNNY BAGS
1687. HDPE WOVEN SACKS
1688. HDPE TARPAULINS USING PLAIN LOOM WITH LAMINATION
1689. HDPE/PP WOVEN SACKS USING CIRCULAR LOOMS
1690. HOSIERY CLOTH (COTTON) PROCESSING (BLEACHING, DYEING, FINISHING OF CLOTH)
1691. HOSIERY INDUSTRY
1692. HOSIERY MERCERISING
1693. HOSIERY PRODUCTS LIKE VEST, BRIEF, T-SHIRTS & SOCKS
1694. JACQUARD FABRICS
1695. JUTE COIR, GRASS ROPE/ SUTLI MAKING
1696. JUTE FELT
1697. JUTE TWINES
1698. KNITTED FABRICS
1699. LAMINATED JUTE BAGS
1700. LAMINATION OF HDPE WOVEN CLOTH (JUTE,COTTON, PAPER)
1701. NYLON YARN CRIMPING, DOUBLING AND BLEACHING
1702. PIGMENT BINDER FOR TEXTILE PRINTING
1704. POLYESTER RESIN FOR WIRE ENAMEL
1705. POLYESTER RESIN
1706. POLYESTER YARN FROM WASTE POLYESTER ZIP FASTENERS
1707. POWER LOOM
1708. READYMADE GARMENTS & HOSIERY
1709. READYMADE GARMENTS MERCHANDISE
1710. READYMADE GARMENTS & COVERS
1711. READYMADE GARMENTS & EMBROIDERY OF GOWNS, SHIRTS, BLOUSES, T-SHIRTS ETC. (ONLY LADIES)
1712. READYMADE SALWAR SUIT
1713. RECOVERY OF NYLON FROM NYLON WASTE
1714. ROTARY PRINTING AND DYEING ON COTTON, SYNTHETIC TEXTILE
1715. SANITARY NAPKINS
1716. SCREEN PRINTING ON COTTON CLOTH
1717. SEWING THREAD REELS & BALLS MAKING INDUSTRIES
1718. SCREEN PRINTING ON COTTON, POLYESTER & ACRYLIC
1719. SHAWLS (WOOLLEN)
1720. SHOE LACES
1721. SILK FABRICS ON HANDLOOM
1722. SOCKS KNITTING
1723. SPINNING, DOUBLING DYEING MERCERISING & BLEACHING OF COTTON YARN
1724. SPINNING & CARDING OF WOOL INTO YARNS
1725. STARCH BOOK BINDING CLOTH
1726. SURAT JARI
1727. SURGICAL COTTON & BANDAGE
1728. SYNTHETIC TEXTILE INDUSTRY(SUITING, SHIRTING, SAREES) TERRY CLOTH
1729. T-SHIRTS
1730. TOWELS, BED SHEET COVERS
1731. TERRY TOWEL
1732. TERRY FABRICS WEAVING UNIT
1733. TEXTILE AUXILLIARIES & CHEMICALS
1734. TEXTILE BLEACHING, DYEING & FINISHING & PRINTING OF COTTON FABRICS
1735. TEXTILE (HOSIERY)
1736. TEXTILE MILL
1737. TEXTILE DYEING & PRINTING
1738. TEXTILE PRINTING (JOB WORK)
1739. TEXTILE PIGMENT PRINTING BINDER
1740. TOWEL (TERRY)
1741. VELVET CLOTH BY FLOCKING PROCESS
1742. VISCOSE STAPLE FIBRE
1743. WADDING OIL (100%) FOR WADDING OF COTTON HOSIERY CLOTH IN THE DYEING PROCESS
1744. WEAVING OF DASUTI CLOTH WITH PRINTING, DYEING, EMBROIDERY & FINISHING
1745. WASHING OF JEANS & OTHER GARMENTS
1746. WORSTED WOOLLEN YARN CLOTH
1747. ZARI GLITTER SALMA SITARA OF PLASTIC FILM

INFOTECH/IT, HOSPITALITY, HOSPITAL, COLLEGE, SCHOOL, MEDICAL, ENTERTAINMENT CLUB, WARE HOUSING & REAL ESTATE, PROJECTS

1748. AMUSEMENT PARK
1749. AMUSEMENT PARK CUM WATER PARK
1750. BANQUET HALL
1751. CALL CENTER (DOMESTIC)
1752. CALL CENTER (INTERNATIONAL)
1753. CHILDREN RECREATION CENTRE
1754. COLD STORAGE
1755. COMMUNITY HALL
1756. COMPUTER EDUCATION INSTITUTE
1757. COMPUTER SOFTWARE
1758. COLLEGE
1759. CYBER CAFE
1760. DENTAL CLINIC
1761. DENTAL COLLEGE
1762. DIAGONOSTIC CENTRE
1763. E-COMMERCE/BUSINESS
1764. E-SCHOOL (Rs. 5000/-)
1765. ENGINEERING COLLEGE
1766. ENTERTAINMENT CLUB
1767. ENTERTAINMENT CLUB, HOLIDAY RESORT, 4 STAR HOTEL, AMUSEMENT PARK CUM WATER PARK, MUSHROOM & ITS PRODUCTS, FISH FARMING, LAKE FOR BOATING, DEER PARK
1768. FASHION TECHNOLOGY INSTITUTE
1769. FAST FOOD PARLOUR
1770. FIVE STAR HOTEL
1771. FOOD PARLOUR
1772. FRANCHISE TRAINING PROGRAMME FOR IIT & ENGINEERING ENTRANCE EXAMS
1773. GOLF COURSE
1774. HEALTH CLUB, BEAUTY PARLOUR
1775. HEALTH CLUB AND FITNESS CENTER
1776. HEALTH RESORTS
1777. HOLIDAY RESORTS
1778. HOLIDAY RESORT CUM

ENTERTAINMENT CLUB WITH 4 STAR HOTEL
1779. HOSPITALS
1780. ICE CREAM PARLOUR
1781. INTERNET SERVICE PROVIDER (I.S.P.)
1782. MEDICAL COLLEGE
1783. MEDICAL COLLEGE, HOSPITAL & RESEARCH INSTITUTE
1784. MEDICAL TRANSCRIPTION CENTRE
1785. MENTAL RETARDATION HOSPITAL & CEREBRAL PALSY
1786. MOTEL/SMALL HOTEL
1787. MULTISTOREY COMMERCIAL COMPLEX
1788. MULTISTOREY RESIDENTIAL COMPLEX
1789. NURSERY SCHOOL
1790. NATURE CARE CENTRE
1791. NURSING HOME
1792. ONLINE SHOPPING MALL (RS. 5000/- REPORT)
1793. PORTAL
1794. REHABILITATION CENTRE FOR AGED & NEEDY PERSONS
1795. RESIDENTIAL CUM COMMERCIAL COMPLEX
1796. RESTAURANT
1797. RESTAURANT WITH PUB
1798. SCHOOL (PRIMARY)
1799. SCHOOL (HIGHER SECONDARY)
1800. THREE STAR HOTEL
1801. TOURIST CLUB
1802. TRAINING INSTITUTE FOR MEDICAL TRANSCRIPTION
1803. VIDEO FILM STUDIO
1804. WARE HOUSE
1805. WEBSITE DESIGN & E-MAIL REGISTERING

AGRO BASED INDUSTRIES

1806. COAL BRIQUETTES FROM AGROWASTE
1807. FURFURALFROM RICEHULL
1808. MUSHROOM CULTIVATION & PROCESSING (BUTTON)
1809. MUSHROOM GROWING & PROCESSING WITH AIR CONDITIONING
1810. MUSHROOM CULTIVATION & PROCESSING UNIT DEHYDRATION & PACKAGING OF OYSTER & PADDY STRAW MUSHROOMS
1811. ORGANIC MANURE
1812. PAPAYA CULTIVATION
1813. PAPAYA & TOMATO CULTIVATION
1814. PROCESSING & UTILISATION OF COCONUT
1815. PROCESSING OF SHEEP HAIR TO PRODUCE WOOL

BAKERY, CONFECTIONERY & FOOD PRODUCTS

1816. AGROLACTOR SOYAMILK
1817. APPLE FRUIT JUICE WITH CANNING BOTTLING
1818. AYURVEDIC SHARBAT
1819. BAKERY UNIT (PASTRIES, BREAD, BUNS, CAKE, TOFFEE ETC.)
1820. BAKING POWDER
1821. BANANA & ITS BY PRODUCTS
1822. BANANA POWDER
1823. BANANA WAFERS
1824. BANANA CULTIVATION
1825. BEER INDUSTRY
1826. DEHULLING OF JAUN FOR BEER
1827. BEER & WINE
1828. BEER, ALCOHOL, IMFL
1829. BESEN PLANT
1830. BISCUIT PLANT
1831. BREAD & BISCUIT PLANT
1832. BOTTLING PLANT COUNTRY LIQUOR FROM RECTIFIED SPIRIT
1833. BRANDY
1834. BREAD RUSKS
1835. CANNED FRUITS & VEGETABLES
1836. CANNING & PRESERVATION OF MEAT
1837. CANNING & PRESERVATION OF VEGETABLES
1838. CANNING OF MANGO PULP & MANGO SLICES
1839. CARBONATED BEVERAGS
1840. CASHEW FENI
1841. CASHEW NUT (DRIED & FRIED)
1842. CATTLE BREEDING
1843. CATTLE BREEDING & DAIRY FARM TO PRODUCE MILK
1844. CATTLE FEED FROM TAPIOCA
1845. CHEWING GINGER & AMLOKI
1846. CHEWING GUM
1847. CHILLI SAUCE
1848. CHILLI POWDER
1849. CHOCOLATE
1850. CIDER PLANT
1851. COCOA POWDER
1852. COCOA BUTTER & COCOA POWDER
1853. COCONUT SHELL POWDER
1854. COCONUT WATER
1855. COCONUT SWEET (WATERY)
1856. COCONUT MILK POWDER (DEHYDRATED)
1857. COCONUT PRODUCTS & BY PRODUCTS (INTEGRATED PLANT)
1858. COLD DRINK
1859. CURRY POWDER
1860. DAIRY FOR MILK PROCESSING (GHEE, BUTTER & PANEER)
1861. DAIRY PRODUCTS
1862. DAIRY PRODUCTS MILK PACKAGING IN POUCH (GHEE, BUTTER, ETC.
1863. DAIRY FARM TO PRDUCE MILK WITH PACKAGING (COW)
1864. DAIRY FARM TO PRDUCE MILK WITH PACKAGING (BUFALLOE)
1865. DAIRY FARM & MILK PRODUCTS
1866. DAL MOTH, CHANACHUR & BHUJIYA
1867. DEHYDRATION OF FRUITS & VEGETABLE
1868. DESICCATED COCONUT POWDER FROM COCONUTS
1869. DEHYDRATION & CANNING OF FRUITS & VEGETABLES
1870. DRY FRUIT ROASTING & PACKAGING
1871. DRYING OF RED CHILLIES, HALDI, DHANIYA, PEAS & GROUND NUT
1872. EGG POWDER
1873. FISH CANNING IN TIN & POUCHES
1874. FISH DEHYRATION (DRYING OF FISH)
1875. FISH MEAL
1876. FISH PROCESSING (BEAST FREEZING PROCESSES)
1877. FLAVOURS FOR FOOD INDUSTRIES
1878. FLOUR MILL (ROLLER)
1879. FROZEN MEAT
1880. FOOD DEHYDRATION (FRUITS & VEGETABLES)
1881. FRIED & ROASTED GROUND NUT, GRAMS, PEAR ETC.
1882. FRUIT JUICE MAKING & PACKAGING IN PLASTIC CONTAINER
1883. FRUIT JUICE IN TETRA PACK (DRINKS)
1884. FRUIT JUICE, SQUASHES, SAUCE & KETCHUP, JAM, JELLY, VINEGAR ETC.
1885. GARLIC FLAKES
1886. GARLIC POWDER
1887. GHEE & BUTTER
1888. GINGER (PULVERISED)
1889. GINGER GLAZING & PRESERVATION
1890. GINGER STORAGE
1891. GINGER PROCESSING
1892. GINGER OIL & GINGER DUST
1893. GINGER POWDER (DRY) & OLEORESIN
1894. GRAPE DEHYDRATION
1895. GRAPE CULTIVATION
1896. GRAPE JUICE
1897. HONEY PROCESSING & PACKAGING
1898. ICE CREAM & ICE CANDY
1899. ICE CUBE
1900. INVERT SUGAR
1901. IDLI MIX, DOSA MIX SAMBHAR MIX, VADA MIX, GULAB JAMUN MIX
1902. INSTANT COFFEE & INSTANT TEA

1903. INSTANT NOODLES
1904. INSTANT SOUPS
1905. IODIZED SALT FROM CRUDE SALT
1906. JAM CHUTNEY PICKLES & SQUASHES
1907. KATHA MANUFACTURING
1908. LECITHIN (SOYA BASED)
1909. LEMON & ITS PRODUCTS
1910. MACARONI MANUFACTURING
1911. MACARONI, SPAGHETTI, VERMICELLI & NOODLES
1912. MAIZE & ITS BY PRODUCTS MALTING PLANT
1913. MANGO PAPPAD (AAM PAPPAD)
1914. MANGO POWDER RIPE
1915. MANGO POWDER
1916. MANGO PROCESSING & CANNING (MANGO PULP)
1917. MEAT PROCESSING (CHICKEN MUTTON)
1918. MEAT PROCESSING (BUFFALO)
1919. MENTHOL BOLD FROM MENTHOL FLAKES
1020. MILK POWDER
1921. MILK POWDER & GHEE
1922. MILK POWDER, GHEE & SPICES
1923. MILK PRESERVATION & MARKETING TO WHOLE SELLERS
1924. MILK PRESERVATION & MARKETING TO WHOLE SELLERS (IN POUCHES)
1925. MILK TOFFEE MANUFACTURES
1926. MINERAL WATER
1927. MINERAL WATER IN POUCHES
1928. MINI FLOUR MILL ATTA MAIDA, SUJI & WHEAT BRAN
1929. MITHAI/HALWAI (SWEET & NAMKEEN)
1930. MUTTON PROCESSING
1931. PAN MASALA (MEETHA, SADA, ZARDA) MAKING & PACKING
1932. PAN MASALA AND POUCH MAKING
1933. PANEER (CHEESE)
1934. PAPAD & BARIYAN
1935. PAPAD PLANT
1936. PEPSICOLA IN POLYTUBES
1937. PETHA PACKAGING
1938. PICKLES
1939. PIGGERY/MEAT/CHICKEN PROCESSING
1940. PINE APPLE JUICE CANNING
1941. POTATO & ONION POWDER
1942. POTATO & ONION FLAKES
1943. POTATO CHIPS
1944. POTATO GRANULES
1945. POUCH FILLING FOR SAUNF SUPARI ILAICHI ETC.
1946. PRESERVATION OF RAWS MANGO JUICE
1947. PROCESSED CHEESE & MARINE PDTS.
1948. PULP FROM TARMARIND
1949. READYMATE PROCESSED FOOD
1950. RICE & CORN FLAKES
1951. RICE BASMATI (TRADING)
1952. RICE POLISHING & PACKAGING IN POUCH
1953. ROASTED/SALTED/MASALA/ CASHEW NUTS ALMONDS & PEA NUT
1954. ROLLER FLOUR MILL

INFOTECH/IT PROJECTS

1955. MEDICAL TRANSCRIPTION
1956. E-COMMERCE
1957. CYBERCAFE
1958. INTERNET SERVICE PROVIDER (ISP)
1959. COMPUTER EDUCATION CENTRE
1960. PORTAL (WEBSITE DESIGN)
1961. CALL CENTRE

TERMS AND CONDITIONS

FOR INDIA

1. Please ask for Quotations/ Proforma Invoice for Each *Market Survey Cum Detailed Techno Economic Feasibility Report.* Payable in advance through Draft/M.O./Cash in favour of 'ENGINEERS INDIA RESEARCH INSTITUTE', Delhi. Delivery by Regd.Post/Courier within 2 Days. (Postage Free)

2. Ask for a Hi Tech Projects, monthly magazine. Each issue covers approx. 75 project profiles.

FOR OVERSEAS

1. Please ask for Quotations/ Proforma Invoice in US $ for Each *Market Survey Cum Detailed Techno Economic Feasibility Report.* Payable in advance through Bank Draft in favour of 'ENGINEERS INDIA RESEARCH INSTITUTE', Delhi. (Payable in India). Delivery by Regd. Air Mail Post/Courier within 3 Days. (Postage Free)

2. Ask for a Hi Tech Projects, monthly magazine. Each issue covers approx. 75 project profiles.

ENGINEERS INDIA RESEARCH INSTITUTE

4449, Nai Sarak (D), Main Road, Delhi - 110 006 (India)

Phones: 91-11- 2391 8117, 2391 6431, 2384 0361

Fax: 91-11- 2391 6431 E-Mail : eirisidi@bol.net.in Website:www.eiriindia.org

Also at : 4/54, Roop Nagar, Delhi - 110 007 (India)

Ph:. 23840361 Mob: 098114 37895

PATRON: YOU CAN ALSO DEPOSIT THE AMOUNT IN "EIRI" ACCOUNT WITH UTI BANK LTD. CA-05401020006248 OR ICICI BANK LTD. CA-022705000598 OR UNION BANK OF INDIA CA-307201010015149 AND JUST SMS US ON PH. 09811437895